Mirror in the Shrine

MIRROR

Harvard University Press

Cambridge, Massachusetts, and London, England   1988

in the SHRINE

American Encounters

with Meiji Japan

Robert A. Rosenstone

This book is printed on acid-free paper, and its binding materials
have been chosen for strength and durability.

Library of Congress Cataloging-in-Publication Data

Rosenstone, Robert A.
Mirror in the shrine.

Bibliography: p.
Includes index.
1. Japan—Civilization—1868–1913. 2. Griffis,
William Elliot, 1843–1928. 3. Morse, Edward Sylvester,
1838–1925. 4. Hearn, Lafcadio, 1850–1904. 5. Americans
—Japan—Biography. I. Title.
DS822.3.R67   1988   952.03'1'0924 [B]   87-31053
ISBN 0-674-57641-1 (alk. paper)

Photographs on title-page spread
top left, Lafcadio Hearn
bottom left, William Elliot Griffis
right, Edward S. Morse

For Sakura

You lived it too

Contents

Five: REMEMBERING

Prologue:
Who and Why

The purpose of all interpretation is to conquer a remoteness, a distance between the past cultural epoch and the interpreter himself. By overcoming this distance . . . the exegete can appropriate its meaning to himself; foreign, he makes it familiar, that is, he makes it his own. It is thus the growth of his own understanding of himself that he pursues through his understanding of the other.

—PAUL RICOEUR, *The Conflict of Interpretations*

The historian can claim a voice in the contemporary cultural dialogue only in so far as he takes seriously the kind of questions that the art and science "of his own time" demand that he asks of the materials he has chosen to study . . . when many contemporary historians speak of the "art" of history, they seem to have in mind a conception of art that would admit little more than the nineteenth century novel as a paradigm.

—HAYDEN WHITE, "The Burden of History"

This is a book about the American encounter with Japan. About Americans who have lived in Japan. About three Americans who chose to work in Japan and whose lives were altered greatly by that choice, often in ways they did not fully understand. Few people in the United States now recognize their names, but in their own time—the late nineteenth and early twentieth centuries—William Elliot Griffis, Edward S. Morse, and Lafcadio Hearn were widely known as experts on Japan, acclaimed for their articles and books on the history, society, politics, and culture of that nation. Were they alive now, we would call them Japan-hands or Japanologists, and interviewers would seek their opinions as to why the Japanese are currently beating us so badly in the great trade wars of the late twentieth century. And though they mostly knew that nation in its preindustrial state, they would be able to provide more useful answers, I suspect, than most of those we get from current pundits.

In Japan, Griffis, Morse, and Hearn are remembered in much the way we view the Marquis de Lafayette or Baron Kosciusko, foreigners who aided the nation at a crucial period of history. The three are part of a much larger group of foreigners who are doubly honored as people who both helped in the process of modernization and were sensitive enough to recognize and promote the values of traditional Japan. For their efforts, each has been memorialized in a variety of ways. In Fukui, where he was a teacher in what was then a feudal realm, you can find a stone monument to Griffis, and artifacts and photos from his era are a highlight of the Municipal Museum. In Matsue, where Hearn married, taught, and wrote, his house is now a kind of shrine, and next to it stands a museum dedicated to his life and work. At Tokyo University and throughout Japanese academia, Morse is remembered as the mentor of Japan's first generation of life scientists, the man who brought the teachings of Darwin to Japan, the creator of the first museum of natural history, the leader of the first archeological dig, and the inspiration for the nation's first academic press.

By contrast, few in the United States ever hear of them. Graduate students and professors of Japanese studies may occasionally mention Griffis. Or do a few days of research in the rich collection of his papers—fifty-two boxes and twenty-eight scrapbooks—at the Rutgers University library. Or refer to *The Mikado's Empire*, the best of his ten volumes on Japan, without always acknowledging the fact that for many decades it was considered the best single interpretation of Japan by an American. People with an interest in the domestic architecture and crafts are likely to come across Morse's *Japanese Homes and Their Surroundings*. But how many who find their way to the Peabody Museum in Salem to see the enormous assemblage of Edo period folk arts know that they were collected by Morse? And how many people make the necessary advance reservation at the Museum of Fine Arts in Boston that will allow them into that dimly lit attic with its display of five thousand pieces of Japanese pottery—once boasted of as the finest collection in the world—that Morse so laboriously purchased and catalogued? Of the three, Hearn may be the best known, for teachers of literature and casual readers still occasionally succumb to the spell of the gossamer world of *Glimpses of Unfamiliar Japan*, or one of the other twelve volumes he produced. But to do so is to admit to a distinctly unfashionable taste for the precious, the exotic, the anachronistic, the Orientalist.

In telling the stories of Griffis, Morse, and Hearn, I take an opposite approach from that of most works about Westerners in nineteenth-century Japan. My aim is not to show how We changed Them by bringing the benefits of technology and republican institutions, but how They taught Us in ways much less easy to specify. Using this theme as a focus, I want to recapture the meaning that these three lives still have for us. Certainly the process in which Griffis, Morse, and Hearn were involved, that of living in and attempting to understand another culture, is in our late-twentieth-century world more important than ever. Surely today we are still deeply concerned with the questions of what and how we can learn from other traditions.

History, itself, can be seen as one of those other traditions. This means that like all works of history, this book is also about the present. About the concerns of the author who wrote it. About his relationship to the story he tells. About yours to the story you read. It is a book that explores the consequences of living in Japan in part because the author had something of the same experience himself, if a hundred years later than his subjects. It is a book about the search for continuities between then and now. A recognition of how past and present always interpenetrate. An act of reconstruction and representation. And an attempt, like all interpretive acts, to pursue an understanding of oneself and one's own world through an understanding of the lives and worlds of others.

The quotation from Paul Ricoeur and its companion from Hayden White are used to help suggest the way this book creates its world. They situate my endeavor as one touched by many of the theoretical issues that today stir the realm of criticism. Part of my aim is to break with some of the conventions of narrative history, to move beyond the "realistic" nineteenth-century novel as a paradigm for the historian's "art." To do this is to raise questions about historical narrative and modes of representation that have been acknowledged by some historians in theory but have yet to touch the way history is conceived or written. My purpose is to raise such questions not in a theoretical way, but within a narrative.

This goal accounts for certain aspects of the book which will not shock any reader of modern novels, but may seem odd to some academic historians—the use of different voices; the montages and moving camera and quick takes; the direct address to readers and characters; and the self-reflexive moments. These methods originated as part of an effort to render as fully as possible my encounter with the subject of Americans encountering Japan. Some of them will, no doubt, seem familiar. The notion of writing as a motion-picture camera is hardly new. My own use of it arose from the startling recognition that I could visualize scenes that included samurai only in terms of Japanese historical films—and that such films have been highly important in determining how I (and no doubt most other Westerners, and perhaps Japanese) see and therefore understand that warrior class. Yet the filmic metaphor does more than acknowledge the historian's debt to the visual media. Motion pictures have given us the notion of quick takes; short, disconnected scenes that by image and juxtaposition can make a point more quickly and in a different way than an extended explanation. Using the word as camera also is a way of focusing on details of landscape, building, and artifact as if in close-up, which helps underscore an implicit theme of the book: that the visual impact of Japan, the very shapes and colors of that visual culture, were a major part of the experience that helped to alter the beliefs, ideas, careers, and lives of my subjects.

The occasional use of a reflexive mode may, to some readers, seem strange in a work of history, with its supposedly objective, third-person view of the past. Yet historical works, for all their "objective" research methods, are also a record of a subjective encounter between human beings and the residues of the past. When a character named "the biographer" enters this work to reflect on the problems of creating his narrative, or the gaps in the historical record, or the dull and repetitive and obdurately uncommunicative nature of the diaries and letters he must for the sake of historical completeness read, the intent is to open out the world of the narrative; to break its ostensible "realism" by highlighting the constructed nature of this or any historical effort; to underline that all such encounters—the historian with the past, or the reader with this text—must of necessity include an act of interpretation.

Another way to call conventions into question is to use the second-person form of address. Within this book you will meet a kind of floating "you"—a "you" which may be the author directly addressing the reader, or talking to one of his characters, or mulling over the problems of writing the book which you are reading, or doing more than one of these things at the same time. The ambiguity is intentional, a conscious questioning of an often spurious clarity claimed by some historical narratives. At the same time, this "you" allows me to collapse some of the rigid distinctions that mark historical narrative; distinctions between past and present, and between author, character, and reader; distinctions which suggest that history is a one-way street, the imparting of knowledge from an author down to a reader, rather than a meeting in which the realities of both become implicated and enmeshed with notions of the past.

These narrative methods are no doubt overdetermined, a result of personal history and taste, the problems of rendering the subject at hand (how to express the wordless otherness of Japan), and disciplinary concerns—a recognition that although history has in recent years enormously expanded its boundaries of research, it has remained stuck with a model of representation well over a century old. My goal has involved a simultaneous attempt to do a number of things—to make a history which is more conscious of itself as an artifact, more ambiguous and open-ended; to introduce a reflexive note into narrative, one which points to the structural problems of the story being narrated; to achieve the density, specificity, and ease of temporal movement of a novel without sacrificing the integrity of data on which any work of history must be based; to create, in short, a piece of historical writing suited to the literary sensibility of at least the middle, if not the late twentieth century. Surely all who are interested in the past have a stake in this experiment, or in any such effort to extend the representational possibilities of the history we both write and live.

Mirror in the Shrine

Quotations are in italic. They are taken from the published and unpublished writings of the main subject of the chapter in which they appear, unless another source is indicated in the text. Sources of all quotations appear in the Notes. For ease of reading, diacritical marks on transliterated Japanese words have been omitted.

Before

It is because the Far-East holds up the mirror to our civilization,—a mirror that like all mirrors gives us back left for
right,—because by her very oddities, as they strike us at first,
we truly learn to criticize, examine, and realize our own way
of doing things, that she is so interesting. It is in this that her
great attraction lies. It is for this that men have gone to Japan
intending to stay weeks, and have tarried years.

—PERCIVAL LOWELL, *Choson*

How and where to begin? With the personal or the historical?
The history or the historian? With Townsend Harris standing in
front of the temple of Gyokuzenji in the fishing village of Kakisaki
late on the afternoon of Thursday, September 4, 1856? Or with
the author at the rail of the S.S. *Philippine Mail* in Yokohama
Harbor on the rainy morning of September 16, 1974? Harris
looks at Shimoda Bay, circled by pointed hills that resemble
breasts (and are called just that in Japanese), watches the steam
frigate *San Jacinto* dip its flag in salute and then steam away
towards the open sea. The author gazes at a misty world of gray
docks, trucks, forklifts, and giant cranes, and laments (to himself)
the quick destruction of that cherished travel-poster image of
Mount Fuji, snow-covered cone against a blue sky, framed by
branches shimmering with cherry blossoms. Harris goes inside the
temple—his new home—and turns to the journal where just a few
days before he noted in triumph: *I shall be the first agent from a
civilized power to reside in Japan.* Now his mood is more sober:
*Grim reflections—ominous of change—Undoubted beginning of
the end. Query,—if for the real good of Japan?*

1

I do not encounter these words until sometime in late 1975, after returning home from a year of teaching at two Japanese universities. Reading Harris's journal was part of a larger undertaking. From the very first day back in the United States, a sense of discontent, uneasiness, and dislocation had gripped me. Home did not look or feel the same as it did before this sojourn in Asia. Nor were my feelings the same as when I had returned from earlier years spent abroad in Western Europe. Something strange had happened to me in Japan, and in an attempt to understand what it was, to learn why my eyes and mind had apparently been altered and my own culture made to feel more than a bit alien, I turned (like a good academic) to my own discipline, history, and began to delve into writings by and about other Americans who had lived there before me. Harris seemed particularly important because he was the first American to reside in Japan legally. Those who preceded him—some shipwrecked sailors, a group who jumped ship from a whaler, and Ranald Macdonald, the half-Chinook who got himself to Hokkaido in 1848 in the belief that American Indians had originated in Japan—were not exactly residents. All were taken prisoner by government authorities, sent off to Nagasaki, and held until they could be shipped out on Dutch vessels from Deshima, the sole Western trading post in the land during Japan's 250 years of self-imposed seclusion.

Working in lonely and difficult conditions, Harris negotiated an agreement on trade that made access to Japan easier for all who followed him. And follow they did. During the remainder of the nineteenth century, some two thousand Americans came to live in this newly opened ancient land: merchants looking for profits; missionaries wanting to convert the heathen; and o-yatoi, foreign helpers—teachers of English, engineers, scientists, doctors, attorneys, military advisers, agricultural and business specialists—hired by the Japanese government to help with the process of acquiring Western civilization. All, or all who left significant records of their stay, were quite certain that the science, technology, government institutions, and morals of their own tradition were far superior to those of any Asian land.

To read the articles and books, diaries, journals and letters of these men and women was to enter a land in which the physical landscape, especially of urban areas, was vastly different, but the human landscape—the social, religious, and aesthetic attitudes and behavior patterns of the people—surprisingly similar to the Japan in which I had resided. The discoveries, the wonders, the joys, the difficulties, the beauties, and the misunderstandings I had experienced as a teacher and traveler had been experienced in much the same way by my predecessors a century ago. Despite their persistent feelings of cultural superiority, a goodly number of these early sojourners had—though this was usually phrased indirectly—been disturbed by the same questions that troubled Harris: Were their skills, values, or ideas really good for this ancient culture? Might they not be destroying something of value by introducing modern ideas and practices? The reverse question, the one which interested me more, the question not of what we do to another culture but of what it does to us, did not seem to be part of their consciousness. At least none of them ever rendered it into words.

No wonder. This kind of question is likely to arise only in a self-conscious age, among self-reflective (and reflexive) people, and nineteenth-century Americans—especially the kind who sought careers in Japan—were anything but that. Obviously my question was both a modern and a personal one; but after several years back in America, and after much reading by and about my predecessors, it began to seem a social question as well. Was there not, I wondered, some challenge—one that, by living there, I had obviously internalized—which Japan (and perhaps Asia at large) was issuing to American (and Western) culture? Would it not be possible to launch a powerful critique of the West from the perspective and premises of Japanese culture? And might not such a critique address the many issues that our own modern critical tradition seemed to me to fumble or ignore?—the importance in human life of aesthetics, faith, morals, manners, harmony; the possibility of finding human fulfillment, even happiness, within the confines of a hierarchical, even repressive, social order.

Somewhere between my questions and wishes, my continuing view of America in part through the eyes of another culture, and my ongoing research into the lives of Americans who had lived and worked in Japan, this book was born. Because I am a historian, it is set in the past, among the first generation of Western sojourners in Japan, when the cultural contrasts were most stark and clear. Because I am no theoretician, but someone who likes to tell stories set in the past, and who believes that the openness and ambiguity of a story is the best method for attempting to represent the complexity of human experience, this work is a narrative. Because I wished to deal with the most subtle shifts in perceptions, attitudes, and world views, the book takes the form of biography, or, to be more accurate, three biographical tales that highlight the Japanese experience of their protagonists.

These three men—the missionary William Elliot Griffis, the scientist Edward S. Morse, and the writer Lafcadio Hearn—were hardly chosen at random. I selected them to represent different parts of the American sensibility, and their stories to highlight different aspects of the American encounter with Japan. Though all three were well-known Japan experts in the latter half of the nineteenth and the first decades of the twentieth century, and though they read each other's books, they never met in person. Their relationship within the covers of this book—indeed, their very lives as recounted here—may be seen as beginning in the mind and words of the historian.

This book itself—where does it begin? At so many times and places: with the author sitting at his desk, green Fulbright Fellowship forms before him, deciding to write *Japan* rather than *Italy* in the space that says *Country of First Choice*. In Kyoto at the historic Tawaraya Inn, with its wooden tubs, dark corridors, serving-women in kimono, and exquisite flower arrangements, all out of a historical film by Kurosawa. At the famed rock garden of Ryoanji, where attempts at contemplation are interrupted by a shrill, amplified voice, explaining in detail that the garden is inexplicable. During a delicious dinner prepared with great delicacy by three huge and bashful sumo wrestlers. On visits to dozens (hundreds! thousands!) of temples, shrines, castles, cemeteries, pottery villages, and sushi bars—where, even though I was obviously relishing the food, someone always asks "Do you like raw fish?" At a performance of Noh, when boredom at the slow pace turns suddenly into a powerful feeling of love for an entire culture. On a midwinter day in a coffee shop when two bulky, hairy creatures push through the door and I draw back in momentary horror before realizing that they are nothing but bearded fellow Americans. While standing on a railway platform, shivering with memories of World War II movies as a hundred voices join to shout *Banzai! Banzai! Banzai!* Or looking from the window of a bullet train as it rockets away from a platform and seeing students, colleagues, and friends vanish in a blur of tears. Or at that instant five years later when, after so many worries, fears, and doubts, and after more than a few false starts, I finally sit down at the desk and type the name of the sacred mountain that I still have never seen.

One

LANDING

I reach the altar, gropingly, unable yet to distinguish forms clearly. But the priest, sliding back screen after screen, pours in light upon the gilded brasses and the inscriptions; and I look for the image of the Deity or presiding Spirit between the altar groups of convoluted candelabra. And I see—only a mirror, a round pale disk of polished metal, and my own face therein . . .

—LAFCADIO HEARN, "My First Day in the Orient"

1

Seductive Temptations

Mount Fuji. There it is. So pure, so startling, so white with snow. Just the way it looks in all the pictures. Surely it demands a response from William Elliot Griffis as he stands at the rail of the S.S. *Great Republic* on that chill morning of December 29, 1870, his eyes full of things both familiar and alien—fishing boats with odd-shaped sails; thatched huts sagging along beaches; a rolling countryside quilted with rice paddies; ranges of hills; and soaring above everything else that splendid cone, that image of perfection glowing in the rosy light of dawn. Such a powerful vision must be named, described, rendered into Christian terms. Japanese deity the mountain may be, but then (or later) it becomes a *fitting temple of the Creator's architecture*, a mighty signpost for His children to admire *while their hearts pour out in gratitude for kindly guidance through the perils of the deep.*

On placid waters the ship steams past inlets, and outcroppings of rock, and jutting green headlands named, with casual Western arrogance, Webster Isle, Cape Saratoga, Treaty Point, Reception Bay. In Yokohama Harbor the sky bristles with the masts of junks and sampans, and the water is thronged with steamers from the ports of Shanghai, Hong Kong, Marseilles, Southampton, and Rotterdam, and warships flying the flags of Great Britain, France, Holland, Prussia, and the United States. The shoreline shows no impressive docks, imposing warehouses, or tall structures. Only small breakwaters, and behind them a spread of low buildings framed by hills thick with greenery.

Excitement. Wonder. Disbelief. Those must be the feelings, but words can hardly capture the sensations that belong to Griffis as the engines fall silent, the great side paddle wheels stop churning, and—after four weeks of shuddering, rolling, and creaking—the ship lies still in the water. Small boats surround the *Great Republic*, and well-dressed Europeans swarm onto the decks and into plush salons, looking for friends and business associates, giving advice on hotels, asking for news. Are the Germans and French still at war? Are the British and Russians about to declare one? Among the visitors, no females are in evidence, save for those few *fancy creatures in velvet and diamonds, with gold on their fingers and brass in their faces . . . on board to see if any of their guild had arrived from San Francisco.*

The descent to the gangplank leads through steerage, a realm of close-packed Chinese passengers where local merchants do a brisk business in fish, mandarin oranges, dried persimmons, and huge brown bottles of *sake*. From the lower deck, Westerners get a first good look at the native workers, standing in punts—small, muscular men clad in the *clothing mother Nature provides for her children*, with only a tiny loincloth for protection. Like Venetian gondoliers, two of them work a scull in the stern of the shallow craft that skims across the harbor to shore, where a short flight of stone steps leads up into a customs shed. Forty-four days after saying goodbye to friends and family in Philadelphia, Griffis sets foot on the soil of what for the next half century he will call *The Mikado's Empire.*

<>

Yokohama is not quite that. To land there in 1870 is to enter a place in but not wholly of Japan, a little bit of the Western world grafted onto the edge of Asia. Hastily constructed in 1859 as the first of the nation's ports open to world trade, Yokohama is a boom town, the scene of solid investment and high-risk enterprise, of major European trading agencies and shady firms that spring up one week and vanish the next. Fifteen hundred Westerners, three thousand Chinese, and twenty-five thousand natives call it home, and the population continues to grow. The original plan— a two-square-mile rectangle bounded by rivers and canals meant to isolate the foreigners from the rest of the nation—has already been abandoned. No longer do Japanese soldiers guard the bridges over the waterways, and many people, both foreign and native, reside in valleys and hills beyond them. Now the only troops to be seen are from British and French battalions, here to ensure the extraterritorial rights of all Europeans.

Like any treaty port in Asia, Yokohama is a meeting place for merchants, sailors, missionaries, drifters, adventurers, and globe-trotters from a score of nations. The city boasts four newspapers; two hospitals (British and American); three churches (Episcopal, French Catholic, and Union Protestant); a Public Garden; a Men's Club; a race course; a cricket field; and a theater, the Gaiety, used more for charity bazaars and boxing matches than for stage productions. In the lively streets, Westerners mingle with a variety of natives: vendors, jugglers, samurai, farmers, girls in bright kimono, many of them drawn from Tokyo or even farther points to do business, shop, and observe the odd behavior of the foreigners who have torn their nation from seclusion.

Business, pleasure, and curiosity may bring a cosmopolitan population together in Yokohama, but only in public. Private life, like the arrangement of the city quarters, remains largely segregated. To the left of the customs building lies the Settlement. Facing the harbor across a stone Bund (embankment) are the rambling structures of important Western commercial companies, along with two fine hotels, the International and the Grand. Behind them, on streets plotted at right angles, stand homes set behind iron fences, stone-fronted banks, restaurants, barber shops, livery stables, warehouses, and auction rooms. The best stores, clustered along—what else?—Main Street, reveal through glass windows a variety of products: watches, dresses, suits, shoes, and sewing machines. Farther back, on a patch of land reclaimed from swamp, are the lanes of Chinatown, jammed with stalls selling fruit, vegetables, and herbs.

To the right of the customs shed lies the native town. No stone or brick here, no fenced yards, or plate glass windows, but two-story wooden structures with sliding panels that open the lower floors to the world. On broad Honcho-dori (*Curio Street* in the guidebooks), bargains in silk, painted scrolls, lacquerware, porcelain, baskets, carved dolls, paper fans, bronzes, and ivory-inlaid cabinets are displayed on platforms covered with soft white mats. Nearby is the most famous and infamous of institutions: the licensed pleasure quarter, Miyosaki. In the tea shops and restaurants of this district, young women can be hired to play the *koto* or *samisen*, to dance and sing and entertain men in more intimate ways. Most celebrated of all Yokohama's establishments is the Gankiro, an elegant house complete with fish pond, red lacquer bridges, wide balconies, and large banquet halls. Its aim is the foreign trade; its prices are three times those of similar places catering to Japanese.

<>

Twenty-seven-year-old Willie Griffis—part missionary, part teacher, part opportunist—is not the sort either to ignore or to sample such fleshly pleasures. A just-completed year of study at Rutgers Theological Seminary has strengthened his moral and religious convictions without either banishing a taste for attractive women or blinding an eye always open to economic opportunity. Griffis is on the way to a teaching position in Fukui, capital of the feudal domain of Echizen, at a salary so large that he expects to save a good deal of money. Brimming with literary ambition, he is already full of plans for articles and books on the oddities of this little-known empire. Cautious, too, and well aware that conservative samurai occasionally use their swords on foreign *barbarians*, Willie has a small Smith and Wesson revolver tucked into a pocket of his coat.

Intruding barbarians have good and rational reasons for being here: Japan needs the commerce, the science, the Western languages, the true religion of a tradition with *treasures of knowledge and wisdom higher* than Asia can provide. This last point is a bit sticky, for the government has yet to repeal a 250-year-old ban on the preaching and practice of Christianity. So Griffis must be prepared to be subversive, not just to teach but also to show—surreptitiously—how progress in industry, commerce, technology, medicine, and government are intimately connected to the spiritual values of Western civilization. That is the way to soften up the natives, to help Christianity spread among them like a *silent conquering force.*

That the need is great cannot be doubted. A *land of seductive temptations of the most fearful sort*, Japan has thirty million souls who desperately need to be educated and saved. That this is no simple task begins to become apparent to Griffis shortly after he leaves the customs office. For the next four days he sleeps in the homes of missionaries; dines, prays, and strolls the streets with them; tags along to New Year's receptions at four Western consulates; and delivers a Sunday sermon in the Union Church. From breakfast until bedtime each day, he listens to the small triumphs and large complaints of these men and women who seem hungry for a sympathetic audience.

The situation of Protestantism in Japan is not at all what Griffis imagined. The view from America made missionaries appear to be exalted beings, but here in Yokohama they seem, at least in their own eyes, more like a *neglected set of peculiar people*. Leaders of local society, Griffis is told, those prosperous merchants and professionals who live in large, elegant homes up on the hilly area known as the Bluff, scorn the missionary endeavor. Far too few Westerners attend church; far too many take economic advantage of the locals; and some act with a most un-Christian brutality, beating, kicking, and blaspheming the native servants. Worse yet is the behavior of the soldiers, sailors, and drifters who carouse, gamble, and brawl in the grog shops and taverns of Blood Town. Add to this the number of tourists who flock to the Miyosaki district, and the foreigners who live openly with native concubines, and you have disturbing hints that the presence of the West here is tinged with ambiguity, and the light of progressive social change shadowed with darkness.

<>

January 3, 1871. The Yankee ready to invade the *Land of the Gods*. A frosty day, the air keen as a razor—Willie's pocket thermometer reads twenty-eight degrees Fahrenheit. The colors of the morning are sharp, painful: *Blue sky, blue water, blue mountains, white Fuji*. On the Bund waits a stagecoach, two restless ponies in harness. Cost to the capital city: two Mexican silver dollars. Estimated travel time: two and a half hours. The huge Australian on the driver's bench cracks his whip and off they rattle along the waterfront, turning right at the British Consulate and then heading along Benten-dori into the native quarter. Shop-boys raise curtains on storefronts. Bathhouses overflow with people. And there, nonchalant as if on a Sunday stroll, goes a man *naked as when he stepped out into the world. His copper hue, like a lobster's, is intensified by the boiling he has just undergone. He walks in a self-exhaling cloud of auroral vapors, like a god in ambrosia. He deigns not to make his toilet while in sight, but proceeds homeward, clothes in hand.*

Rumbling over the nation's first iron bridge, the coach speeds toward the Tokaido, the high road that joins Kyoto and Tokyo. Europe lies behind them now—ahead is the *real Japan.* How much it seems like *a wonderful picture book;* how it makes him want *to be a poet to express it, and an artist to paint all I see*—the tiny villages strung along the road; the weathered houses, shutters open, where families devour bowls of rice; the groups of youngsters at play; the women with rosy-cheeked babies strapped to their backs; the priests with shaved heads; the laborers with bare legs; the samurai, hair in lacquered topknots; the pilgrims, clad entirely in white; the beggars, young and old, dirty, ragged, and covered with sores.

Kanagawa slows the coach to a walk. Where in this *flourishing* town are the *splendid stores,* where the wealth that Griffis expects to find in the Orient? Not here, in these poor streets full of fish and vegetable stalls and shops displaying umbrellas, straw hats, grass cloaks, knives, and tools. Better to forget such preconceptions. Better to enjoy the scenery as the vehicle climbs into hills, then dashes along a *splendid road beneath an arch of pines* to a stop at a teahouse for refreshments. For the horses, water; for the driver, brandy from a flask; for the travelers, tea and sweetmeats carried by pretty girls who come forward with downcast glances and softly voice a word of greeting: *Ohayo.* Stunned by a pair of dark eyes, Willie places a tip on the tray *for beauty's sake.* This brief encounter is memorable, worthy of description, of generalization. Three years later he will write: *The maid is about seventeen, graceful in figure, and her neat dress is bound with a wide girdle and tied into a huge bow behind. Her neck is powdered. Her laugh displays a row of superb white teeth, and her jet-black hair is rolled in a maidenly style. The fairest sight in Japan are Japan's fair daughters.*

Deep bows and cries of *Sayonara* send the coach onward, past thatched villages where iris blazes purple along the ridgepoles. Instead of neat Pennsylvania fields of winter wheat, the eye encounters an endless series of muddy rice fields, vast ditches edged by dark stands of pine and the bright green of bamboo. At Kawasaki, where they stop to await a flat-bottomed boat, a yet unused railway bridge spans a shallow river. Griffis goes into a warming hut and a dozen ill-clad *coolies* step back to allow him access to the fire. How considerate they are, how polite for men who lack schooling, political freedom, or the true faith. Yet never forget a fundamental fact: here in Asia a man is no more than *a wheelbarrow, a beast of burden, a political cipher, a being who exists for the sake of his masters or the government.* At home *A man is a man.*

Beyond the river, paddies give way to villages and more villages, the far-flung suburbs of the capital. Just before the Shinagawa barrier, the coach passes an execution ground where, from a six-foot pole, the severed heads of two executed samurai stare coldly back at travelers. This ghastly welcome seems a fitting example of this despotic nation's *bloody code of edicts, misnamed laws, by which she terrifies her people into obedience.* Inside the great gates, a bright view of the vast spread of the city, its leafy hills and distant castle walls. There is Fuji once again, and the blue bay of Tokyo with its chain of tiny forts. And there, at anchor, the half dozen vessels of Japan's navy. Each floats the new national flag, a rising red sun on a white field, the symbol of a reborn nation whose growth Griffis hopes to speed.

<>

For six weeks Willie lives at the home of Guido Verbeck, head of Daigaku Nanko, Japan's first Western-style college. Like all of the school's twelve foreign teachers, this Dutch Reformed minister has a bungalow in a compound hidden behind *high and hideous* walls, just across a bridge from the old castle. So powerful is the initial impact of the city that for the entire first week the single word *Rambles* marks the pages of Griffis's journal. Not until January 13 does he begin to describe his activities—the mornings in Verbeck's library, where he studies Japanese; the hours given to tutoring students in English; the two weeks he substitutes at the college for a teacher who is ill; the afternoons he explores the crowded streets of this *wilderness of a million souls*, or lingers in the *monotonous and gloomy* grounds of the old castle. Griffis is an avid tourist. He rides on horseback into the suburbs to see temples, shrines, and gardens; visits Tokyo's first hospital and the Western school run by Fukuzawa Yukichi; watches the Emperor review his troops; attends a sumo wrestling match; and begins to turn what he has seen, done, and learned into articles for the *Christian Intelligencer*.

Even in this short period, the fresh can edge toward the routine, the unusual toward the common. If most of his daily moments quickly vanish, or blend too easily into that smooth narrative called memory, some images from those early days will retain their sharp edge of meaning for years. Picture Griffis as he later will see himself. At Nihonbashi, the humpbacked bridge from which all distances in the empire are measured, he shrinks away from *loathsome beggars* and mendicant priests who chant *doleful prayers*, and gazes at the *kosatsu*, the signboard of edicts whose mysterious (to him) characters proclaim, among other things, *The evil sect called Christian is strictly prohibited. Suspicious persons should be reported to the proper officers, and rewards will be given.* On a street lined with shops, he glimpses a girl sitting in an open window, washing her hair, and thinks, *the human form divine, bare to the waist.* At the end of a day at Daigaku Nanko he watches hundreds of young men thrust swords into sashes and stalk off carrying slates and copybooks in ink-stained hands. At the great temple of Kannon at Asakusa, he finds the atmosphere of a country fair—rows of curio shops, and refreshment booths, and hordes of people eating and drinking. *Religion and innocent pleasure join hands in Japan. Are the Japanese wrong in this?*

The pleasures of Tokyo do not keep Griffis from successfully bargaining with Echizen officials for a 50 percent increase in the salary so recently agreed to in America. A bilingual contract names him teacher of chemistry and natural philosophy at the Meishin-ken, or College at Fukui, for a three-year term at an annual salary of $3,600, and specifies that he will be provided a house *built in European style* and allowed to keep Sunday as a day of rest. To celebrate this agreement, Prince Matsudaira Shungaku, former ruler of the domain, hosts a banquet for Griffis and Verbeck in the feudal splendor of his Tokyo palace. In a room where the sliding screens are papered in silver and gold and covered with delicate paintings of cherry blossoms and graceful birds, they feast on a ten-course European meal complete with ale, sherry, claret, and champagne. The single jarring note is provided by two Japanese, who loudly slurp their soup and take occasional refreshing swallows from finger bowls.

Not all of Willie's daily moments are tasty, pleasant, or joyous. Fear hovers over horseback rides to suburban shrines, rambles through streets where no European faces are to be seen, formal dinners in the Western compound. It is impossible to forget that fifty foreigners have in the last decade fallen beneath the sword, or to ignore the rumors of plots, threats, and plans for uprisings that speed through the nervous capital of a government only two years in power. When encountered in the streets, bands of retainers for the *daimyo*, the great provincial lords, appear haughty, swaggering, insolent, and threatening enough to make Griffis feel for his pistol.

Fear becomes reality at 4 a.m. on Saturday, January 14, when a knock on the door rouses the household and brings a messenger with word that two English teachers have been cut down. Behind Verbeck and a servant carrying a lantern, Griffis hurries through a maze of dark streets and enters for the first time into a native house, its dim rooms hung with *emblems and tokens of Japanese religion, enjoyment, and superstition*. In the following days, he plays nurse to the wounded men and talks over the meaning of the assault with Verbeck until the older man's opinion becomes his own. Certainly it is a sad affair, but not much different from what regularly happens in the Five Points area of New York City. Besides, the victims are not entirely blameless. They were out past the curfew; they had dismissed their native guards; they were with prostitutes when the attack occured. Their actions must be seen as a kind of provocation, an instance of the sort of injustice foreigners regularly perpetrate here, part of a sad story that includes insolence, insult, and exploitation.

Such an insight—achieved or adopted—may hint at a new perspective on Japan, but does not touch Willie's belief system. Yet at the end of his stay in the capital, his usual judgments have become a bit confused, and some of them point in an unexpected direction. In six short weeks he has experienced *paganism, feudalism, earthquakes*; has seen *how long contact with heathen life and circumstances slowly disintegrates the granite principles of eternal right, once held by men raised in a more bracing moral atmosphere*; has met *scores of white men* who have *long since forgotten the difference between right and wrong*. Before leaving for the interior in mid-February, Griffis confesses that the foreign worker in Japan faces a serious problem: *For a man's own salvation of morals and as a surety of duty, it is almost absolutely necessary that he must be either a Christian or a married man.* Although he can take comfort in being one of these, there is little doubt Willie would prefer to be both.

2

Christian Virtues

A rush of pleasure. The swelling excitement of waking for the first time in Japan. Sharp images burst through the window, sharp feelings stab Edward S. Morse as he gazes from the Grand Hotel into a pale Yokohama morning. Outside lies a *world of delight*. Only the color of the sea, fading slowly from black to blue, the frigates and steamers in the harbor, and the trees on a nearby hill are familiar. Everything else in view is novel—the quaint shapes of native craft slipping down the narrow canal to the right; the people streaming by on the Bund, some in robes, some in loincloths, a few sporting an odd, jarring item of Western clothing—a pair of trousers, or boots, or a top hat; the line of rickshas, enormous baby carriages on tall wheels, waiting at the iron gates of the hotel. It all seems a marvelous birthday present. Today, June 18, 1877, he is thirty-nine years old.

Morse takes up a sketchbook. No artistic motive drives his pen, no desire to capture scenic views or to render the fullness of a moment. His passion is the small and practical. Neither darkness nor sea swell the night before could prevent him from making sketches of the curious oars and locks of the boat carrying passengers ashore. Now he concentrates on the primitive pile driver worked by eight laborers engaged in building a seawall at the entrance to the canal. They stand on a staging lashed together with rope and straw, join voices in an odd, monotonous chant, and, at the end of each stanza, tug mightily on ropes that connect through pulleys to a heavy weight which rises quickly and then

drops with a heavy thud. What a *waste of time to sing the chanty
. . . without exerting the slightest effort to raise the weight.* How
ridiculous to devote nine-tenths of the time not to labor but to
singing!

Wasting time is for others. A hurried breakfast and Morse is
off on a brisk walk into the native quarter. His first impressions
are strong, disorienting, pleasant: the odd architecture; the signs
with their suggestive characters; the sounds of the people; the
pervasive odors of tea and cedar; the sight of women nursing
babies in public; the use of men rather than beasts of burden to
drag carts. Attractive wares pull him into stores. No matter how
small the stock, no matter how poor the shop, there is no sense
of hurry. Morse sits on the edge of a platform while male and
female attendants bow, smile, bring forth cups of green tea, and
light up their pipes. Visible through wide-open panels are the
rooms where family members eat, drink, read, doze, or work in
domestic spaces that are startling in their emptiness: *No chairs,
table or other articles of furniture are seen, unless it might be a
case of drawers; no chimney, no stove, no attic, no cellar, no door
even, only sliding screens.*

An eye for detail pulls Morse onward. Every item for sale—
teacups, tools, curtains, fans, toys, ceramics, lacquerware, cakes—
seems a marvelous blend of design, decoration, and craftsmanship.
Soon his sense of time vanishes, for there is always another shop
to enter, another sketch to make, another cup of tea to drink. By
the time fatigue and hunger enter his consciousness, Morse is lost.
But not alone. A ricksha man, waved aside at the Grand Hotel,
has followed him all morning, gazed into the same shops, echoed
each smile and bow. Now the American, good democrat and
egalitarian, hesitates, experiences *a sense of humiliation* at the
idea that a human being is to be his horse. Aching feet conquer
scruples. Morse climbs into the frail vehicle and the barefoot,
barelegged, bareheaded man grasps the shafts and starts to run.
The pleasant up-and-down motion turns embarrassment to exhilaration. Dwellings, shops, restaurants, midday crowds flash by
*like various pictures we had seen on fans and . . . thought were
exaggerations.* By the time they reach the hotel, he is a convert to
this new mode of transportation: *You really travel at a good speed,*

your horse never runs away, and when you stop he guards your property.

<>

As a visitor to Yokohama, Ned Morse is an odd duck. Nobody invited him to Japan. No private organization or government agency on either side of the Pacific suggested the journey, arranged passage, or paid his way. Other Westerners arrive here in the seventies as tourists, teachers, technical experts, missionaries, or businessmen. Morse is none of these. His profession is science. So is his religion. He is a natural scientist, known equally well for undertakings scholarly and popular. On the lecture platform he can entertain audiences with stories about butterflies, birds, spiders, grizzly bears, glaciers, and redwood trees, but his research interests have long focused on a single animal. For fifteen years, on collecting and dredging expeditions from the Carolina coast to the Bay of Fundy, he has been on the track of minuscule mollusks called brachiopods. He has come here because of reports that Japanese waters contain many more varieties of these creatures than are known at home.

Morse is a Yankee, with the traits of the stereotype. Life for him is real and earnest, and its many forms are waiting to be studied, described, and classified. This means that a single day of sightseeing is enough. By June 19 he is itching to work. Access to a boat and to some kind of structure to house specimens are his only needs, yet in Japan such aims border on the quixotic. Here the study of natural science is unknown and the movements of visitors drastically circumscribed. Except for those in government employ, foreigners are restricted to within twenty miles of the treaty ports—Yokohama, Nagasaki, Kobe, and Hakodate—and forbidden to spend the night away from them. Only government permission will allow a Westerner to jaunt along the coast in search of a suitable site for a marine laboratory.

A fifty-minute train ride takes him to Tokyo to meet with David Murray, a Rutgers mathematician who serves as Japan's superintendent of educational affairs, and Tanaka Fujimaro, vice-minister of education. Their offices may have Western tables, chairs, and rugs, but the flavor is distinctly native. No American rooms would contain such spare arrangements of flowers, or earthenware vessels with live coals to use in lighting pipes or cigars. Nor would tea be brought before business can be discussed, and certainly never by a servant who bows so close to the floor. To talk with the minister, an interpreter is necessary. Conversation is slow, formal, and stiff, and yet oddly pleasant. Somehow the hushed tones of Japanese comfort Morse. Compliments on America and Japan flow back and forth and are punctuated by smiles, nods, and feelings of goodwill. But getting down to specifics proves to be impossible. Requests seem to vanish into a cloud of words, hazily affirmative and insubstantial. When it is time to go, Morse has received no direct answers to his questions about the possibilities of research.

No doubt Murray counsels patience, for Ned spends the next ten days shuttling between Yokohama and Tokyo, playing tourist. The train he rides is only one sign of Japan's rapid adoption of Western ways. Telegraph lines along highways, gas lamps in the streets, the occasional paved streets and brick buildings—all speak the pleasant word progress. So does the current political situation. In 1871 feudalism was abolished and the old domains turned into administrative prefectures, and just a year ago samurai were forbidden to wear swords. Assassination of Westerners is now a thing of the past, and if the several hundred foreigners in Tokyo must still reside in compounds, they at least no longer worry about walking the streets at night.

Political developments are of less concern to Morse than progress in science and technology. To pass the time, he seeks facts and figures on Japanese advances in sanitation, health, engineering, and education. Every scrap of evidence proclaiming the end of superstition and the advent of science is a joy. The sight of university students in kimono performing experiments in a chemical laboratory is one happy sign. So is the familiar clicking sound of American sewing machines, issuing from traditional houses. Most heartening is the attitude toward medicine, a realm in which people often cling tenaciously to traditional beliefs *no matter how crazy and idiotic*. The Japanese are different. They have dropped the old Chinese *medical cult* in favor of more *rational* practices, and in some aspects of public health are beginning to surpass

Western nations. At home one can still find *incredible idiots* who oppose vaccination for smallpox, while here the government is inoculating the entire population.

Change comes in a context. Even the practical Morse cannot wholly ignore history and tradition. Yet when not on the track of recent developments, he remains an idiosyncratic tourist who never purchases a guidebook to Yokohama or Tokyo (such volumes have been written by William E. Griffis) and neglects to visit popular places of interest like the tombs of Tokugawa Shoguns at Shiba or Ueno; or to climb Atagoyama for its view of the city and Mount Fuji; or to stop at Sengakuji, burial site of the famed forty-seven *ronin*. Temples, shrines, and gardens pull him less than sites of little concern to the average foreigner: a factory where tea is fired, the Yokohama fish and vegetable market. Often he simply strolls the streets, an inquisitive eye catching details of local life. Morse fills pages with offbeat information—he explains how night soil is collected and used as fertilizer; rhapsodizes over the design and durability of workmen's tools; lists the way chopsticks are skillfully wielded not only at mealtime, but in a variety of tasks and in many different sizes by jewelers, cooks, street cleaners, and ragpickers. This focus on the humble and practical is perfectly in character; his lifelong way of understanding the world has now shifted to the task of taming the experience of a foreign civilization.

<>

Four o'clock on the morning of June 29. Rickshas roll through the hushed streets of Tokyo; stars fade above curved roofs. Morse, Murray, and several other Westerners (their exact number and names never recorded in his notes) are off on a ten-day jaunt. With them go an interpreter from the Department of Education and two attendants to do the cooking, packing, lugging. The aim of the trip is sightseeing; the main destination, Nikko, with its great complex of shrines and temples surrounding the tomb of Tokugawa Ieyasu, unifier of the nation in 1600. Morse has other things in mind. Eighty pounds of equipment—insect nets, shell scoops, collecting bottles, specimen cases, small microscopes—are packed into one of the vehicles. If live sea creatures are currently out of reach, insects, ancient shells, and unusual plants will have to do instead.

For two days the weather is mild, the mosquitoes hungry, the movement in ricksha and horse-drawn wagon constant and jarring. Morse's eyes grow weary with too many sights: rice fields with workers in straw hats so broad they seem from a distance like *animated toadstools*; a landscape scattered with wooden *torii*, framing paths that lead to weatherbeaten shrines; a Buddhist temple, open as a pavilion, where a teacher stands before a blackboard covered with Chinese characters and Arabic numerals and reads aloud from a book to a crowd of students who repeat his words in a singsong drone; groups of blind girls, moving slowly along the road, plucking *samisen* and singing; rude countryfolk in village streets, concentrating over the stones and square boards of Go, a game *more complex* than chess. At rest stops, no matter how primitive the *tavern*, the walls are hung with scrolls of characters executed in bold calligraphy. Translations show these to be *proverbs, good precepts from the classics*, and *appeals to the beauty of nature*, all of *a high moral character*. How different from home, where similar places are decorated with pictures of *prize fighters, burlesque, horse races or naked women.*

At Hasha-ishi, a mountain town with wild forest pressing close, they sleep on the floor of an inn where two kerosene lamps in the room are the solitary sign of Western life. The wide balconies, the swept courtyards, dwarf pines, and stone lanterns here speak of a tradition that flowers in the complex of buildings and gardens of nearby Nikko. To visit there is one thing, to capture it in words or drawings something else again: *I must confess the utter inability of doing the slightest justice to the temples and tombs, so wonderful are they, so elaborate, so vast and magnificent.* Retreating from this glut of shape and color, from pagoda, carved roof, and ornamental gate, Morse turns to more familiar activities: he gathers frogs; he studies the webs of spiders; he pins moths and insects to a board. To judge from many detailed sketches, he also begins to take an interest in architecture. How restful the emptiness of the inn; how beautiful the unfinished wood; how tasteful the scroll in the *tokonoma* (alcove); how refined, discreet, and attractive the treatment of the latrine in the courtyard, a structure that *in a*

New England village usually forms an unsightly and conspicuous object.

From Hasha-ishi they climb on foot into boulder-strewn mountains where moss-covered stone Buddhas crumble along narrow paths. The oppressive afternoon heat is only made worse by the repeated cries of *atsui, atsui* from every passing traveler. At a spring in full view of a teahouse, they watch two girls bare their tops and slip into the water: *On discovering that we were looking at them, they shyly, but laughingly drew their dresses up again, having heard that foreigners consider such behavior immodest.* When they reach a two-mile-wide sheet of water named Lake Chuzenji, Morse undertakes a vain, afternoon-long search for living mollusks, then climbs the steep sides of Mount Nantai to a peak more than eight thousand feet above sea level. On the summit stands an ancient shrine, its open platform strewn with rusty coins, broken and corroded sword blades, and queues of hair, all offered to solemnize special vows. The mind of the nonbeliever is impressed, and even more so when he learns later that most mountains in the land have similar shrines: what *a wonderful conception*, what *devotion to their religion.* Admiration proves different from reverence: he cannot resist the temptation to take some sword fragments as souvenirs.

The way back to Tokyo is down through forest and meadowland, through waist-deep fields of blazing red azalea, through swarms of dragonflies, along paths alive with beetles shining in a rainbow of colors, across rickety bridges that span plunging streams. Alone in the countryside on the afternoon of July 4, Morse strips down to drawers and an undershirt, dons a broad straw hat to shade him from the fierce sun, goes into action with his butterfly net, and raises his voice over and over in "The Star-Spangled Banner." At Nowata, a wretched village where the children are dirty and the faces of the poverty-stricken adults coarse, Ned is pleased to find no *trace of brutality or maliciousness in their looks or any expression of haggard despair such as one sees in the slums of our great cities.*

One sequence in these days is well worth recording. Yumoto. A spa high in the mountains. The unpleasant smell of boiled egg, of sulfur hot springs. Along the street, the bathhouses, no more than rude sheds open at the side, where people of both sexes and all ages sit half a dozen to each wooden tub, sunk to their shoulders in steaming water. Enter two Americans, Murray and Morse, a vaudeville team bearing a thermometer. The pursuit of science never ceases. Water temperature?—ah, that is certainly worthy of study. So here they go. Morse leans over the tub, averts his eyes from the bathers, dips the thermometer into the water, and is startled to hear girlish voices saluting him with cries of *Ohayo.* He looks up, sees two young travelers encountered the day before, notes they are naked, notes they look *like little children,* and moves on to the next bathhouse to repeat the performance. Soon a crowd gathers, following the Americans from one bathhouse to another until the task is complete. Later, in his journal Morse will insist on the relativism of standards: *What would be immodest for us is not for them.* But nowhere in any of his notes does he report the temperature of that bathwater.

<>

Good news in Tokyo. The request to dredge for brachiopods has been answered with the startling proposal from the Ministry of Education that he accept a position as professor at Tokyo University, organize a Department of Zoology, and create a museum of natural history. For this he will be paid $4,200 a year and be provided with a house and a stable. The offer is too good to refuse, but that does not prevent a little bargaining to raise the salary to $5,000. Nor is this the end of potential benefits. Some are scientific, others financial, so closely mixed that in a letter home they run together: *I hope to get up lectures on Japan which will go like hot cakes, but above all I will have unparalleled facilities to study tropical life and shall make some important scientific contributions. Then I hope to write a book on Japan.*

Lectures on Japan. A book on Japan. Surely these are odd ideas for a scientist who has never before strayed in word or print from natural history. The decision to accept the job is certainly a rational one, an example of economic and professional self-interest; and surely there can be no doubt that this land presents a rare opportunity to exploit the exotic for financial gain. But something else is already at work here, something that involves the very nature of the things he wants to write about, the values they imply, the questions they raise, the feelings of discomfort and pleasure they arouse.

All this is to suggest that even as Ned has focused on science and progress, Japan has been impressing him with lessons in the practical, the aesthetic, the human values of its tradition. The beauty of line and color in pottery, baskets, and utensils, and the *exquisite taste* shown in homes and gardens, have served to highlight the overstuffed rooms, vulgar prints, gimcrack decorations, and bedraggled lawns at home. The clean seawalls of fishing villages, the immaculate houses of the poorest farm communities, the swept and well-watered streets of Tokyo have all brought to mind the heaps of clamshells, ashes, and rubbish that mark the outskirts of New England towns, including the *refined* community of Cambridge. The orderly, good-natured behavior of the audience at sumo wrestling matches has called up the image of rowdy, uncouth sports crowds at home, and the sight of ricksha men, smiling their apologies after collisions, has made him remember too many scenes of American cabmen shaking fists and hurling threats.

Such contrasts vibrate with hints and possibilities beyond the power of Morse to convey. He is no poet. His words can only be blunt: *Thus far in my few weeks in this country I have come in contact, with few exceptions, with the laboring classes—the farmers and working people—and yet what a record of sobriety, artistic taste and cleanliness it has been . . . A book might be written on . . . their honesty, frugality, politeness, cleanliness, and every virtue that in our country might be called Christian.* Now, with the new status of professor, he looks forward to sampling the way of life of *the higher classes.* But he cannot forget that it has been the common people who, in less than a month, have taught him a most sobering lesson: *Little by little the realization of why the Japanese have always called us barbarians is dawning upon us.*

3

Demons and Gods

Elfish. Everything, everybody, small, queer, mysterious. Little houses under blue tile roofs, little shop fronts hung with blue curtains, little people in blue costumes, funny little streets. The image of *fairy-land* comes to mind. So hackneyed, the worn-out view of every globetrotter, every second-rate journalist who has ever done Yokohama for a day. Lafcadio Hearn knows this, but cannot help himself. In the cozy, swaying ricksha, viewing the world over the bobbing mushroom of his runner's hat, he cannot banish storybook language. Better to make a virtue of necessity, to forget any sense of personal vision, and to insist that cliché is reality. So say it. Here is a realm in which everything is daintier than at home, one whose people seem kindlier and gentler, one where movement is slow and soft and voices hushed. Land, sky, and life are so unlike what one has known that this is *surely the realization . . . of the old dream of a World of Elves.*

The day helps. April 4, 1890, is full of the sweetness of spring. Pleasant sun, cool air, limpid sky. Every object, distant and close, appears in sharp focus. Chinese characters, full of hidden messages, dance across signboards, doorposts, shop curtains, paper screens. Beauty greets the eye even in the tiniest of objects: a decorated paper bag holding a pair of chopsticks; a package of toothpicks, bound in a wrapper lettered in three colors; a sky-blue towel with a design of flying sparrows, used by the ricksha man to wipe his face. Inside every shop, the wares seem enchanted. But cheap as they are, Hearn dares not begin to buy. His appetite is too great. What he wishes is not a single item, but a store full. And more than that: he wants the shop and its owner, the whole street, the city and bay, the mountains, the land and its people. He wishes to purchase the moment, put it in a box, wrap it up neatly and keep it inviolate forever.

To sink into tradition is Hearn's aim. He can accept the signs of modern life—the white telegraph poles, the sewing machine store, the photography studios—as Occidental innovations *set into an Oriental frame*, but his desire is for something older. *Tera e yuke* are the words to make the runner plunge between rows of ark-shaped houses, across a canal and to the foot of a steep hill with an immense flight of stone steps. Halfway up, Hearn rests on a terrace with a huge gate, where dragons swarm in carved stone beneath a tilted Chinese roof. At the top there is a second gate, then a low, wooden building flanked by stone lions. Shoes off. A young priest bows him inside. Dim light, soft matting underfoot, the sweet smell of incense. At the far end of a large, square room, a high, dark altar glows softly with the shapes of unfamiliar metal objects. But where is the image of Buddha? In halting English the priest explains that the temple's statue is shown only on festival days. A disappointed Hearn makes an offering anyway, over the polite demurral of the priest, makes it though he admits to being neither Christian nor Buddhist, but only one who reveres *the beauty of* [Buddha's] *teaching, and the faith of those who follow it.*

The day of sightseeing grows long, with visits to sacred spots on hilltops from which one can look down on Yokohama Bay, speckled with sails, and see Mount Fuji in a flawless sky. Towering *torii*, colossal models *of some beautiful Chinese letter*, lead to shrines surrounded by gardens that dazzle with the white mist of cherry blossoms; to miniature landscapes with groves of dwarfed trees and tiny lakes; and to occasional hints of other tourists in the form of signs in English warning *It is forbidden to injure the trees.* Late in the afternoon he rides along Mississippi Bay, where natives gather sea creatures from a gleaming low-tide landscape. The last flight of steps is so long and steep that his leg muscles are aching when he reaches the top. In a small, gray building, Hearn gropes toward the altar and finds himself looking into a mirror, a round polished disc of metal that gives back the reflection of his face. He is much too literary not to recognize it as a symbol. But of what? *Illusion? or that the Universe exists for us solely as the reflection of our souls? or the old Chinese teaching that we must seek the Buddha only in our own hearts?* Later, he claims, the mirror mocks him, leads him to a thought that—however meaningful—certainly will also look good in print: *I am beginning to wonder whether I shall ever be able to discover that which I seek—outside of myself!*

<>

Lafcadio Hearn specializes in unanswerable questions. An odd mixture of the romantic and the practical, he is a man who, two months short of his fortieth birthday, views himself as *a creature of circumstances*, a person who drifts *with various forces in the direction of least resistance*. Like any such characterization, this one contains a blend of insight and self-deception. In the last twenty years he has lived in Cincinnati, New Orleans, Martinique, Philadelphia, and New York, and has supported himself by working for half a dozen newspapers. But these moves seem less the result of drift than of inner drive, a desire to find and capture something that can never quite be put into words. Easy it is to see Hearn—and many have—as a restless wanderer, a seeker of the exotic, but this is only the most visible part of his story. He is also a man in search of some thing or place or person that will make him feel at home.

Writing is the activity that gives meaning to his days. That was one of the reasons for the many moves; that is what brings him to Japan. In the last couple of years, Hearn has begun to achieve national recognition. Critics have linked him with authors like Joel Chandler Harris and George Washington Cable as part of an important movement in Southern literature, and William Dean Howells, America's leading novelist, has hailed him as a literary force. That judgment has recently been confirmed with the publication of a novel and a book of essays, both reflecting his two years in Martinique. Indeed, the promise of these works made an editor at Harper's suggest the trip to Japan. Lafcadio was ready. An interest in Oriental culture had been his for a long time. So had a desire to travel to the East.

From the first moments in this land that reeks with charm *intangible and volatile as a perfume*, Hearn knows Japan to be at once a perfect and a difficult place for him. The problem is familiar: his artistic and practical goals are at odds. His ambition is no simple travel book but a volume that will describe Japanese life from the inside, as if by someone *taking part in the daily existence of the common people, and thinking with their thoughts.* This implies a detailed study of the language and a stay long enough to steep himself in the customs, beliefs, folkways, and habits of the natives. But Yokohama is as expensive as New York; his money supply is limited; and he will receive no pay from Harper's until he produces acceptable work. To accomplish his larger goal, there is no way around the unpleasant fact that he will have to find a job.

A few days after landing, he knows that the most likely employment will be as a teacher of English. The language, one of Japan's windows into the Western world, is required at all levels of the educational system, and native speakers are in demand. A letter of introduction written by a Harper's editor brings him into contact with Basil Hall Chamberlain, an English-born professor of Japanese language and literature at Tokyo University, who luckily proves to be an admirer of Hearn's writings. A second piece of luck is that the single native personally known to Hearn, Hattori Ichizo, manager of the Japanese exhibit at the New Orleans International Exposition of 1885, is now vice-minister of education.

Even with two such powerful allies, a good position is not easy to secure. In 1890 the boom days are over. No longer is this a land of golden opportunity for Western scholars, teachers, technicians, and administrators. A generation of native experts has been trained, and the Meiji government is drastically cutting back on jobs for foreigners. The mania for Western ways has peaked. The importation of foreign technology and institutions may continue unabated—Tokyo now boasts both electric and telephone service; a written constitution has just gone into effect; and the first elections to a national legislature, the Diet, are in the offing. But in cultural and social matters the swing is back to tradition. The advocacy of intermarriage with Westerners to improve the race, the cries for a simpler written language like English, the

conversions to Christianity—all these are largely of the past. With
the nation beginning to recover and revere its heritage, this is not
an opportune moment for a hungry Westerner to arrive.

A newcomer like Hearn is hardly in a position to understand
these developments. Just as well. For a man who always feels on
the edge of financial ruin, such knowledge could only intensify
the mounting impatience and fear as days stretch into weeks and
no job offer arrives. To husband his small resources, Lafcadio
lives cheaply at a small waterfront hotel frequented by sailors,
and supplements an occasional royalty check by giving English
lessons to a boy of mixed Japanese-American parentage. But it is
largely his surroundings that help to keep money worries at bay.
Those first-day impressions, so overwhelming *that the mind refused to digest them*, may begin to fall into patterns, but as the
weeks pass he continues to see this as a *land of dreams*, one full
of *strange Gods* which he seems to *have known and loved* in
some other place, or time, or life. That kind of feeling is what he
wants to comprehend. Maybe here his quest will end. Maybe here
he will reach the goal of understanding himself. Maybe everything
will become clear if he can attain this single aim: *to see into the
heart of this mysterious people.*

<>

Gods and demons. Hearn is on their trail, an endless job in this
land of Buddhism and Shinto, so curiously mixed together for a
thousand years. So many manifestations of the divine that nobody
has ever attempted to count them. Buddha in his many forms: as
Fudo, the unmoved, the immutable; as Amida, the teacher; as
Yakushi, the all-healer, the physician of souls. Kannon, who re-
nounced Nirvana to remain available to humans as the goddess
of mercy; tender Jizo, protector of children; Emma-O, of the
terrible countenance, King of the Dead; Inari, the fox, god of rice;
Benten, goddess of the sea; Hachiman, god of warfare; Koshin,
overseer of roads and highways; and Kishi-bojin, mother of demons. Difficult it is to keep them straight, for they multiply, they
vary and change forms, they intermingle. But Hearn knows this:
monstrous as *Christian bigotry* may find such a sprawling pan-
theon, it expresses the *infinite Unknown* that underlies all religion.

Temples and shrines. His focus in notes to himself, letters to friends, and articles that chronicle those manic days when he mingles *with crowds of pilgrims to the great shrines*, rings *the great bells*, burns *incense rods before the great smiling gods*, and begins to learn that the Buddhism he knows from books is nothing like the living faith, *something infinitely tender, touching, naif, beautiful*. His constant companion in sightseeing is Manabe Akira, a young English-speaking student of Buddhism who guides him to out-of-the-way places, translates old inscriptions, interprets conversations with priests, and recounts legends and folktales. When Yokohama holds no more surprises, they are off to Kamakura, the thirteenth-century capital of the first great shogun, Yoritomo, now a country village, its air heavy with the aroma of seaweed soup, *daikon*, and incense. And then on to the sacred island of Enoshima, with its storybook town of steep, crooked steps; high, peaked houses with balconies; multicolored flags slapping in the sea wind; and streets alive with pilgrims in clean white dress and broad hats, refugees from a half-remembered romance.

So much in this land to see, to learn, to understand. Lessons are everywhere, in each new experience, but it is difficult to specify their nature. Hearn climbs the steps to so many shrines; views countless sculptures with multiple arms and multiple heads in wood, bronze, and stone; peers at scrolls and Sanskrit texts in the dim candlelight of temple rooms; breathes the stillness of memory in cemeteries thick with splintered stone shafts; hears tales of warriors who become gods, and gods who become beasts, and beasts who become men; rests in gardens of rock, moss, and sand, of carefully trimmed bush and blooming tree; dreams on afternoons in a blaze of sea and sun, beneath a sky so full of clouds that he likes to think them souls *about to melt forever into some blue Nirvana*. In Kamakura, he tolls the great bell of Engakuji; on Enoshima, visits the dragon cave of Benten. At Obon, the Festival of the Dead, he moves with crowds through dark streets to a Shingon temple blazing with rows of paper lanterns. On Buddha's birthday, he buys three fortune slips and finds that two predict a lucky future.

The past concerns him more. Today is the laughing, playful crowds at Yokohama's popular temples, the happy sign of a people who do not *fear the gods which they have made*. Today is the steel rails which carry him to Kamakura, the late-afternoon whistle of a locomotive that calls him away from a sagging shrine and punctuates a solemn truth: the old gods are dying. He understands this, fears it, knows it cannot be helped. Not the major gods. Not Benten or Kannon, for reverence for the sea and for the power of mercy will outlive all temples. But the lesser, local, simple gods, those who have eased so many troubled minds, gladdened so many simple hearts, heard so many innocent prayers. Their dusty, neglected shrines vibrate with a spirit congenial to his soul. Pagan he may call himself, but he is a man of the nineteenth century, one who accepts the *'laws of progress' and the irrefutable philosophy of evolution*. But for a moment—for more than one—he can wish to set such laws aside, or decree them out of existence so that these deities *of a people's childhood* might continue to live on.

<>

In June he receives a job offer. The position: teacher of English at a middle school and a normal school. The place: Matsue, a former castle town, three hundred miles southwest of Tokyo and on the side of Honshu that faces the Asian mainland. The compensation: $100 a month, to be paid in yen—certainly no fortune, but a decent enough salary in a rural area little touched by the inflationary thrust of industrialization. His reaction has to be relief. For some obscure (unconscious?) reason, Hearn has, since landing, turned some old resentments at Harper's into a series of angry letters. The result has been a break, which means no possibility of money for articles from his sole American publishing contact. Now he is wholly on his own, and with such small resources that he must apply for an advance against his salary in order to get through the period until the opening of school in September.

For the next three months the spell of Japan still holds him: *I've been living in temples and old Buddhist cemeteries, making pilgrimages and worshipping astounding Buddhas*. But difficulties and potential problems, like tiny clouds on the horizon, are beginning to appear. The midsummer climate is much too hot and

humid, and stories of the rigorous winter are not exactly promising. A bit of study has shown the language to be *extraordinarily
difficult*. This means a stay of *at least five years to write a book*.
Since the Japanese seem *the most lovable* people in the world,
such a long residence is not a problem, except in those many
moments of insuperable loneliness. To live in a remote area may
be the best way to get to know the land and culture, but that
prospect cannot prevent moments of doubt and self-pity: *I must
resign myself to melt into this Orient and be bound in it—out of
the hearing of European tongues or the sight of European faces,
in a little village where no stranger ever goes.*

He is beginning to write now, to turn hastily scrawled notes
into short pieces that will capture the special feeling of those first,
bright April days. He is also rendering some of the legends, folktales, and ghost stories recounted by young Manabe into words
that will convey their enchantment to Western readers. Fairy-tale
language comes naturally from his pen—words like *strange,
charming, mysterious, magic, witchery,* and *dreamy* pervade both
the personal accounts and the traditional tales. Few hints appear
either in articles or in letters to friends of any visits to Tokyo.
And aside from a few fleeting references, there is no indication
that he is living in a rapidly industrializing nation, or residing
among several thousand Westerners in a treaty port wide open to
the maritime commerce of the world.

The choice not to mention such things is conscious. They are a
violation, a threat to those feelings Japan has aroused, feelings he
believes to be not part of the self but embedded in outside reality.
While viewing the giant bronze Buddha at Kamakura, Hearn feels
wrapped in a blanket of gentleness, of tender and calm and perfect
repose that seems to be the *Soul of the East*, the reflection of *the
higher life of the race that imagined it*. Here is acceptance and
boundless understanding. Repayment for this glorious experience
comes in words that express love for everything Japanese—for the
domesticated Nature of both rural landscapes and urban gardens;
for the traditions of art *as far in advance of our art as the old
Greek art was superior to that of the earliest European art-grop-
ings*; for the people, *the poor simple humanity of the country. It
is divine . . . I love their gods, their customs, their dress, their*

*bird-like quavering songs, their houses, their superstitions, their
faults.*

Such strong feelings lead to a desire that aims beyond love to
fusion: *I only wish I could be reincarnated in some little Japanese
baby, so that I could see and feel the world as beautifully as a
Japanese brain does.* If this statement reeks of literary posturing
and conceit, it also reveals an aching recognition of his own
limitations. Familiar with love and its consequences, Hearn has
been involved in a painful pattern: *I resolve to love nothing, and
love always too much for my own peace of mind—places, things,
and persons—and lo! Presto! Everything is swept away and becomes a dream—like life itself.* Now Japan hints at another possibility. Perhaps the cycle can be broken, continuity created, an
enduring commitment be made. Perhaps one can become part of
this tradition, vanish into it, blend with something larger than
that small self which for forty years has suffered pain, loss, and
separation. Three weeks after landing in Yokohama he can
calmly—hopefully?—suggest the possibility of a stay that will
never end. Perhaps someday he will permanently rest *under big
trees in some old Buddhist cemetery, with six lathes above me,
inscribed with prayers in an unknown tongue, and a queerly
carved monument typifying those five elements into which we are
supposed to melt away.*

Two

SEARCHING

You must write the history of the passions, without which the
history of money, labor, and power is incomplete.

—Carlos Fuentes, *Terra Nostra*

4

With the Help
of the Lord

Providence so ordered that I should see, when almost a baby, the launching . . . of Commodore Perry's (some time) flagship, the frigate Susquehanna; that I should have as a classmate the son of our American minister, Pruyn, who had been in Japan; that I should during my four years at Rutgers College . . . teach the first Japanese students in America; that I should spend another four years in educational work in the interior and capital of Dai Nippon; that my sister, Margaret Clark Griffis, should be principal of the first government school for girls; and that I should remain on constant terms of intimacy with Nippon's sons and daughters ever since. . . .

Ultimately, the mind demands completion, wholeness, and continuity. One's own days turn into a novel. Fact, fiction, and exaggeration blend together into a comforting story, and never mind if that is exactly what happened—who really remembers or knows? Certainly Japan was the major adventure of Griffis's lifetime, so of course it should have been anticipated with appropriate events and ideas. Listen: at the age of eighty, truth can hardly be the issue. Neither is memory. For Griffis, acceptance and understanding are far more important. Only the will of the Lord can account for the blessings received over the decades. To believe that is to see the past radiating with a sweet glow. Just once does he attempt to chronicle his personal accomplishments. The resulting volume consists mostly of sermons preached over a period of thirty years. Its title is *Sunny Memories of Three Pastorates*.

39

◇

Griffis is born twice. He enters the physical world on September 17, 1843, and *the Kingdom of Heaven* fourteen years later. From an economic point of view, the first date is not the best of years to emerge, at least not in Philadelphia, a city still gripped by a depression that began in 1837. Griffis prefers happier omens. He likes to remember September 17 as the anniversary of the adoption of the Federal Constitution, a day when the streets of his hometown are alive with celebration. His spiritual birthday, December 20, 1857, is quieter but more significant. So complete is his acceptance of Christ that in the following seven decades his faith will never waver. Everything good and bad, all joys and disappointments, accomplishments and failures, will be seen as part of some larger plan. He will tackle doctrinal disputes, personality conflicts, and the pettiness of congregational politics secure in the knowledge that Christ's church is strong enough to surmount all problems of this world.

Between these two dates the life of Griffis remains a blank, save for the launching of the *Susquehanna*. This is just the kind of portent he cherishes. Certainly no one on April 7, 1850, can guess that this vessel will three years later carry Commodore Matthew Perry into Edo Bay and play a role in America's chief diplomatic triumph of the century. Yet the crowds are there, six-year-old Willie among them, standing with relatives and friends on a temporary wooden structure erected in his father's coal yard on the Delaware River. On nearby dry docks and the roofs of warehouses, masses of people gather, and as the vessel slips down the chute to float on water for the first time, the moment freezes into an image of brick buildings, pale sky, figures in silhouette, hats waving and sailing through the air, and mouths open in a silent chorus of cheers and shouts.

It is a simpler age. People speak the phrase "manifest destiny" in happy, optimistic tones. Expansion, even warfare, come at little cost. The recent military victory over Mexico has doubled the territory of the United States and brought the West Coast of the continent into the Union. Now the Pacific beckons. Any new merchant ship speaks of exotic ports, distant islands, and economic growth; any new warship, of conflict and triumph in far-off waters, of the Stars and Stripes circling the globe. Both kinds of vessels are propelled not only by sail and coal, but also by a powerful, weightless notion: the idea of Mission. The wings of the Eagle are spreading. America is helping to carry civilization, that subtle blend of Christianity, steam engines, trade, and powerful cannon, to less fortunate nations. Griffis will be an enthusiastic agent of this enterprise.

The domestic turmoil of the period will touch him less. His early years are the tag end of an era now labeled Jacksonian, a period of political, social, economic, and intellectual ferment. Debate swirls around schools, asylums, prisons, and factories; experiments in communalism dot the landscape; stormy revolts mark the worlds of literature and philosophy. Yet little of this penetrates into the milieu in which Griffis is raised. His reading lists remain innocent of names like Thoreau, Emerson, Bronson Alcott, or Margaret Fuller. In his world, temperance is more important than abolition, and these are the only social issues of much concern.

That he grows up with conventional attitudes should be no surprise. Willie's mother, Anna Maria Hess, the better-educated of his parents, has always believed that the teachings of the Good Book contain the full sum of wisdom. The dame school he attends between the ages of five and seven, the public elementary school, even the well-regarded Central High School of Philadelphia—none of these are institutions dedicated to producing a critical intelligence. Griffis may learn to spell and figure, and become acquainted with the geography and history of Europe and America, but never is he taught to question economic, political, or intellectual verities. He acquires a taste for reading, but never learns to focus on anything very serious. Years later he will lament over all the time wasted as a young man upon *acres of trash . . . in the New York Ledger.*

Reading is a necessary escape. In a society where success is the measure of a man, Willie—the fourth of seven children and the second son—is raised in an atmosphere of failure and defeat. His father, John Limeburner Griffis, followed a family tradition by joining the merchant marine as a youth, but after twenty years at sea came home in 1837 to settle down. Somehow, he never acquired land legs. To tell stories of the fogbound ports of the Old World and the sunny ones of Africa, of the jungles near Manila and the odd men in pigtails who trade for opium along the China coast, was far easier than to support a family. Once the coal yard vanished in a business reversal, John never again managed to hold a steady job. An atmosphere of deprivation pervades the Griffis household and the children must begin to work at an early age, but the family is never destitute. Their poverty is the poverty of expectations. No Griffis ever goes hungry, but Willie's sisters perpetually complain about dingy linen, creaky furniture, and threadbare rugs.

Mother is another refuge. The disappointment the young man feels toward his father will eventually become contempt, but Anna always remains on a pedestal. One measure of their closeness may be found in his 1865 diary entry that notes *Mother's twenty-eighth anniversary today* and fails to mention Father at all. Anna is deeply religious; she takes the children to church every week and, when they are away from home, sends them letters which hide all the pain of separation beneath the blessings of the Lord. Family story has it that she once vowed that if any of her sons was called to the ministry, Rutgers would be his college. That Griffis chooses to repeat this tale says a good deal about the relationship of mother to son.

Not until he begins to keep a journal at the age of sixteen does Willie's world come into focus. For decades, he will record his daily activities and then, when older, return to the bound volumes to make corrections, emendations, fuller explanations, as if his relationships to people and events should be preserved accurately for posterity. To read his words after the passage of a century is, for the historian, to be disappointed. One is stuffed full of details and left hungry for substance. At once informative and flat, the journals are a repository of events that exist in a world almost devoid of ideas, emotions, doubts, or aspirations. Here you may learn that he rises early and likes donuts for breakfast; that it rains in spring and snows in winter; that he attends church and Bible study class, visits friends, and walks with them up Chestnut Street and down Walnut; that he sometimes stays in his room reading all day or goes out to parties that end past midnight; that he makes one trip to Niagara Falls, another to Washington, D.C., and a third to Valley Forge; that he indulges a sweet tooth at an ice cream parlor; and that at the age of twenty-one he weighs one hundred nineteen pounds. Occasionally, in the description of a sunset or a landscape, you may sense a soul stirred by beauty. But pain, love, hate, and desire are all absent from his pages, save for a love of the Lord so often professed that it, too, carries little emotional charge.

So resolutely pedestrian are the journals that the motives for keeping them remain obscure. No doubt tradition plays a part. They seem to represent an attenuated legacy of Puritan forebears, those men and women whose diaries are harrowing records of inner struggle, anguished chronicles of despair over the closeness of hellfire eternal. How far from such storms is Griffis; how secular by comparison; how much less savory to modern taste. His is a world of surfaces. No inner man is ever acknowledged, except on those few occasions when, under the stress of an extreme situation, unexpected emotions erupt into consciousness. Usually he will attempt to deny those feelings by refusing to put them into words; during some of the most crucial moments of his life, the journals remain blank. Griffis is not only unknown in the way the modern mind would like to know him, he is also largely—in our terms—a stranger to himself.

One of the earliest entries in the journal chronicles the end of childhood. Two months after Willie graduates from high school in June 1859, he begins work as an apprentice in a jewelry company. The transition from the relative freedom of school to a five-day, sixty-hour week must be painful. For the next five years, Griffis will sit at a bench in a small factory building, learning to use tiny tools to create rings, studs, collar buttons, pendants, pins, and badges out of silver, gold, coral, pearl, and precious stones. All feelings about the experience remain hidden. His comment on the first day—*time passed heavy, but six o'clock came at last*—is not underscored until five years later: *Rose up at 6:15 and went forth to my last day of bondage.* In between, silence, save for the frequent notation *Went to the F.* The solitary recorded moment of satisfaction at the job comes during the very last week of the contract, when Willie brags about *performing the prodigy of making a diamond ring in 1 hr. 15 min.*

Real life takes place away from the factory. Gregarious and fun-loving, Willie is always ready to attend a lecture or a band concert, to stroll downtown, picnic in the country or jaunt over the Almshouse Meadows at twilight to snare frogs for a dinner treat. Natural enough it is for him to be among the jostling street crowds on June 9, 1860, when seventy-one samurai arrive in Philadelphia for two days of sightseeing. These members of the first Japanese Embassy to the United States in their formal silk kimono are a startling sight as they go from the Mint to the gas works to Independence Hall. Yet the occasion does not warrant an entry in Griffis's diary until fifty years later, when history can be updated with a faint pencil note in the margin: *As the strangers rode in carriages up Walnut Street . . . I was impressed with their tasteful costumes, the exquisite workmanship of their swords, but above all by their polished manners . . . From the first I took the Japanese seriously.* Perhaps. But not seriously enough to be moved to read a single book about Japan in the decade before going there.

Church is the center of Willie's life. Raised a Presbyterian, called to Christ under the aegis of the pastor of the First Independent Church of Philadelphia, Griffis at the age of twenty finds himself drawn towards the Second Dutch Reformed Church. Active in both congregations, he is off to religious activities five, six, seven times a week. On Sundays he teaches an early Sabbath Class to youngsters, then attends morning and afternoon services and an evening prayer meeting. On weeknights he goes to young people's meetings, Bible study classes, and gatherings to hear reports on missionary endeavors. Lists of sermon titles and names of visiting ministers crowd his journal. With gusto he evaluates oratorical styles and judges preaching ability, but rarely does he mention anything that is said.

Not until he is seventeen do political affairs impinge upon Willie's world. In debate at the Shakespeare Lyceum in mid-March 1861, he argues the negative side on the question of whether the new Lincoln administration should reinforce Fort Sumter. Three weeks later, on April 13, he writes, *Civil War commenced today*

. . . I spent the evening at the YMCA Room. Retired at 11:30. The following days are full of excitement as he joins crowds milling about in downtown Philadelphia, watches angry groups of men demand that *people show their colors,* and hears ministers reach heights of rhetorical splendor in sermons asking the Lord to bless the Union. This militant mood does not last long. For most of the next four years—except for those moments when Confederate armies draw close to Philadelphia—a tone of distance marks his reactions to the conflict. Twice he joins the military for ninety-day terms—in April 1861 with the Pennsylvania Cadets, and in July 1863 with a company of the regular Union army. These actions give no indication of attitudes towards the larger issues of the war. Never does Griffis express in writing any feelings about states' rights, or the sanctity of the Union, or slavery. At a packed meeting in Concert Hall, he can be deeply moved by the fiery words of the abolitionist Charles Sumner, and at the same time note with disdain that the audience is one-quarter *quakers and niggers.*

If Griffis during the war years seems limited and self-centered, it may be because the passions of the conflict rage at a time when Willie's own life has begun to take on a new sense of direction and purpose. Later, he will recall May 24, 1863, as the major turning point of his life. The occasion is a Sunday sermon; the place, the Dutch Reformed Church; the speaker, William H. Campbell, president of Rutgers; the text, "If any man will be my disciple, let him take up his cross and follow me." The message can hardly be new, but this time the familiar, insistent words trigger something that makes the young man decide to enter the ministry.

The following two years are a period of enormous effort and sacrifice. To study for entrance examinations in four fields—Latin, Greek, algebra, and geography—Willie must rise early, stay up late, and forsake almost all social activities. Dedication and hard work pay off when Griffis goes up to New Brunswick to enter Rutgers in the fall of 1865. The century-old college of his (mother's?) choice, which has long boasted a curriculum balancing the sacred and the secular, has recently entered a period of rapid growth and change. Trustees have decided to supplement the traditional curriculum with a Scientific School, and new buildings with well-equipped laboratories are rising next to ivy-covered halls. During Willie's years there, the college will add several scholars to its twelve-man faculty and the student body will double to one hundred and fifty.

Rutgers unleashes in Griffis a new eagerness and curiosity. To a professional interest in religion and the classics, he adds a passion for science. This poses no intellectual conflict. Darwin's *Origin of Species*, in print since 1859, is not yet a fighting issue, and the leading scientist at Rutgers, an elder of the Reformed Church, can call his discipline *the handmaid of religion*. Records do not indicate whether Griffis elects the classical or scientific curriculum, but they do show his appetite across a broad spectrum of fields. His studies in the Bible, Christianity, and moral philosophy are supplemented with courses in mathematics, astronomy, chemistry, physics, botany, geology, Latin, Greek, Hebrew, German, French, logic, political economy, and history. His list of books read for pleasure is weighted heavily toward the writings of contemporary scientists like Louis Agassiz, Thomas Henry Huxley, and Baron von Humboldt, and the epic historical works of William H. Prescott and John Lothrop Motley that celebrate European expansion and empire.

College is not all books and classes; it is also social life and student organizations, debate contests and athletics, and weekend jaunts to Manhattan. Willie joins the Delta Upsilon fraternity, becomes active in two literary societies, and, along with Robert Pruyn, conceives and edits *The Targum*, a monthly magazine that features his first appearance in print. He develops a passion for sports, often slips down to the Raritan River to boat or swim, jogs for miles along country lanes, and plays on the football team. High-spirited, but never frivolous, he can at least appreciate frivolity in others. When the faculty condemns four students for the prank of pulling down a fence, Griffis joins in protest against a punishment that seems overly severe. He also can, on occasion, show a sense of humor. In February 1867, the famous New York editor Horace Greeley comes to campus to deliver a lecture on *Self-Made Men*, and is assigned to sleep in Willie's chambers. When a minister insists on knowing whether the freethinking

Greeley made his devotions at night, Griffis explains, *I heard considerable snoring, but no praying.*

Even during the headiest of student days, finances are never far from his mind. Tuition at Rutgers is close to $80 a year, and room and fuel cost another $15. Most of his education has been underwritten by subscription from church members at home, but in his junior year Willie has to supplement that fund by taking a teaching position at the Rutgers Grammar School. The difficult part is that now he must spend fourteen hours a week drilling students in the rudiments of Latin and Greek; the rewarding part is the opportunity to deliver an occasional lecture on topics such as Greek mythology, science, natural philosophy, and political economy. Several of his students are from Japan, and occasionally one of them rates a journal notation as *bright* or *gentlemanly.*

Four years at Rutgers open Griffis to *new worlds of knowledge* without in any way altering his beliefs. He graduates fifth in his class, wins prizes for composition and oratory, is elected to Phi Beta Kappa, and remains a deeply moral and religious young man who perceives the world largely in terms of right and wrong, good and evil, Christian and nonbeliever. An unreflective sort, he is never moved to sum up the personal meaning of his college experience, but once, as a junior, Griffis does reach for a perspective on higher education. College students, he thinks, are members of a group at once privileged and burdened, people who lead an *exhilarating and joyous* life full of the excitement of encountering new ideas. Yet college is also a deadly serious place where one forges *the weapons for the life-long fray of duty and profession.* In this realm, *social pleasures* have their place, but one must learn to *use them sparingly.* The aim of education—of life itself—is self-improvement. To fail in this sacred duty is a sign of *ingratitude to God, to friends, ourselves.*

The months following graduation in June 1869 are hectic, trying, troubled, and filled with uncertainty. School may have been a demanding world of trial and preparation, but at least its requirements were clear. Now everything seems confused. To choose the ministry as a career is only the first step into an adult realm whose dimensions can be but dimly perceived. This is America, the land of opportunity. In religion, as in any field, all kinds of positions are available at all kinds of salaries. One can serve the Lord in many ways—in rural or urban congregations, ministries to the wealthy or to the poor, churches for the middle class or for working people. And no one can deny that the affluent need the Lord's word just as much as (some might argue more than) the indigent.

Three years of Divinity School may lie between him and the start of a career, but already Griffis is caught up in such considerations. Without doubt he is ambitious, though it would be difficult for him to admit openly to worldly motivation. Probe beneath his brash exterior and you will find a defensive young man. No wonder: Willie carries a heavy burden of personal and family debt, compounded by the continuing failure of his father to provide a steady income. Yet this alone cannot wholly explain his hunger for success. At college Griffis tasted the world of high culture and found it savory. Genteel manners, knowledge of art, good books, and travel abroad are very much part of his image of the minister, a man who—he feels—must set an example not only in the realms of faith and morality, but in those of learning and taste as well.

To follow the dilemma of Griffis in the months after graduation, to see him wrestling with the problem of his future, to understand how his choice of a position in Japan grows out of difficulties both financial and personal, it is best to turn to his letters to his older sister, Maggie, his confidante, supporter, and chief source of consolation. To her he can confess doubts and secrets hidden from the rest of the world. If the words are often oblique and circumspect, hinting at juicier revelations to be delivered face-to-face, they also vibrate with emotions never recorded in the journals. Carefully he provides details of his accomplishments—sermons preached, lectures given, praise received, money earned—and then launches into complaints about expenses, debts, and future costs. Money is always a sticky point; obviously Willie worries that the family will become too dependent upon him.

The period begins brightly enough, with brother and sister joining together for a three-month journey to Europe. To make the trip, Griffis has to borrow $300, and he is determined to make good use of every penny. They sail late in June, land in England, hasten through the Low Countries to France, Germany, and Switzerland, then go east to Austria and south to Italy before doubling back to Great Britain to catch the ship for home. On October 11 they land in New York City, and that very afternoon Griffis begins to attend classes at Rutgers Theological Seminary and to teach at the grammar school. The pace set this first day back will hardly slacken for a year. Divinity school proves to be at once more difficult and more inspiring than undergraduate study, but Willie never has the luxury of devoting his full attention to classwork. The European travel debt weighs heavy on him, and family requests for money never cease. With the grammar school salary little more than adequate for daily needs, Griffis must begin to hustle.

Words are his single commodity. To a longtime skill in delivering the message of the Lord he now adds a secular message in the form of lectures about Europe. Engagements are not hard to come by, for in that pre-electronic era guest speakers are always in demand, especially if they will work in out-of-the-way places for whatever donations the public cares to make. Not for Griffis the world of wealthy congregations, large auditoriums, and travel by train. His is a humble circuit of farming communities, lengthy hikes along muddy roads, and lectures delivered in drafty halls. The take varies widely. On a *good week pecuniarily*, he may leave Rutgers for half a dozen appearances. Here is one of his best: Friday night at Raritan, $15; a stormy Saturday at a country church, $5; Sunday, morning and evening lectures in Whitehouse, donations unrecorded; Monday, a long walk through *horrible* weather to Griggstown, $7.75; Tuesday, at Newmarket, $8.25. Total for the week after deducting expenses: $31.25.

The grinding routine—*study, teach, lecture and preach*—takes a heavy toll. Usually exhausted, subject to severe colds, Griffis falls into dark moods. The *debt cloud* does not easily dissipate; the lament *I wish I could raise cash* becomes a litany. Pain stabs him when he discovers that a preacher he knows has a salary of $5000 a year, or learns that the post of minister at a New York congregation at a salary of $3000 could have been his were he already ordained. In February he speaks to the head of the seminary about a possible *short course* to ordination and is sharply rebuked. Explanation to Maggie follows: it was a *penny-wise plan. . . . My aim is high. I shall not spoil it by haste . . . He that believeth shall not make haste*. Two months later, Willie entertains the fantasy of quitting school for a year and moving to New York to devote himself entirely to lecturing and writing. Once again prudence—or reality—prevails. By May the $300 debt is paid off. Now he can look forward to two more years of seminary with a mind *better prepared* to study.

Money is not his only worry. For the first and apparently only time in his life, Griffis wrestles with theological problems. Delicious he finds it to describe himself as *grappling with doctrines that shake my old faith to the very foundations and demand of me all my powers of mind*. The chief issue is the Unitarian challenge to the notion of Trinity. A serious problem, no doubt, but something less than soul-shaking, or Willie could hardly follow his confession with this: *Whatever the result of my deliberations . . . on my theoretical belief, certainly my preaching will not be dogmatic, but practical, earnest, positive and cultured*. At another point during the year Calvinism attracts him, its gloomy doctrines evidently suited to his current frame of mind. But this can be no more than a temporary infatuation for a mentality that normally basks in good works and the sunshine of divine love.

This same powerful emotion, in its earthly guise, is another part of his personal turmoil. Willie cannot visit Manhattan without noting that Broadway is *thronged with pretty girls*, yet his heart is elsewhere. Even since college, a *passion* for one particular young lady has been *the purest and strongest power in my nature, save my religion*. For many months she flits through his journal, a shadowy figure always referred to as *E* until a January 29, 1870, note to Maggie headed with the words *VENI! VIDI! VICI!: Love's labor won. I have heart won fair lady! I have won her. Ellen Johnson is my Ellen . . . I am loved in return*. No, she is not what the world takes for *pretty*, but something far better—a creature with *a quick and brilliant mind, a deeply affectionate nature, a cheerful religion, a full flow of spirits*, a woman who thinks *no home brighter and happier than a ministers*.

Brushing aside evidence of Ellen's reservations—she does not want the engagement made public—Griffis rushes home to Philadelphia, takes up his old tools, and fashions a gold wedding band for her. When in April she begins to prepare for a six-month trip to Europe, Willie offers a reluctant blessing. Separation is not to his taste. He can accept it only because she promises *freely all that I could desire—not to forget me, to love me more, and to be my wife*. That will be a blessed state. Life without the love of a woman *would be hard, stern and dark*, but his days shall be *sunny, glowing and joyful*. No firm date is set, but in a year or two at the most, *marriage and its train of joys* will belong to them.

The prospect of marriage makes the apprentice minister feel more mature and worldly, better prepared to handle both the outside world and *the subtle workings of the human heart*. In June 1870 he begins a job at Knox Memorial Chapel, a Methodist church in a working-class district of Manhattan. The salary is $100 a month and the work pleasant. Ellen's absence may be felt, but his health is good, his debts paid off, his days full, and his future bright. During the summer Griffis sleeps long and well, studies and writes sermons in the morning, attends to church business in the afternoon, sees college pals at night, and often spends weekends visiting friends in the country. Two days a week go to pastoral visits. The tenements of New York confront him with a kind of *inexorable and hopeless* poverty, a struggle for existence that makes his own monetary complaints seem, by comparison, a *sin*. Yet Willie cannot keep from boasting that his own *experiences of poverty and the struggle for bread* fit him to be a messenger of comfort to the poor.

September is a cruel, disturbing month, a time when life suddenly veers in a new direction. Hints of change arrive on the sixth when a letter from the president of Rutgers brings Griffis a *dazzling* job offer. The position is teacher of natural science; the place, Fukui, Japan; the term, three years; the salary, $2400 a year plus a house, a horse, and travel expenses. Only one thing keeps Willie from accepting the job: *Were it not for the fact that E.G.J. exists I should not hesitate five minutes*. If any resentment touches this comment, there is no time for it to grow. One week later Ellen returns from Europe. Willie meets with her on the fourteenth, but no record of their conversation exists, and no hint other than the mute letter *E* that graces his journal on this most serious occasion. Two weeks later, he confesses to Maggie: *There is no present likelihood that E. and I will ever be husband and wife. Do not ask me for details or explanation.* His heart is *almost broken . . . yet all is right, and E remains in my mind purer, nobler and more worth living for than ever.* The rest is silence.

Willie is free now—more than free. He is a man who desperately needs to do something, and Japan is waiting. Yet to take the plunge is still not easy. For two weeks he hesitates, consults with people, worries the decision. Up he goes to Albany, where Robert Pruyn, father of his classmate and former minister to Japan, urges him to accept the *splendid offer*; stresses *money and travel advantages, society, health, knowledge, usefulness and good to be accomplished*; and offers to advance $800 to cover the cost of the journey. The Reverend John Ferris, secretary of the Board of Foreign Missions of the Dutch Reformed Church, makes it seem *a duty to God, the church, my country and Japan to go.* And all of Willie's professors at Rutgers but one (who sees the offer as *a temptation of the devil*) are highly positive about this *glorious opportunity* for Griffis and for God.

Family reaction to the decision to go, made at the beginning of October, is predictable. Willie's sisters dissolve in tears; his mother writes, *that you believe yourself called of Him is sufficient to me*; his father remains silent; his two brothers begin to hope that he will be able to find equally lucrative positions for them. An angry Maggie lays the blame squarely on Ellen: that young lady's change of mind is sending Griffis off *to a land without God, without the Bible, without a Holy Sabbath.* Yet even this horrible prospect is an opportunity. Instead of borrowing $800 for the trip, she suggests, *It would be just as well to get $1,000* and use the balance to buy new carpets for the house.

Sister and brother are much alike. Griffis is a man equally committed to himself and to duty, to the practical and the religious, the worldly and the spiritual. Nowhere is this more apparent than in the decision for Japan. September's *chain of events* surely come from God, and though the decision may lead to calamity, disease, or death, he is not afraid. That he looks forward to carrying the Gospel to a heathen land cannot be doubted; that he would not do so were the price not right is equally true. He is a good American, which at the very least means that he wants it all: *I can study and be ordained there, and God willing, return to my native land only one year later than if I staid. Beside the grand opportunities and culture, travel and good climate . . . I can not only study on my theology, but collect materials to write a book. I can support my family at home, at least, pay the rent, and carpet the floors, and send handsome sums home, too.*

The word "rationalization" in its modern psychological sense is unknown in the mid-nineteenth century. If a later generation wishes to apply it to Willie's words, it must be with the realization that to gain understanding is to lose immediacy. Insofar as the concept illuminates his behavior, it obscures his experience. For us it may be—undoubtedly is?—difficult to believe, but Griffis is sincere when he places responsibility for this new direction on a power higher than the self: *Unable to do anything else, now, by the help of God, I go forth to new duties, with a conscience clear and a path as plain as when I first started in the work of the ministry.*

5

The World of Nature

Begin with shells. That makes the most sense. They lead to everything else—the career in science; the years in Japan; those five thousand pieces of pottery hidden in a dimly lit attic of the Boston Museum of Fine Arts; that enormous collection of folk art and crafts owned by the Peabody Museum in Salem; this very chapter. Shells fill the earliest entries in the diary of teenage Edward Morse. Six decades later they can still be the chief topic of a letter to a friend or the subject of an article for a magazine. By then, his reputation as an expert on Japan far surpasses his fame as a scientist, but something in him never lets go of shells. It is as if this first and most enduring passion is a model for all later passions, as if collecting, studying, and classifying the remains of small, inarticulate creatures is a way of giving voice to the voiceless, as if by understanding shells he can understand everything, including his place in the universe.

Not that Morse can ever express such thoughts. He is a man whose prose, like his mind, tends toward the tangible. Self-made, practical, down-to-earth, instinctively democratic, he has little interest in the artistic, the historical, the literary, or the philosophic. Few flights of imagination ever disturb his consciousness. Morse is content to believe in what he can see, touch, smell, dissect, and sketch. The surfaces of the world are his reality. Seashells, bird wings, roof tiles, utensils, latrines, works of art—

all are equally interesting. For him it is easier, more pleasant, to deal with solid objects than with people, emotions, ideas, beliefs.

<>

Fifteen years old, a skinny lad who earns $4 a week as a draftsman for the Portland Company—that's Ned Morse of the earliest remaining diaries and letters. It is 1854 and shells are already his major preoccupation. At work he dreams of them; away from work he pursues them. In fine weather or foul, he wanders along the seashore scanning tidal pools, digs in the clay banks of the Kennebec River, pokes into crevices of stone walls, examines mossy stumps and the undersides of rocks in the woods that edge Portland, Maine. Sometimes he wheels a barrow to the market and returns with it full of fish entrails that may yield rare deep-sea shells. He haunts the wharves, where sailors are willing to share huge pink-and-white conches that sound with the roar of far-off seas. He listens to the talk of lustrous, shimmering shells dredged from the coast of Egypt or the mouth of the Amazon, to be sold to collectors in great cities like Liverpool, New York, Marseilles.

The romance of such places, the dreams of adventure they inspire in youngsters, never reach the pages of Ned's diary. His desires are matter-of-fact: Morse specializes in small, homely land shells that bring nothing from stores or dealers. But neither beauty nor money is his aim. Satisfaction comes from studying shells through his three-dollar microscope, drawing them, sorting them into groups, arranging them neatly in the drawers of his cabinet. His goal is a complete collection of Maine shells; his fondest wish, to discover a new species. This happens for the first time when Ned is nineteen. A piece of the shell of an earth-colored land snail, one thirty-second of an inch in length, goes off to the Boston Society of Natural History, where the region's foremost conchologist proclaims it *a distinct species . . . the most minute of any yet observed.* The official proceedings term it *Helix asteriscus, Morse.*

Sweet recognition to a lad with scientific ambitions, but just another source of discord at home. His father, Jonathan Kimball Morse, deacon of the Baptist church, partner in a company that deals in beaver furs and buffalo robes, sees no profit in shells. They interfere with everything important—school, work, church. His son is too irresponsible. Ned has been thrown out of more than one school for talking back to the headmaster. He regularly picks quarrels with his boss at the Portland Company; he has been fired more than once, and only rehired because his older brother is a company official. Worse yet, his mortal soul is in danger. On Sunday, Ned often claims illness to stay home from church and spend the day puttering among the shells in his cabinet. Here is ample cause for the angry eruptions between father and son that can end with Jonathan intoning prayers and Ned toying with the idea of suicide and confiding to his diary, *Must I give up the only things I care to live for and turn to support of this body, gross and low?*

Despair is not a common mood. The pain of conflict with father is eased by the love and support of his mother, Jane Beckett Morse, a woman romantic enough to claim descent from Thomas à Becket and scientific enough to win recognition from the Portland Society of Natural History for assembling a comprehensive collection of local plant life. When he is twenty-two, Ned describes her as an *accomplished lady* who has studied Greek, Latin, German, French, and Spanish, who understands conchology and botany, and who can *skate, dance, ride a horse, a locomotive and forty other hobbys.* She also is a hell of a cook. His lifelong taste for roast turkey, baked beans and, above all, fresh doughnuts begins in mother's kitchen.

Along with an interest in science, Jane passes on to Ned her sunny temperament. Jonathan Morse may relish an orthodox world of hellfire and damnation, sin and punishment, but his wife has turned her back on such painful doctrines to dabble in spiritualism, hoping to communicate with the shade of a deceased son. Ned accompanies her to seances, devours tracts, argues the topic with friends, labels nonbelievers *darn fools*, and once is deeply moved to hear the voice of Edgar Allan Poe, through a medium, urge an audience on to higher moral values. When an experiment to see if his own *Guardian Spirit* can accurately transmit information from a friend in another town ends in failure, his belief is not shaken, and with good reason. Spiritualism provides an alternate worldview to the gloomy doctrines of his father's church, a universe brimming with sweetness and hope: *God teaches us to smile. Nature, the flowers are all smiling and beautiful.*

Were Morse himself narrating this story, he would agree with the sequence: shells first, parents second. But he would not share the impulse of the biographer to put siblings third. So rare is any mention of his older brother or three younger sisters that a reader of his journals could take him for an only child. Yet almost any page will tell you he has a close friend named John Gould. Together they are students at the Bridgton Academy in 1854. When Morse is sent home for carving school desks with a penknife, a correspondence that will last for seven decades gets underway. Shells are the initial basis of the relationship and the chief topic of letters in which they exchange data about new finds. That Morse is the more single-minded of the two begins to show in 1856 when John returns to Portland and goes to work, conveniently, in a bank. For the next thirty years, Ned will shamelessly borrow money from John—to live in Cambridge, to finance scientific ventures, to go to Japan. Gould's reward will be an unceasing flood of letters that detail Morse's scientific accomplishments and financial woes.

Friendship is part of the world of activities typical of any small-town New England youngster in the forties and fifties. You may see this life as if in a series of watercolor illustrations—boys and girls with red cheeks on a berrying party in the woods; young men in a sailboat heeled against gray swells; heaps of youngsters bundled in coats, hats, and blankets, riding a horse-drawn sleigh through a landscape of snowy fields. Ned learns to bang tunes on an upright piano; enjoys a good game of whist; dances the cotillion at sociables; flirts with young ladies; proposes to a girl named Lutie, and when gently rejected, decides *I will be a brother to her.* He acquires a taste for beer, wine, cigars, and a pipe, regularly vows to give each up and just as regularly breaks those vows.

By the age of twenty Ned is part of a circle of *free thinkers and Deists* who share meals, wine, and conversation unhindered by *stiffnecked orthodoxy.* Despite having found this niche in Portland, he is often restless, moody, full of desires for things not easily defined. He wants to leave a job that drains his energy into drawings of locomotives, machinery, and bridges. He wants to be on his own, to work full-time on shells. Yes, he is something of a local luminary—secretary of the local Society of Natural History, host to scientists from Boston or New York, who solicit his opinions on local fauna, praise his cabinet, admire his drawings, and ask him to go on expeditions. All this has an effect. No single act leads to the decision, but one day it has to enter Morse's consciousness that his hometown is not the right place for anyone with yearnings toward a career in science.

<>

To Portland eyes and ears, Boston—with a population of more than a hundred and fifty thousand in 1858—is congested and noisy. It is also expensive: $4 a week for room and board. That includes the first indoor plumbing Ned has ever seen—a toilet, *which saves the travelling down two or three flights of stairs and the inconvenience of being half frozen in the attempt,* and a tub that brings forth a solemn pledge: *I intend taking a bath every week.* The main attraction of the city is not the plumbing; nor the job as designer and draftsman with Bricher and Russell, Engravers on Wood; nor the Parker House where young men splurge on claret, ale, oysters, and charlotte russe; nor the theater where you can see *Our American Cousin*; nor the Everett Gallery, where the latest Albert Bierstadt landscape is on sale for $800; nor the *most magnificent* Public Library. No, for him the heart of the city is the Boston Society of Natural History.

A place where amateurs mix with professionals, the society mirrors the low state of science in pre–Civil War America. Research has declined drastically since the days when Benjamin Franklin was elected to the French Academy. In the first half of the nineteenth century, Americans excel only in that most democratic of fields, natural science. The case of Morse is not unusual. He has never completed a secondary education; his knowledge of technique and theory derives from a few books bought or borrowed, meetings with equally amateurish local investigators, and scraps gleaned from visitors with more formal training. Yet Ned is bright and energetic, and his eye and mind are keen. These are just the qualities necessary to seek out and classify the dimly known plant and animal life of the continent.

Hints of change are in the air when Morse is elected a corresponding member of the Boston Society of Natural History in October 1859. At the biweekly meetings, there is a sense that science is becoming more important. A good part of this stems from the presence of Louis Agassiz, who a decade earlier abandoned a major research center in Switzerland to take the first chair in geology and zoology at Harvard's new Lawrence Scientific School. The world-renowned scientist is a superb promoter who has convinced New England's elite that scientific research is worthy of support. With the backing of wealthy industrialists and the Commonwealth of Massachusetts, Agassiz has begun to construct the world's largest museum of comparative zoology.

Just one year after leaving home, Morse joins a dozen young men who eagerly begin to work in the half-completed building in Cambridge. Financial compensation for Agassiz's first assistants is small, $30 a month plus free room and board, but the real reward is educational—all are admitted as students to the new Museum School. Acutely aware of his poor background and *superficial knowledge*, Ned turns into a serious student. The first year he takes careful notes at more than one hundred lectures on zoology, paleontology, ichthyology, embryology, and comparative anatomy, and supplements these with a home reading program that includes French and German. Agassiz is quick to recognize his talents and expertise. On New Year's Day, 1860, Ned notes in the diary: *Prof has given me the most unlimited control over Shells in the Museum.*

This is a major task. As one of the four great divisions of the animal kingdom, mollusks—to give shelled creatures their proper scientific label—form one of the four main sections of the museum. In a single year Ned studies, arranges, classifies, catalogues, and bottles thirty thousand specimens that belong to four thousand species. To determine accurately their proper categories is a matter of endless study and the delicate dissection of soft, minuscule bodies. Hours, sometimes days can be spent in a search for the lingual ribbon, anus, or reproductive organs of a creature so tiny it must be viewed under a microscope, but the results can be worth all the labor. More than once Morse finds that a genus should really be a family, or that a single species can be subdivided into several.

Student assistants are valued for brawn as well as brain. They haul, lift, and unpack the barrels, boxes, kegs, cans, and crates that pour in almost daily from Agassiz's buying trips, expeditions, and contacts around the world. Here are fossils and creatures living and dead from the American West Coast, Brazil, Australia, and Africa. *Prof*—for so Agassiz is always called—works with them, jolly as a birthday child pulling forth presents, or in this case rare varieties of fish, turtles, crabs, birds, and mammals as large as deer and moose. Some familiar items end up on the students' dining table; others are almost impossible to identify. On one occasion Morse finds something that looks like an animal without its shell and studies it seriously for quite some time before recognizing it as a stray leaf. In the ensuing general merriment, Agassiz exclaims, *You need not laugh, gentlemen, for I, not long ago, puzzled over a pair of old breeches for two hours.*

Prof is like that, and the students love him. His influence extends far beyond zoological matters. Full of stories about the great men he has known—Georges Cuvier, Dominique François Arago, Alexander von Humboldt—he speaks of science not as a profession, but as a sacred calling. Young men must be dedicated, ready to forgo economic gain in the pursuit of knowledge. But they also must avoid being too narrow and single-minded. History, literature, and philosophy are important for a *cultivated* person. So is a well-rounded social life. Warning against any tendencies toward misanthropy, he urges the young men to associate with well-bred people and to seek especially the company of *intellectual and refined women.*

Mentor, companion, hero, role model, Agassiz is for Morse the ideal male parent that has been missing at home. The journals and letters brim with references to him as *a Father* and comments like *There is no better man in the world.* When he is sharp with Ned—*Prof spoke to me about the manner I had of jumping from one thing to another*—the young man vows to do better. He even attempts to follow Agassiz into the realm of culture by making a stab at Dickens, attending the opera, and going to an occasional art exhibition. Little surprise that his taste runs to landscapes, or that he will judge a work as a masterpiece because the artist draws with the fidelity of *a close student of nature* and renders perspective so well *that one can guess the distance of any object.*

Such an opinion reveals much about Morse's relation to the world: everything is judged through the eyes of natural science. Into this sphere goes all his sense of wonder. Elsewhere his mind is pedestrian, conventional, and limited. Never does he read a book of history, philosophy, or political economy, or study the civilization of Greece or Rome. He dwells in Cambridge in 1859, but his detailed journal remains innocent of words like abolitionist or transcendentalist, and his eyes never encounter the writings of those nearby residents Emerson, Thoreau, Bronson Alcott, Hawthorne, Longfellow, Holmes. For Ned, a political opinion is to call Great Britain *the most stupid conceited nation on this earth*; a literary one is to rate *Two Years before the Mast*, by Richard Henry Dana, a *good thing*. Under Agassiz's supervision he can become a scientist, but even Prof cannot make up for his barren background, for the fact that Morse is a man largely cut off from the high Western tradition in humanities, literature, and the arts.

<>

Freshness, excitement, group spirit, camaraderie, the contagious joy of working toward a common goal — this first phase at the museum lasts a year, maybe a few months more. Then, perhaps inevitably, problems begin to surface and Agassiz's luster to dim. For some students, discontent with Prof is triggered by the intellectual conflict that begins to undermine his position in the nation's scientific community. The issue is evolution; the initial battleground, the Boston Society of Natural History. Morse is an observer rather than combatant, but the struggle will affect the course of his life, lead to his major scientific accomplishments, and eventually take him to Japan. Skirmishes over this most important scientific theory of the century began in the spring of 1859, before Ned's arrival in Cambridge, when the Harvard botanist Asa Gray clashed with Agassiz over the idea of the development of species. In November, when copies of *Origin of Species* arrive in the United States, the battle is fully underway. The son of a minister, Agassiz believes species to be fixed and immutable, an affirmation of God's coherent plan for the universe. Nothing Darwin can say, no evidence, no arguments however logical or coherent, can change his mind.

Debates at Society meetings in early 1860 are sharp and acrimonious, as Ned and his comrades watch Prof struggle with the proponents of evolution. Agassiz's knowledge of geology, paleontology, and zoology is vast, but the bedrock of his argument is an unshakable faith in the discontinuity of epochs, a belief that there is no relationship whatsoever between fossil species and living ones. To bolster this position, he gives Morse a special assignment: *There are thousands of species of shells found fossil in England and France which authors consider the same as recent living species. Prof. don't believe they are the same and he wishes me to examine closely and make comparisons of those species in order to prove their difference.* Sometime later Ned will begin to call these shells by their proper name—brachiopods.

Because Agassiz's resistance to evolution is shared by many scientists, the real issue is open-mindedness. By holding to *a priori* assumptions, and by insisting that any resemblance between fossils and living species proves only that after each ice age destroyed much of the world's animate life, the Almighty stepped in to recreate some of the same species, Agassiz begins to tarnish his reputation in scientific circles. Other scientists return to laboratory studies; their assent to evolution may come years later. Morse himself takes such a path. Like Agassiz, he initially objects to Darwin from a vaguely theological viewpoint. *Don't you perceive,* he writes to Gould, *that if his theory is true it would leave one without a God? . . . for the origin of species according to his idea would be simply chance and nothing else.* More personal is his vision of evolution as too much like his father's orthodoxy: *Darwin's chapter on the struggle for existence smacks too strongly of Calvinism . . .* [his] *picture looks a good deal like Calvin's drawing of us poor worms.*

A mind shut against Darwin proves closed to other viewpoints as well. The loving father can also be autocratic, harsh, unjust. No doubt this has been true from the beginning, but only in the fall of 1860 does Morse's idealization give way to criticism of Agassiz. Yes, he is a great man, but several angry, unfair tirades against students—set down to his *foreign temper*—make it clear that this applies only to the realm of science. And here, too, doubts can surface. It is annoying to find his second-year lectures are often word-for-word repetitions of those already delivered. Some are far worse: *Stupid lecture this afternoon from Prof. I went to sleep.* Toward the end of his second year at the museum, Ned can summarily dismiss Agassiz's public presentations at the Lowell Institute: *He regarded cats and dogs as belonging to the same family. Walked out.*

<>

In January 1862 Morse is back in Portland to pursue a new career as an independent zoological draftsman. Disillusionment with Prof is not the only reason for the move. The world has changed greatly in the last year. Jonathan Morse has died; Lincoln has been elected president; the South has seceded from the Union; guns have fired on Fort Sumter; troops have marched into battle at Bull Run. At the first call to arms in April 1861, Ned rushed home to enlist, only to encounter a foe too strong to overcome: mother. Pages for the crucial two weeks are later cut from the diary, but Jane Morse's arguments are not difficult to imagine: she is a widow of little means; she has three daughters to support; brother Fred is already doing all he can. Defeat on the home front serves only to increase Ned's jealousy as he watches friends like John Gould don uniforms, parade through the streets, board trains for the journey to war. No way around it—being a man has something to do with shouldering arms for one's country, and here he is at twenty-three, still a boy, a student, and an assistant at a meager salary that can barely support one person. By the close of 1861 there is an added complication, another reason to leave the museum: Morse wants to get married.

Love has taken him unawares. Ned has always enjoyed the company of women at dances, sociables, and group excursions, but the early rejection by Lutie made him certain that he would always remain *an old batchelor*. Still, he desires *an honest female friend*, a kind of sister, and one appears at a dance during his trip home to Portland in February 1860. Her name is Nellie Owen. She is a young lady who attends church regularly, suffers from severe headaches, and keeps a diary that chronicles a life so uneventful that the daily weather report provides most of its drama. In June they embrace for the first time; in October Ned tells his mother, *Nellie is just like you.* During the following months he regularly confesses that he cannot *do anything but think of the moment that I shall clasp her in my arms again.* The question of whether he is worthy nags at him, but after their engagement at the end of the year, it is answered with a solemn resolve: *She is the one to whom I will look for advice, one who will lead me to a higher scale of thought, and one I shall love to please by my good behavior.*

Easier to say than do. He does occasionally attend church with her, irksome though it proves to be. And when Nellie asks him to forsake tobacco for health reasons, Morse makes a brief effort to comply, while confiding to his journal that she is *ignorant regarding the effects of the use of it.* At first he attempts to share his usual passion, hauling her off to the zoology museum in Cambridge, but Nellie proves to be more interested in Morse than in mollusks. Not until June 1863 can they afford to marry. Their diaries for the thirty-month waiting period suggest—despite a chaste, restrained vocabulary—the emotions of love in any age: desire, yearning, concern, doubt, caring, regret for an ill-spoken phrase, resolve to be more careful with the other's feelings. On the eve of the wedding, Ned takes a step peculiarly his own—he asks John Gould to join them on a *marriage tour* that will consist of a snail-collecting trip: *What a delightful time we should have!*

His friend cannot accept, but the invitation may be seen as a symbolic key to the marriage. Collecting, science, and career will always take precedence over home and family. Nellie is a good wife in the most traditional sense; for forty-seven years she will silently take care of the household, raise the children, and stay out of the way so that Ned can get his work done. Her headaches continue and are especially severe on Sundays, birthdays, and anniversaries. On his many extended jaunts away from home, with the single exception of Japan, Morse will always leave Nellie behind.

<>

Fifteen years of steadily growing success follow the departure from Cambridge. Prof's training has turned the amateur into a professional, but talent, dedication, and hard work are necessary to create a career. By the seventies, Morse has a reputation as a scientific researcher, curator of mollusks at the Peabody Institute of Science in Salem, founding editor of *The American Naturalist*, lyceum lecturer, visiting faculty member at Harvard College, and writer for journals, magazines, and newspapers. During this period, Bowdoin College confers an honorary doctorate upon him; the American Academy of Arts and Sciences and the American Association for the Advancement of Science both elect him to membership; he is asked to deliver the Lowell Lectures in Boston; a new normal school in New York City offers a chair; and Asa Gray recommends him in 1872 to the president of Princeton as *just the man* to start a new School of Natural History.

Most of his income derives from the popular side of his career. A witty, energetic speaker, Morse becomes a favorite with audiences that do not sharply distinguish between education and entertainment. On annual swings through the East and Middle West he lectures on insects and animals, shelled creatures of the land and sea, ancient glaciers, flowers and their friends. Livelihood may be the major reason for such activities, but they also represent a tacit expression of faith in the educational potential of ordinary people. The same attitude fills his publications. Ned's newspaper articles encourage readers to enhance the pleasure of mountain and seashore trips by observing and learning more about the world of nature, and his *First Book of Zoology* urges students to seek the animal kingdom in the snails, worms, and frogs of their own backyards.

Morse's own investigations retain a similar flavor. Other researchers may specialize in embryology or comparative anatomy, adopt new vocabularies and move toward the experimental laboratory, but he sticks with natural science into the seventies and never loses a taste for the outdoor pleasures of collecting in forest, field, river, and sea. No surprise that his major discovery grows out of shells. A decade of tracking brachiopods up and down the Eastern seaboard indicates that they have been incorrectly classified. Until now the creatures have been considered mollusks because, like clams and oysters, they are bivalves with two shells. But the resemblance is not a true one, for the valves of a mollusk are left and right, while those of a brachiopod prove to be dorsal and ventral, or front and back. Indications to this effect are not conclusive, and research must continue for years, with detailed examinations of the internal organs—liver, stomach, ovaries—of creatures only one-eighth of an inch in length. In 1870 his major scientific publication is ready. *The Brachiopoda: A Division of Annelida* proves conclusively that they are not mollusks, but worms.

More than a century later this discovery may seem a trifle tame, routine, even pedestrian. But in nineteenth-century natural history nothing is more important than accurate classification. No wonder that Morse's findings thrust him to the pinnacle of his career and bathe him in glory as praise pours in from scientists in both the United States and Europe. Most delicious is the letter from Charles Darwin that commends the strength and clarity of the presentation: *What a wonderful change it is to an old naturalist to have to look on these 'shells' as 'worms.'* Words like this are ample repayment for all the years of tedious study; they underlie Ned's own shout of triumph in a letter to John Gould: *It isn't every day that a prominent class of animals is walked out of one branch and into another.*

Brachiopods do more than bring an international reputation; they also help to turn Morse into a follower of Darwin. His public endorsement of evolution comes in 1873 at a meeting of the Essex Institute in Salem. By then the issue has become a touchy one in religious circles, and being too outspoken may endanger Ned's career as a lecturer. At least that is the opinion of Gould, who may be growing weary of lending money to help support his friend. But to the suggestion that he tone down future statements, Ned has a sharp reply: *I should rather come down to one meal a day and lumber along in debt*—one can almost hear Gould sigh—*than to follow so humiliating a path.* Truth is truth. The public is ignorant of Darwinism and it is his duty to spread enlightenment. His changed view of evolution is only the mark of a careful scientific mentality: *My chief care must be to avoid that 'rigidity of mind' that prevents one from remodeling his opinions; there is nothing* [more] *glorious . . . than the graceful abandoning of one's position if it be false.*

This attitude does not extend beyond the realm of science. However open his mind, Ned in his late thirties remains uncurious about the social, political, and artistic premises and practices of his nation and culture. Over the years his beliefs have been remarkably consistent. He is a scientist and an American; he believes honesty is the best policy, and that the early bird gets the worm. Evolution may provide a new way of rejecting the church of his father and such distasteful doctrines as original sin or eternal punishment in an afterlife, but it does nothing to affect a faith— shared by Darwin—in the *wisdom and goodness of the creator*. Nor does it free Morse from the values and habits of a culture rooted in the Puritan tradition. Work is his life, his pleasure, his duty, his reason for being. It justifies man's ways to man.

How distressing, then, to feel that one's important work is done. Following the fame that derives from the culmination of a life devoted to shells, Morse the researcher loses direction and purpose. Mollusks no longer tug at him. In the mid-seventies he complains to friends that the field has become routine and threatens to abandon shells because nothing more can be done *aside from describing new species*. Surely this is an odd assertion for a man whose life has been devoted to just such activities! Were Morse self-conscious, he might find in such a remark an indication of some psychic alterations. Had he the benefit of late-twentieth-century psychological insight, he might see himself as sliding into a midlife crisis. Barring such insight and foresight, he is left with the daily routine of a life that seems less satisfying than before— studying shells, preparing and delivering lectures, attending scientific gatherings, writing articles and papers.

The way out comes through shells. A lecture tour in 1874 takes Morse to California for the first time, where San Francisco provides not only the flavor of Asian culture, but also a most important chance contact. Someone with a taste for natural history and a knowledge of East Asia informs him that the waters of Japan are rich in species of brachiopods unknown in the United States. Immediately Morse decides that he must go there as soon as possible to continue his old studies in a new setting. For the next three years, he will work to arrange free time and raise the necessary money for the expedition. What he cannot earn, he will, of course, borrow. For Ned—or for his closest friend John Gould—no price seems too high nor any distance too great when it is a matter of learning more about creatures who live in shells.

6

Leucadia to Martinique

Self-consciousness makes the difference. Unlike the others, Lafcadio Hearn knows how to place his days in a context of words, can admit to those peculiarities of belief and behavior that set him apart from contemporaries. He says: *Real life is something I spend my whole existence in trying to get away from*, and we think of his childhood and nod in understanding. He explains: *The wish to become is reasonable . . . while the wish to have is . . . foolish*, and we are tempted to take this as a way of interpreting the curve of his days. Supporting evidence is not difficult to find. Those many sharp breaks with friends and editors; the sudden abandonment of good jobs; the moves to new locales where he is unknown; the stories of ghosts and spectral lovers; the cloudy, quasi-philosophic speculations that blend Herbert Spencer and Buddhism—all this can seem part of a flight from materialism and toward a world of the spirit.

But wait. Best not accept the too-easy explanation. The man who claims to turn his back on reality makes more than one successful career by doing so; the man so concerned with becoming also needs to have. Hearn is a paradox, a case study in how the word can at once obscure and illuminate. Not that his writings are the entire problem. To his more than twenty volumes, scores of articles, and hundreds of letters must be added all those other interpretations: the many biographies and critical studies, the reminiscences of friends and family members, the dozens of pieces in academic journals. Read them all and you will be reminded of how far removed we are from what the flesh once knew and the heart once felt. Hearn would agree. Elusive, hidden, ultimately inexplicable to himself, he devotes a lifetime to seeking words for what can never be said.

<>

Blame imperialism.

The meeting is unlikely; the marriage unlikelier still. He is thirty; Anglo-Irish; a graduate of Trinity College, Dublin; third-generation army; a surgeon; a nominal Anglican. She is twenty-five, Greek, uneducated, untraveled, devoutly Orthodox. Neither is political, but revolution brings them together. It is 1848 and Europe is in turmoil—barricades in Paris; republics in Naples, Florence, Turin; a parliament in Frankfurt; Prince Metternich driven from Vienna; stirrings in Prague, Brussels, Geneva. Far off in Cephalonia, that windswept mass off the west coast of Greece, a local assembly resolves that the Ionian Islands should no longer be a British protectorate. In response, Her Majesty's troops fan out through the archipelago. The small detachment that lands on the isolated, barren island of Cerigo has as its physician one Charles Bush Hearn.

We do not know exactly where or when Hearn meets Rosa Cassimati, or what language they speak together (though passion needs few words), or how they are discovered, or if it is true—as Hearn family story has it—that her brother attempts to avenge his sister's disgrace by waylaying the surgeon and stabbing him. We do know this: in June 1849, when Charles is transferred to the island of Leucadia, Rosa goes with him; on July 24 she gives birth to a son; on November 25 the couple are married in a Greek Orthodox ceremony; and in February 1850 he sails for England on the way to a new military assignment. Four months later, the wife left behind gives birth to another son, named Patrick Lafcadio in recognition of his mixed heritage. Joy is tempered by tragedy when, at the end of August, the firstborn dies of some unrecorded affliction.

We do not know (but can easily guess) why Charles conceals

his marriage from the War Office until he is fully two years into a West Indian tour of duty; or why (more difficult) he finally admits to having a wife and child; or why (almost impossible) he has Rosa and Patrick Lafcadio brought to his mother's home in Dublin in August 1852. We do know that Rosa's charms do not transfer well from Greece to Ireland. Charles arrives home in October 1853 to find an intercultural war in progress. Moodiness, hysterics, bouts of insanity—all kinds of instability are attributed to the Greek interloper. More than half a century later Lafcadio's early biographers are ready with explanations: Rosa, you see, is dark of hue and distinctly Mediterranean (some suggest Oriental). To an early twentieth-century Anglo-American biographer, that alone has great explanatory power.

The details of the next five years are far less important than the devastating pain, never directly expressed, that they must cause the child. Certainly we can do without the names of aunts, cousins, and summer estates, without the scenes that take place between Charles and Rosa during his few months in Dublin. It is easy to divorce a foreign wife whose illiteracy has kept her from properly signing a marriage document. By late 1857 the young boy has become an odd kind of orphan—his parents are alive, but he will never again see either of them. Charles is off in India with a new wife; Rosa is back in Cerigo, wed to an islander; and Patrick Lafcadio is residing with Sarah Brenane, a great-aunt and childless widow who expects to make him heir to her considerable fortune.

The absence of parents and the promise of wealth, the conjunction of deep insecurity and wild dreams—these emotional legacies will never be shaken. Some friends will later insist he was born *overly sensitive*; others that his delicate, morbid streak goes back to that Eastern background. Patrick Lafcadio will, in a way, agree. As an adult he will disdain his northern European heritage (there goes his first name) and call himself Greek, or identify with Latins; he will detest cold climates and yearn for warmth and sun as if for home. Of one thing he is certain: whatever happened between mother and father, Charles is to blame for his loneliness. At the age of forty, Lafcadio will recall seeing his father on only four or five occasions; will remember fear in the presence of a taciturn man with a *rigid, grim face*; will confess never to have felt any love for Charles Bush Hearn.

Mother is quite the opposite—a lovable victim, impulsive and full of warmth. Any anger or early feelings of abandonment are by adulthood rationalized away: her situation in Ireland was cruel; she spoke no English, had no means of support, was first isolated and then betrayed. But she was loving, so loving that whatever he later finds good in himself—a desire for justice, a sensitivity to beauty, a capacity for faith—will be attributed to Rosa. All through life he will see the female as creator: *It is the mother who makes us,—makes at least all that makes the nobler man: not his strength of powers of calculation, but his heart and power to love.*

The next fifteen years could be out of Dickens. How one would like to see him handle the characters: fussy, meticulous Aunt Sarah, dressed always in black, equally passionate about cleanliness and salvation; Cousin Jane, who looks like an angel and luxuriates in talk about the pains of hell; the tutor who with a pen crosshatches bathing drawers and shirts onto the pictures of nymphs, graces, and goddesses in a book on Greek civilization; the various maids, cooks, butlers, and footmen who take the place of young companions; and Henry Molyneux, the smooth, distant relation who wins Sarah Brenane's confidence, moves from managing her money to having himself declared her principal heir, and is instrumental in having Lafcadio sent away to various schools, the farther from Dublin the better.

No doubt the novelist could do the locations justice, too: that tall, gloomy house in the suburb of Rathmines, with its shadowy ceilings, long staircases, and dusty attics, and the chilly, narrow room where Lafcadio is locked every night; the country manors where, in the bright weeks of summer, the youngster learns the joys of seaside and field, of tidepool and flowers; the Institution Ecclésiastique, near Rouen, which former student Guy de Maupassant describes as smelling *of prayers the way a fish-market smells of fish*; the stone pile and green playing fields of St. Cuthbert's, near Durham, England, where Hearn briefly takes the name Paddy, specializes in pranks, denounces religion, and shocks a confessor by expressing a strong desire to yield quickly and completely to any and all fleshly temptations the Devil might care to send his way.

Such overt rebellion is hardly characteristic. The real world of this frail lad is inner. His pleasures are solitary, his imagination so vivid that sometimes he cannot distinguish between daydreams and nightmares. Swimming is his sport; reading his joy; writing his talent, one that is rewarded with many prizes for composition. Chances that he will emerge from a cocoon of introversion are crushed at the age of sixteen when he is struck in the left eye with a rope during a playground game. Doctors in London cannot save his sight, and Lafcadio is permanently disfigured: white tissue scars the surface of his cornea, and something less visible scars his psyche. The lad who returns to school is quiet, subdued, and withdrawn. Cause or excuse—ever after he will feel self-conscious with new people, uneasy with all males save for a few close friends, and distinctly unattractive to women.

One year after the accident, another cruel twist of fate drastically changes Hearn's life. When Henry Molyneux's investments fail, Aunt Sarah, now seventy-five and feeble, must give up her own home and move in with her new heir's family. Does Molyneux twirl his moustache as he makes plans for the young man he has supplanted? Hearn will later think so. Late in October 1867 the youngster is yanked from school and sent to live with Mrs. Brenane's former maid, a woman now married to a dock-worker in London. For more than a year he vanishes from history, disappears into the fog and roaring streets of the British capital. Decades later he will drop hints about running away, wandering the city's ugliest regions, sharing the hunger and misery of the poor, enduring a session in a London workhouse. One result of this period will be a lifelong distaste for great cities. Never for him will they mean glamour, excitement, or culture—only inhumanity, oppression, the death of feeling and of hope.

Childhood, innocence, even adolescence—whatever remains of these ends abruptly in 1869 when Molyneux sends passage money to America and instructions to seek out a distant relative in Cincinnati who will supposedly help him get established there. Of the Atlantic crossing in the spring, he will never pen a word. But more than thirty-five years later he will vividly recall his instantaneous love for the tall, grey-eyed Norwegian peasant girl who sits facing him on the first day of the train ride from New York to Cincinnati. Only once do they exchange words, but the sound of her accent never fades, and *the shadow, the golden shadow of her* always stays with him. Near death he will sketch this brief encounter as *My First Romance*. It will outlast all the later ones.

<>

Cincinnati in 1869, four years past the Civil War. Call it Boomtown, that oldest and newest of American stories. Give it a subtitle: How to Convert Natural Beauty into Wealth. Mention the great bluffs above the Ohio River, and the view of Kentucky's hills shimmering in the distance. Describe, closer at hand, the stench and blight of pork-packing houses, soapworks, tanneries; the slums sprawled along the waterfront; the hills and valleys scarred with shanties and new suburbs. Lots of life here, lots of hustle; lots of big dreams of trade, industry, and quick wealth. Two hundred thousand people call the city home, and that number is on a rapid rise. A good minority of them speak German; larger numbers carry the lilt of the Irish countryside; thousands of newcomers talk in the tones of the newly emancipated.

Never will Hearn report how the city looks to eyes fresh from London. Maybe the shock is too great for him to remember. Put yourself in his place: you are nineteen, five feet three, slight of body, blind and scarred in one eye and nearsighted in the other, painfully shy, decently enough educated but wholly unprepared for any practical pursuit. At the initial meeting with Molyneux's relative, it becomes clear that he will be of no real help. So suddenly you are on your own, facing that most elemental question: how to live. The answer is never clearly recorded. You write no letters, keep no diary. Only three decades later do you refer to the activities and feelings of those first weeks and months alone, and then in suggestive metaphors rather than concrete details. You were *dropped into the enormous machinery of life*; you experienced the *wolf's side of life, the ravening side, the apish side; the ugly facets of the monkey puzzle.*

Work is the first issue. Anything will do. You try hawking, canvassing for politicians, writing advertisements; you attempt to become an accountant, sign on as a messenger boy for the telegraph office. Maybe the jobs do not pay enough or maybe lack of skill gets you fired. Whatever the reason, none of them lasts very long. Too often you are short of cash, on the run. More than once your bags are seized when you are tossed out of a boarding house. You know what it is to sleep in a doorway or a stable, to dine on stolen food, to be bullied by the police. Only as a servant do you find a resting place. For a year and a half you light fires, shovel coal, and do handy work in a boardinghouse *in exchange for food and the privilege of sleeping on the floor of the smoking room.*

All this is part of a writer's education, one may be tempted to say. But that is the safe voice of historical hindsight, while yours are the fearful moments of wondering about not only the next meal but the next decade, and the ones after that. As if a question has been posed, you begin to haunt the public library at Sixth and Vine, to sample its fifty thousand volumes. Do you find the answer there? Is it in the pages of Charles Baudelaire, Gérard de Nerval, Gustave Flaubert, Stéphane Mallarmé—all those French writers who develop and cater to your taste for the exquisite? Or in those tales of the supernatural, the folklore and mythologies from Africa, India, Oceania; or in the books on the way of the Buddha; or in the poetry and tales of Poe, the single American author whose life and works seem congenial, whose interest in the bizarre matches your own?

Hearn the writer is born in the library. His work will always carry the scent of dusty bookshelves, hints of tales penned in foreign languages, queer notions lifted from distant epochs and remote cultures. The earliest stories, *published in cheap Weekly papers* and lost to history, bring no payment or recognition. Not until November 1872 does he receive money for a piece of writing. Fifteen months and some eighty free-lance articles later, he joins the staff of the daily *Enquirer* at a salary of $25 a week. Already he has something of a reputation as a journalist, but one that has little to do with those staples of the newspaper game—politics, industrial progress, financial scandal, petty crime. Hearn is a feature writer, his choice of subjects always part of a personal desire to explore both the outside world and the self and to examine the relationship between the two.

Spiritualists, prostitutes, ex-slaves, failed suicides, kosher butchers, gravediggers, pickpockets, roustabouts, ragpickers, policemen, pawnbrokers, artists, and murderers—these are the kind of characters that Lafcadio likes to track to their natural habitats, to courtrooms, cemeteries, city dumps, slaughterhouses, wharves, midnight missions, and the gin mills, opium dens, dance halls, and cribs of Bucktown's Rat Row. In pursuit of a good story, he allows himself to be hauled by a steeplejack to the top of the highest church spire in Cincinnati; dons a dress and bonnet to attend a lecture restricted to females (and suffers momentary panic when another man, similarly attired, is discovered, roughed up, and tossed from the auditorium); drinks fresh cow's blood—good for the health!—in a slaughterhouse; sneaks into a studio to view the most voluptuous of local models lying undraped before a roomful of painters; and attends a seance where—to his great surprise—the spirit of Charles Bush Hearn, speaking through a medium, begs forgiveness for the wrong of abandoning his son.

Hearn does not merely celebrate city life. He also plays the critic, exposing fraudulent fortune-tellers, abortionists, dishonest missionaries, corrupt government officials, YMCA leaders who own slum property. Criticism moves toward a new kind of journalism that aims at sensational effects. He begins to call himself a *ghoul* who revels in *thrusting a reeking mixture of bones, blood, and hair under people's noses at breakfast time.* Never is this more true than in late 1874, when a tanyard worker, stabbed with a pitchfork, is stuffed while still alive into a furnace. Hearn's reconstruction of the victim's agony and the descriptions of the remains—*a hideous adhesion of half-molten flesh, boiled brains, and jellied blood . . . crisped and still warm to the touch*—do more than ruin a few appetites. They also make him well known in the community and, through reprints, capture the attention of a national audience.

How far to come in just five years. The once penniless immigrant now enjoys a steady income, an address listed in the city directory, and a circle of friends—journalists, artists, poets, printers, and freethinkers. He also has a woman—Mattie Foley, the cook at a house where he boards. Eighteen, illiterate, and the mother of an illegitimate four-year-old boy, she is *a healthy, well-built country girl* who in soft, melodious tones tells fascinating stories of childhood on a plantation. Mattie may be no darker than the olive-skinned Hearn, but she was born in Kentucky as a slave.

Call the next step a repetition of Charles Bush Hearn and Rosa Cassimati. See it as another way of thumbing one's nose at middle-class conventions. Term it self-destructive, an unconscious identification with the oppressed and scarred of the earth. Marriage between black and white has been illegal in Ohio since 1861, but in June 1874 Hearn somehow gets a license and persuades a black Episcopalian minister to perform the ceremony. Almost immediately, the pressures of living together drive the couple apart. Details are virtually nonexistent, but the problem seems to be temperament—he is too sober and serious, she too playful and irresponsible. Soon Mattie is out on the streets, in trouble with the police, and he is back in a world of male friends, full of guilt over his inability to save her from ruin: *I love her,—more I fancy than I will ever love any woman; and somehow the lower she falls, the fonder I feel of her. I think I have been unjust to her— unjust in marrying her at all—lifting her up only to let her fall lower than ever.*

Not that the marriage does much for him. In the summer of 1875, some local politicos who have been stung by Hearn's pen carry rumors of the scandalous marriage to his editor. The same day, Lafcadio is out on the street, so full of despair that later reports of a suicide attempt cannot wholly be discounted. Or is it only show, the kind of gesture that one good friend will recall as not uncommon: *He would have liked to kill himself spectacularly if he could have written the story for his newspaper.* Whatever the truth, his dark mood cannot last for long. Six days after his final article in the *Enquirer*, Hearn is writing for the Cincinnati *Commercial*.

Success. Surely that is what it means to be picked up so quickly by a rival newspaper. The chance to reject an offer to return to the *Enquirer* a few weeks later only underscores the personal triumph. But Hearn, at the age of twenty-five, knows the difference between the public image and *the inner life . . . which no other eye can see.* Increasingly, the cost of journalistic success seems too high. Work has become a grind—the hours too long (often noon to 3 a.m.), the scope for creativity small. In 1876, bums, convicts, and hustlers have become so familiar that it is difficult to make their stories interesting. Time now to set aside hours for more serious work, to begin to translate Théophile Gautier's elegant stories from French into English. Such endeavors are in part literary exercises, in part escape. Daily he may mingle with the victims and victimizers of Rat Row and gaze at the murky Ohio River, but Gautier takes him to far-off times and places, lets him lie on a silken bed with Cleopatra, stride the streets of Thebes, gaze at the Nile on perfumed nights.

Such work must have an effect, for suddenly one day it is all too much. Or far too little. Weary of the daily struggle in an ugly city, weary of *the American disposition to work people to death, and the American delight in getting worked to death*, he longs for a brighter, warmer world; for a slower pace; for the color of the tropics; for the passion of Mediterranean life. Later he will say: *It is time for a fellow to get out of Cincinnati when they begin to call it the Paris of America.* The city may boast libraries, theaters, concert halls, and gardens, but its soul—if that be the word—lies in the smoky factories and stony bank buildings of a commercial civilization. Abruptly and without warning, he quits his job in October 1877 and boards a boat for New Orleans. He may imagine that he is only going south, but we can see him starting on a much longer journey.

<>

Beginning again. The world newly born; the faces fresh; the pleasure of not being known. Reality still undefined. Anything possible. Or so it can seem when you float in on that great brown river, past the cane fields and the cottonwoods drooping with Spanish moss. The eye stretches; the soul expands. Here is a harbor of ships from ports out of dreams—Constantinople, Smyrna, Marseilles, Hong Kong. Here are miles of levee, warehouses bursting with sacks of cotton and sugar. Here is a city of verandas, porches, and balconies, of gardens, statues, fountains, and flowers. Quickly you come to know that *curious, crooked French quarter*, its houses tinted yellow, green, and blue; the great cathedral in Jackson Square; the open-air markets with heaps of tropical fruit; the rich smell of oriental coffee wafting from cafés; the faces from Italy, Greece, Cuba, and Brazil; the soft tones of Spanish, French, and *the sweetest of all dialects, the Creole of the Antilles.*

Love for New Orleans proves stronger than hunger during seven months that Hearn cannot find work. His savings vanish. He sells off all his books, roams the streets in ragged clothes, comes down to living on *a five-cent meal once in two days.* His twenty-eighth birthday passes in an agony of dread and self-doubt. Ahead lies nothing but *starvation, sickness,* [and] *artificial wants, which I shall never be wealthy enough to even partially gratify.* Heredity is the culprit. In a country where to be a success you need *gigantic shoulders,* he is one of the *small people;* in the land of the practical, a dreamer who will never have the leisure to develop his talents or create *something decently meritorious.* The desire for independence has been thwarted. By late spring of 1878, he feels like *a most damnable failure.*

This harsh judgment is characteristic. So is the unwillingness to give excuses, or to recognize the larger social factors in his predicament. New Orleans, not yet recovered from the Civil War and the occupation by Union troops, has a stagnant economy. The bright side of this, that living is cheap, becomes apparent after June 15 when he lands a job on *The Item* at a salary of $10 a week, enough to let him live in a decent room, eat well, and have enough money to purchase books. Unlike the demanding Cincinnati papers, this four-page daily takes very little of his time. Three hours every morning are quite enough to fulfill all his duties—to *rattle off* leaders on literary or European matters, put together a few articles based on telegraphic reports, cut and paste a column of news from the rural Louisiana press, and take notes from the New York papers for the next day's editorials. By midday he is free. Ahead stretches the *long, golden afternoon,* with *its perfume and its laziness.* How fine a prospect; what a sweet existence this could be for *one without ambition or hope of better things.*

That person is not Hearn. His aim is high, his journalism practice for more serious literature. All his hours point in that direction. New Orleans fascinates him with its feel of the tropics, polyglot population, and multicultural heritage. He becomes an amateur anthropologist, folklorist, linguist. From blacks he collects samples of the street dialect called *gumbo*; from Creoles, who pride themselves on the purity of their Latin blood, he takes recipes, proverbs, tales that closely blend legend and history; from street vendors of potatoes and herbs, he learns musical cries and a patois blending English, Spanish, French, and African tongues. All this is the stuff of feature articles, and not just for the local press. In the pages of *Harper's Weekly*, Hearn begins to share the city, its people, customs, and languages, with a national audience.

A growing reputation lets him leave *The Item* late in 1881 to become literary editor of the more substantial *Times-Democrat*. The man who glories at living in *a Latin city* has little taste for the sentimentalities of most current American literature, so his Sunday pages become a forum for fashionable authors—largely French—from the Continent. With sympathy and understanding he attempts to explain movements like the naturalism of Émile Zola or the impressionism of Pierre Loti. With delicacy, circumspection, and self-censorship, he translates stories or chapters, his pen confined within the limits of what a genteel audience will tolerate. Through Hearn, New Orleans readers sample Nerval, Flaubert, Maupassant, Alphonse Daudet, and Anatole France.

After the publication of his first book, a collection of tales translated from Gautier, in New York in 1882, Lafcadio begins to cut something of a figure in New Orleans. Still elusive and certainly not very social, he favors capes, floppy hats, and soft shirts, and begins to spend time with writers and artists. For a while he is close to George Washington Cable, the local literary lion. Together the two men take meals, drink wine, and stroll the streets of the Vieux Carré discussing literature. When Joel Chandler Harris, creator of Uncle Remus, visits from Atlanta, he seeks out Lafcadio and goes home to write a column in the *Constitution* that calls Hearn a *man of letters who has already made his mark*. When nationally known authors like Charles Dudley Warner, Joaquin Miller, and Mark Twain meet the diminutive writer on swings through the region, they carry back to Northern editors the word that Lafcadio is a writer to be watched.

All this is very nice, but hardly enough to satisfy his growing ambition. Hearn is not content with recognition that comes from turning the writing of others into English prose; he longs to be known for original work. Art—most definitely spelled with a capital "A"—is his reason for being, his true religion. No sacrifice is too great to attain the kind of *grace* that creativity brings: *Could I create something I felt to be sublime, I should feel also that the Unknowable had selected me for a mouthpiece, for a medium of utterance, in the holy cycling of his purpose; and I should know the pride of a prophet that had seen God face-to-face.* This kind of faith and hope keep him at the writing desk for more hours than are good for his health, until his sighted eye grows painful and begins to bulge in a most unattractive manner. Lafcadio now must read with the paper just a few inches from his face, and write with his head bent almost to the desk. When he walks through town, the world is a blur. Only by using a small pocket telescope can he make things come into focus.

A similar fuzziness marks his art. That lusty side of the man, the one who enjoys good food and pleasures of the flesh, appears only in letters to friends. His public prose emerges from disembodied realms of fog and ghosts, where passion lives as an idea in the mind rather than a scream in the throat. Ask his chief fantasy and you get this answer: *I would give anything to be a literary Columbus,—to discover a Romantic America in some West Indian or North African or Oriental region,—to describe the life that is only fully treated of in universal geographies of ethnological researches.* Such kinds of work call for travel that he cannot afford, so he must be content *to find the Orient at home.* Personal desire and practical self-interest blend together in his aims: *A man must devote himself to one thing in order to succeed: so I have pledged me to the worship of the Odd, the Queer, the Strange, the Exotic, the Monstrous. It quite suits my temperament.*

The original stories Hearn begins to produce in the eighties are by his own admission not quite stories nor wholly original: *I have no creative talent, no constructive ability for the manufacture of fiction.* Those frequent feature-page efforts that he calls *Fantastics* are mere sketches—impressions of a landscape, a garden, a cemetery, a hotel room; recollections of dreams, of women seen or imagined; evocations of love, fear, decay, and death. More structured are tales taken from distant traditions—Finnish sagas, Hindu folklore, East Asian chronicles. No simple act of translation is involved here. Lafcadio does not hesitate to change points of view, delete characters, add or subtract moral statements until the tale is more than half his own. Two collections issued by Boston publishers—*Stray Leaves from Strange Literature* and *Some Chinese Ghosts*—encourage him toward something more contemporary. The result is *Chita*, a novella about a girl who is the sole survivor of a hurricane on the Louisiana coast. Like everything he writes, it is short on plot, characters, and moral dilemma, and very long on setting and mood.

The problem is more than literary. Hearn is a divided soul, one who wants to write fiction, knows fiction to be an *expression of real life*, and cannot stop himself from shunning just such life. Far more to his taste are contemplation and reflection, viewing things from afar and meeting people in books. Encounters with flesh-and-blood human beings are problematic, and his desires for intimacy are usually overbalanced by fear. No doubt this is a legacy from childhood, from being abandoned too many times. Now Lafcadio rejects people before they have a chance to desert him. Virtually every close personal relationship will terminate when Hearn picks a quarrel over some imagined slight and then makes a sharp, irrevocable break.

A similar swing characterizes his attitude toward New Orleans. By the middle of the eighties, he is weary of the city and ready to fulfill repeated threats of sailing off to the tropics. Later he will produce reasons enough for this break—annoyance at the editor of the *Times-Democrat* for judging his work scandalous and editing it too much; distaste for *the great number of shitasses whom I was obliged to say 'Goodday' to in N.O.*; realization that even here he is not free to voice beliefs about the equality of the races or to express his real feelings about the importance of sexuality. The decision to leave comes in May 1877, shortly after *Harper's* accepts *Chita* for publication. Never will Lafcadio acknowledge that to abandon New Orleans is to repeat the flight from Cincinnati, to flee once again from the familiar and comfortable toward the risky and unknown. Some may see this as a search for the self; others, for a home. With Hearn there is no need to choose between the two, for both quests are ultimately the same.

<>

Martinique. The tropics at last. The kind of island he has dreamed of all his life. Turquoise sky, great cocoa palms, volcanic hills, an azure sea tilting to the horizon, beautiful brown women. No hustle, no deadlines, no Puritan heritage. A community where people are honest, good-natured, easygoing, and courteous, where the only vices—if that's the word—are erotic: *No one thinks it scandalous even if your housekeeper be young and pretty, and have a baby suspiciously like you.* Just the place to grow fat and lazy, to shed all ambition, to learn the two important lessons of how much rum to drink and how much love to make. No wonder it seems *simply heaven on earth.*

That's the initial reaction, voiced when he visits the island on a Caribbean cruise in the summer of 1887, repeated when he returns in October for a stay that may last months, years, or—as he tells some friends—*forever.* It continues as the public view, remains implicit in later articles for *Cosmopolitan* and *Harper's* and in the chapters of his first really successful book, *Two Years in the French West Indies.* If never quite denied, this bright picture grows shadowy as the months pass. The loveliness of Martinique and power of the tropics present a challenge at once psychic and professional: if you have been raised in purgatory, how do you learn to live in *Paradise?*

Not easily; not over the long run; not if you have—what shall we call it?—a conscience, a soul, a something struggling to express itself. The easy part is falling in love with the vivid colors of the landscape, the soft winds, the graceful movements of the natives, the languid daily round—strong, aromatic coffee brought by a servant before dawn; an hour swim at sunrise; mornings at the desk above the white curve of St. Pierre's harbor; your first meal at noon: fruit, vegetables, tiny fish fresh from the bay. By half past two, the crushing heat has made it impossible to work: *If you try to write, your head feels as if a heated feather pillow had been stuffed into your skull.* So you change to pajamas, sleep through the afternoon, and wake for a *tremendous* sunset—*the blaze of a whole world on fire.* Then supper, a stroll along the quai, and bed by nine o'clock.

Seductive is the word for this existence. Dangerous, too. It can erode the patterns of a lifetime: *Slowly, you begin to lose all affection for the great Northern nurse that taught you to think, to work, to aspire. Then, after a while, this nude, warm, savage, amorous Southern Nature succeeds in persuading you that labor and effort and purpose are foolish things,—that life is very sweet without them;—and you actually find yourself ready to confess that the aspirations and inspirations born of the struggle for life in the North are all madness . . .*

Perhaps. But it's your sort of madness and not so easily shed. Maybe you can give up ideas of success and hopes of fame, but it is difficult to abandon intellectual life. Admit it: writing is a problem here, serious conversation a great effort, reading almost impossible. You can believe *Heaven and Sea make so mighty a poem* that all human poets seem *dullards,* all novelists *stupid beyond endurance,* and not see how this refers to you. At least you can until the editor of *Harper's* finds few of your sketches interesting and then returns a novella that took four months to write. Reveries now must give way to reality, to despair, hopelessness, and fears that something in this land has deranged you: *I am not sure of myself now at all,—maybe mentally out of gear without knowing it.*

Six months after landing, something is definitely wrong with Hearn's writing, something that *bewilders* him. Once the future seemed so easy: get out of journalism, find a lovely island, write a book about native life, some short stories, a novel of the tropics. Now he must reckon the cost of living where beauty is exactly what prevents one from work and where the glorious climate is precisely what *does not allow you to think or . . . to study or to work earnestly.* Feelings of exile begin to surface: *You get tired of the eternal palms against the light, tired of the colors, tired of the shrieking tongue* [that Creole he once considered the sweetest of dialects] . . . *tired of hearing by night the mandibles of great tropical insects furiously devouring the few English books upon the table.*

Enough. The problem is clear—abandon writing or the island. Enough. The choice cannot be in doubt. Yet for fifteen months he lingers, letting that old fantasy slowly leak away. More than nostalgia or an unwillingness to give up paradise keeps him here. Never forget his more practical side. The really good writing will come later. This is the time to gather material on native life, to tour the island, walk through cane fields, climb Mount Pelée; to play with children, listen to the songs and stories of fishermen, female porters, laundresses, East Indian storekeepers; to take notes on flowers, spiders, birds, and snakes, real and legendary; to attend Carnival, dance and drink with the passionate knowledge that something is about to end.

Like tearing my heart out. Those are the words for that day in May 1889 when the ship steams away from the port of St. Pierre. Hearn is sailing toward New York, that frightful city whose stone and iron terrors will make him say *Civilization is a hideous thing. Blessed is savagery!* He is sailing toward six months of living with a friend in Philadelphia while turning Martinique into one book of sketches and another of short stories; toward fears that he may have to return once more to daily journalism; toward hope that he can still find a far-off, exotic spot where the climate does not blur the memory or sap the will to write. He is also sailing toward these words in a letter: *My friends advise me to try the Orient next time; and I think I shall.*

Three

LOVING

The study of the West's Journey to the East is a study of the West; it is of the soul of the West that one learns, rather than that of the East.

—ROBERT S. ELLWOOD, "Percival Lowell's Journey to the East"

7

Feudalism in Fukui

Like a motion picture. Twelve horseback figures in a late winter landscape. From afar, dark shapes along a dirt road through valleys, across low streams, in hills where the naked branches of trees are frosted white. A heavy sky droops with clouds. Bursts of hail, flurries of snow angled by a sharp wind, an occasional shaft of sunlight. Close up, the sweating flanks of horses, mud splattering the camera lens, a flashing view of wooden stirrups, eleven filled with sandals, the twelfth with heavy boots. Pull back and you see warriors in dark robes, faces set in the blank look of the samurai on duty. The expression of the face of the twelfth figure, clad in a Western coat, blue eyes squinted against the weather, is hidden in the folds of a muffler.

Whatever lies behind the blue eyes is not easily read. Excitement, yes, indistinguishable from anxiety. The silent refrain: I am the first European to visit this temple, the first to stay at that inn, the first to see this fold of hill, that stand of trees. Wrapped in a larger notion: I am riding into the past, into a feudal land, into some storybook realm of Oriental despotism. Plenty of evidence for that. The honor guard, swords ready to defend his life. The stops at the great wooden barriers between fiefdoms, protected by squads of foot soldiers with long pikes. In the three days since crossing the border into Echizen, the ceremony in each small town: officials in formal attire bustle forward, make speeches of greeting; silent crowds touch heads to the ground, then stare wide-mouthed at the pale-skinned *tojin*.

Twelve days since leaving Yokohama, the mind crowded with images. You can see them as flashbacks, or as the frozen moments of a wood-block print, the color a trifle faded but still fresh and vibrant to Western eyes. Far behind now the day of seasickness on the S.S. *Oregonian*. Far behind, the great commercial center of Osaka, with its castle, fine restaurants, and extravagant *singing girls*. Six days since leaving the coast for the interior, a journey by flatboat on the Yodo River, steamer on Lake Biwa, then by palanquin, foot, and horseback, fifteen, twenty miles a day. During daylight, a caravan of fifty porters and guards, Hiroshige's lonely travelers, lost in a world of snowdrifts and storms; at night, the dim coziness of inns lit by candle and warmed by the heat of the *kotatsu*, a quilt over the glowing charcoal of a *hibachi*.

Griffis is becoming acclimated. He is learning that it would not do for the servants of a great lord to hurry. He is slowing to the pace of the samurai, to the smoking of pipes, the cups of tea, the lounging that precedes each day's movement. He sleeps on a futon on the floor. He supplements European dishes prepared by his cook with native food, awkwardly wielding chopsticks. He enjoys the attention of the young serving girls with their perpetual smiles. He listens to the pluck of the *samisen* and the *caterwauling* of female voices joined in ancient song, is equally enchanted by the stag dances of the samurai and the graceful slow motions of hand, foot, and fan of the female entertainers. Nothing more *improper* than an excess intake of *sake* has crossed his vision, but the defenses and wariness of a lifetime do not easily drop—he still reckons these people to be *probably the most licentious in the world*.

Now the long-awaited moment is at hand. A view forward from the cavalcade across the plain, the accented voice-over of an interpreter crying *Yonder is Fukui*, and a sudden burst of sunshine flooding the city in *golden glory*. That's the only account we have, take it or leave it. Zoom forward, and there, nestled in groves of trees and tufts of high bamboo, see a dark mass of houses, the curving roofs of two large temples, the tower of a castle small by European standards. No golden spires, no massive walls, no huge buildings. How to show the incipient moment of disappointment, the beginning of the end of a vision of Fukui as *something vaguely grand, mistily imposing.* No time now, for here come the local officers to form an escort and lead their visitor through streets lined with curious faces, then over a bridge and through an imposing gate. Everyone dismounts in a courtyard before the door of an ancient rambling house. Low bows are followed by the hearty if awkward handshakes of men unused to such a mode of greeting.

Griffis enters his new home and inspects rooms and appointments while the Japanese mill about and utter sharp sounds of approval. Two of fifteen rooms in the old-style mansion with high wooden ceilings and neat matting have been partially Westernized. Sliding partitions and windows are of glass, not paper. Rooms scaled to the eye of someone sitting on the floor have been crowded with bulky, foreign objects—a canopied bedstead, dressers, a huge table and chairs, an iron stove fitted with a chimney pipe and glowing with hot coals. Some officials bow out, others sit down to the welcome banquet, European style, a matter of knives, forks, and plates, of soup, fish, meat, and fowl, of wines, ale, and sweet desserts. Then Griffis is alone to unpack trunks and *cozy up* his new quarters with knicknacks, small pictures, familiar books. After dark, an officer calls to offer Griffis assistance in choosing servants, horses, flowers, pictures, curios, and what every young man obviously needs, a fair maiden as a *playmate.* What momentary stirrings of desire, what flashing wayward thoughts, lie behind the curt reaction: *I thanked him, and accepted all his offers but the last.*

To bed alone then, the room silent, the night cold, the body tired, the mind free. Thoughts as pictures. How odd to know the stars the same as those at home, to hear the call of wild geese, to wake to the gentle throb of distant temple bells. In the morning, sun and blue sky. Sunday, March 5, 1871. Sabbath in a land without Sabbath. No church bells call to Griffis, no Sunday school or sermons await him. In the streets of Fukui, merchants, priests, and vendors move with the rhythm of their normal occupations. Midmorning. Guards and grooms arrive with a magnificent horse, the mane and tail knotted in festive tufts, the saddle gilded, the back covered in bright silk. The troupe rides across bridges, through moats, and into the inner precincts of the castle. Pages, attendants, warriors kneel as the foreigner removes shoes at the doorway of a government building and walks in stockings along polished wooden hallways. At the state room, the interpreter drops to his knees, but the freeborn American strides forward. Matsudaira Mochiaki, the ruler of Echizen, and six of his ministers greet Griffis with outstretched hands, then all sit on chairs at a table to share tea, oranges, sponge cake, and conversation.

An hour later Willie rides out through the massive castle gate. The excitement of journey and arrival are over. Time to tour his new domain, to look for what has existed in his mind, to find what two months of Japan's simple villages and frugal people have not yet destroyed: a taste of Oriental splendor. Or so he later claims. Perhaps it is true, perhaps until that morning ride his eyes are clouded with *films of glamour*. Fukui is the end of the line. No more illusions possible now. It is like all the other towns—*The houses of wood, the people poor, the streets muddy, few signs of wealth, no splendid shops. Talk of Oriental magnificence and luxury! What nonsense!* This strong reaction to the world as it is and not as he wishes it to be: *I was disgusted. My heart sank. A desperate fit of the blues seized me.* Homeward he goes to a European dinner in those hybrid rooms. At fadeout he is chewing *the cud of gloomy reflections.*

<>

The letdown is inevitable. Since late September Griffis has been dreaming of Fukui; since mid-November he has been on the road. He has crossed three thousand miles of the American continent, five thousand miles of ocean, and three hundred fifty miles of the Japanese mainland. He has seen *wild Indians* in Nebraska and Chinese temples in San Francisco, has preached in Yokohama and nursed the victims of samurai swords in Tokyo. Now at the long-sought destination, he has reached that instant when the excitement of travel falls away, any notion of the exotic vanishes and you are forced to confront a question with dread implications: what am I doing here, so far from everything familiar, from loved ones, family, and friends?

No easy answer. The rationale voiced effortlessly at home, the beliefs that made life meaningful and launched you onto this journey must now stand a severe test. Against an alien reality, Griffis has layers of protection: a deep Christian faith; an unquestioned commitment to individualism, science, progress, and republicanism; a substantial self-interest in terms of salary. But good reasons do not chase away the blues, and the mood which descends in early March proves to be recurrent. One week after arriving in Fukui, he complains in a letter to his sister Maggie about *homesickness* and *dejection*; two weeks later, he is discouraged at the *magnitude* of his task and *the dirt, the foulness and the vile side* of Japanese life. In the coming months, similar hints of loneliness, doubts, and despair in letters will be checked by such phrases as *I do not, cannot write my feelings to you.*

Such avoidance is only part of a strategy for handling the shock of this unfamiliar society. More positive is that traditional American cure-all—hard work: *From early morn till near midnight I am busy, and I go to bed wearied out. I dare not have time to be homesick.* More interesting and inventive is an elaborate myth that Griffis creates out of his own experience. This unconscious maneuver begins just nine days after his arrival in an article to a Philadelphia newspaper: *Dear Intelligencer: How would one feel, suppose you, if the world were to roll back and the ages with it, and land him into the twelfth century? Doesn't it seem a curious idea to live every day, drawing the breath of life and eating daily food, and walking on solid earth, where there are no railroads, nor snorting locomotive, nor telegraph wires, nor printing press, nor pavements, nor parks, nor milkman, nor newsboy? How 'could' we do without gas, newspapers, glass windows and street cars? How 'could' a nineteenth-century New Yorker live in the twelfth century? We repeat it—how?*

Here is the role Griffis will cherish for a lifetime. An American *at the ends of the earth*, he lives in an age buried deep in the Western past, braves the wilds of a preindustrial social order, endures a primitive existence in the name of duty and a higher power. So proud is he to be a teacher *in a daimio's capital far in the interior, away from Western influence*, that over the years the story will grow ever more elaborate and inaccurate. He will forget the British-born colleague who teaches English in Fukui and remember himself as the solitary Westerner. He will imply that rather than simply asking Verbeck to find a chemistry teacher overseas, the ruler of Echizen had somehow personally selected him to organize a scientific school. A half-century later he will continue to boast, against all evidence to the contrary, that he was the first of thousands of foreigners in government employ to be brought out under the Imperial Charter Oath of 1868.

This myth of an American stranded in twelfth-century Japan is part of a script in which feudalism is a key element. To live in such a social order is to achieve a rare—perhaps unique—distinction, one calculated to entice editors, charm an audience, and promote the self. That Echizen is a feudal domain when Griffis arrives is true; that it is hardly a pristine example of such a social order is more difficult for him to admit. Certainly many elements of the traditional structure are intact. The population is divided into four classes—samurai, farmers, artisans, and merchants—with a fifth, the *Eta*, still untouchable, uncounted, unacknowledged. Sumptuary laws regulate food, drink, clothing, housing, and recreation for each class. The current *daimyo*, who rules half a million people, still reckons his wealth in the traditional manner, at 320,000 *koku* of rice a year. Echizen prints money, maintains an army, censors publications, and has its own legal code, courts, and school system.

To take all this as evidence of feudalism *in full swing* is to ignore the obvious. The hiring of a foreign science teacher is no aberration, no act of whim, but one of many signs that the old order is drawing to a close. Griffis is in Fukui as part of a movement for change that began in Echizen even before the 1853 arrival of American ships in Edo Bay. In the 1840s the regime, then headed by Matsudaira Shungaku, began to encourage change and experimentation in medicine, military affairs, and education. Young men were sent to Nagasaki to attend schools teaching Western medicine and military ways. Vaccination for smallpox was introduced in 1850, and two years later samurai began to practice with rifles as well as swords. New schools were opened in which the traditional Chinese-dominated literary curriculum was supplemented with more practical subjects. With the overthrow of the Shogun and the restoration of the Emperor in 1868, education became a way of supporting the national regime in its efforts to learn the technology and military secrets of the West.

The new science teacher may sympathize with such a goal, but his own notion of how to modernize this nation concerns more than the practical. Occidental civilization is of a piece, and developments in social, political, educational, and religious life all go together. Part of Griffis's self-imposed task is to demonstrate to the Japanese that Western guns, steamships, science, government, and social organization cannot be wrenched out of a context of belief, but originate *in the heart, in the belief, in the life which is guided by* [the] *holy book.* To teach science is ultimately not enough; Willie wants to *help these people upward to God.*

Again—the myth. Not yet ordained, forbidden by Japanese law to preach Christian doctrine, Griffis can thrill readers at home and perhaps titillate himself by indulging in such hopes. To spread Christ's word is the major part of the task that makes life worthwhile. Here in Fukui is work that a man is *proud to perform.* So highly important is this calling, Griffis tells his *Intelligencer* audience, that it allows him to endure the rigors of feudalism; to reside in a realm devoid of *newspapers, Churches or concerts;* to forgo the *society of congenial Christian men and* [the] *refining influence of pure and cultured women.*

Two weeks into his Fukui stay, all of Willie's defenses are well in place. Avoidance, hard work, and mythmaking provide a cushion against extremes of loneliness and at the same time help to release his energy and ambitions. Griffis does not suffer from the virtue of modesty. He sees himself in the vanguard of social change, envisions a major personal role in the coming transformation of the country. Educational and moral reforms are linked together when, in the first letter to Maggie, he expresses his grandiose aims: *to make Fukui College the best in Japan, to make a national textbook on Chemistry, to advocate the education of women, to abolish the drinking of saki, the wearing of swords and the promiscuous bathing of the sexes.*

<>

New shapes, smells, sounds, tastes, behavior. Odd encounters that can startle and delight, strange juxtapositions that perplex and mystify. The shock of the unfamiliar is everywhere. For days, weeks, the world tastes savory, pungent, fresh. That is the time to catch it, fix it clear enough to last a lifetime. Later the same things will happen again, experience will cycle into repetition. The beautiful and the ludicrous will lose their edge, the delicate and the brutal collapse together, the alien become familiar. To focus on the first moments, the initial encounter, is to catch something that will never again recur with the same burden of meaning.

Only once can Griffis awaken in the chill darkness and know that his new life as a teacher is about to begin. Only once can he feel that special nervous excitement as he leaves the house for the first time flanked by an interpreter and a samurai whose two swords protect against those who may hate foreigners. School is only a few minutes away, but the path to it seems to cross the centuries. Through the courtyard the three men walk past the ruins of *an old family shrine*, past the porter who kneels, head to the ground, and into the street along Walking-Wind River. Crowds here: *small boys going to school; officers going to business; coolies going to work, or 'moosmies'* [young girls] *with glittering black eyes, rosy cheeks and pearly teeth*. The men cross three wide moats, pass through gates cut into walls twenty feet thick and thirty-five feet high, made of building blocks *so large that it puzzles one to know how they got there*.

At the heart of the citadel lies the College of Fukui. Housed in the *immense* former residence of the *daimyo*, the school has seven hundred students (*four times as large as Rutgers!*), a library that contains both native scrolls and Western books, and a medical school that boasts a fine life-size pair of dissection models imported from France. Many students have cut off their topknots, but such a visible sign of modernity does not mean tradition is dead. That quickly becomes apparent when the foreigner is welcomed on Monday, March 6, with a demonstration of martial arts—fencing with swords of bamboo, jousts with spears short and long, wrestling and other types of hand-to-hand combat, all punctuated with the most *unearthly yells and exclamations*. The school day ends with another startling sight, *a picture of feudalism I shall never forget*: hundreds of students wrap books, brushes, and inkstones in square pieces of silk, bow to the floor before their teachers, reclaim weapons from the sword room, thrust them into girdles, step into wooden clogs, and, with appropriate swaggers and fierce looks, thunder off over a stone bridge.

The next morning Griffis stands for the first time at a table in a classroom that measures twenty by thirty-five feet. Light pours in through the *shoji*. Seventy students sit on the matted floor. Willie begins to lecture. He makes a distinction between the organic and the inorganic; he mentions several of the sixty-five known elements; he compares the old Western system—earth, fire, water, and air—to the Chinese tradition of earth, fire, water, wood, and metal. He speaks slowly, stops every couple of sentences for the translation. The faces before him are blank, impossible to read. That does not prevent these words from reaching his diary: *First day of teaching, succeeded quite well . . .*

By the end of the week, the phrase *taught as usual* enters his diary. From now on the important entries dwell on excursions—afternoon rides and hikes into the countryside, stops in villages that huddle at the base of snowy mountains, chance encounters with farm women who offer the stranger tea and refreshments. The first weekend brings him a companion—English teacher Alfred Lucy, back from a vacation in Yokohama. This veteran of five years in Japan makes Griffis a trifle uneasy. Lucy is fluent in the language, devoid of interest in the culture, full of contemptuous opinions of the natives and given to saying such things as *Japs speak the truth only by accident.* Like *99 out of every hundred* foreign men, he has been living with a Japanese woman; like many others, he cares little for religion and does nothing to conceal the fact that he is here for one purpose alone, to make money.

Language and the need for company draw the two Westerners together for Friday dinner, a Saturday ride, and, on a *clear and beautiful* Sabbath, a climb into the hills above Fukui. How different from Sunday at home. With no church to attend, Griffis finds himself visiting two large Buddhist temples; instead of discussing the Bible, he watches men with nets on poles moving through brushy hillsides to snare ducks. The afternoon concludes with a stop at a tea house overlooking the river valley. Here Lucy joins the natives in taking hot *sake* while Griffis allows himself no more than tea, flavored no doubt with the taste of moral rectitude. That evening he begins to write a first article about the problems of living in feudal Japan.

<>

The story now becomes difficult to follow. What is needed is a method, a camera that will at once highlight important scenes and capture slow trends, those imperceptible shifts that elude measurement and yet create the texture and meaning of the stay in Fukui. You want to see startling encounters and witness slow adjustments, the acceptance of oddities, the incorporation of notions once considered ludicrous, uncivilized, reprehensible. You want to watch Griffis at home, attempting to make his needs understood to servants who speak no English; in stores bargaining with merchants; on rides into the mountainous countryside. You want to feel his growing confidence in the classroom as he lectures on hydrogen, oxygen, nitrogen, carbon, sulfur, zinc, silver, and nickel to the always quiet, attentive students; to ease with him into feelings of comfort as the rooms of the old mansion become homey; to experience the initial joy and eventual weariness that comes with having to explain still one more time the chemical composition of air or the wisdom of the United States Constitution; to feel the slow-creeping boredom that descends over conversations where no interpreter is at hand and one must limit the vocabulary to that of a child. Yes, you want to become Griffis in Fukui, rather than remaining a spectator, one who views him through that ancient, supple, but ultimately distant camera on life we know as words.

I am very busy here. I must be.
But difficult it is to distinguish boast from lament, to know how much of the *must* belongs to the world and how much to the self. No matter. The days are long and full. Darkness shrouds the stand of tall pines in the courtyard when he rises. Baths and shaves are by candlelight. Breakfast is taken in a pale world, dawn accompanied by the taste of *some sort of omelette and batter cake combined.* Morning lectures are only the beginning of a long workday. No laboratory has yet been built, no textbooks ordered, no scientific equipment acquired. So Griffis must play the role of designer, architect, production manager. After lunch, taken with other teachers, he must discuss with school officials plans for the

lab and meet with blacksmiths to explain the manufacture of various apparatus. After dinner at home, he must pore over catalogues and send letters home requesting Maggie to purchase books and equipment, then write lectures simple enough to pass through the uncertain vocabulary of a translator and think of demonstrations that can be done with the implements at hand— burner, flask, voltaic battery, and microscope.

Exciting work to teach, attend to fire, flask, experiment, etc.
The exhilaration is easy to believe, especially since its opposite is also present: *Very tiresome to teach today.* Yet the human encounter between this Westerner and his students remains hidden. Journal entries are inexpressive: *Began study and experiments on water,* or *Lecture on mercury,* or, simply, *Nitrogen.* And the prose of a letter to a scientific journal at home is stilted and distanced: *In teaching physical science in Japan, one has need to begin at the lowest foundation, to demonstrate everything, and to clear away much rubbish of astrology, Chinese notions of philosophy, falsely so called . . .*

Three or four evenings a week, I hold evening classes in my own house.
You can see them arriving—the rich merchants, doctors, and government officials preceded by servants with lanterns; the teachers, Buddhist priests, and students picking their way through the darkness of the courtyard, pushing aside the sliding doors and crying *Gomen kudasai.* In the room full of Western furniture, they squat silently on haunches, all equal before the knowledge that Griffis has to impart. Monday he lectures on physiology; Wednesday reads and explains David Hume's *History of England*; Thursday speaks about *the governments of the world* and *the laws of civilized countries*; Friday teaches German to half a dozen medical students. On any evening, he may informally lecture on industry and culture, or describe the glories of American history, or speak as a world traveler and share firsthand knowledge of Europe. Sundays bring another, subtler form of instruction. With members of the household, with guards, interpreters, live-in students, and visiting priests, he reads and explains chapters from the Bible.

Industry is my happiness.

No doubt. But the definition of work is wide enough to include what others might consider recreation. For the missionary and writer, anything and everything may be part of the broad task of communicating truth. When he takes an afternoon to ramble through Fukui and poke into shops, it can be justified with the excuse of studying custom and character *under all the lights and shades of city life.* Daytime rides into the countryside or weekend jaunts out of town are portrayed as investigations into the state of local industry. He visits the stone quarries, pottery factories, the cottonseed mill, the oil press, the *sake* distillery, the paper-making villages, the copper mine, and the rifle factory. He visits the gunpowder mills, where a shrine to five workers killed in an accidental explosion elicits the comment, *Buddhism and gunpowder, what a combination.*

It never satiates me to see the life of this simple people in their rude villages.

The senses absorb and enjoy valleys terraced with rice fields, quiet groves that shelter shrines, temples, and tombstones. Never on such journeys is Griffis alone. Always a guard at his side, an interpreter, and sometimes a colleague or two. Everywhere a foreigner is the object of curiosity and attention. Crowds follow him; dogs whimper and bark; children cry *tojin, tojin,* then race off as if a fiend might be in pursuit. In remote villages *where no European has ever set foot* the population falls to its knees as the entourage approaches. Such behavior can hardly please a democrat: *I feel more disgusted and amused than honored by it.*

I spent the evening with several of the scholars . . . and about half a dozen or more principal men of the village.

On weekends away, Griffis stays at the house of the richest man in town, usually a merchant who deals in tea, or paper, or oil. Never is there any indication that the host is a man of business. The house is old, elegant, and full of art treasures—scrolls, inlaid boxes and swords, brushwork poems hundreds of years old. The garden is a wonderland of trees, bushes, falling water, fish ponds and stone lanterns. Banquets in his honor always feature professionals performing traditional dances and songs, but for the Japanese the highlight of the evening is talk. Local scholars and government officials ask questions that allow Griffis to expand upon science, manufacturing, and all the other *wonderful things* America has to offer Japan.

Mr. Lucy and I on Saturday were invited to meet the Prince in his summer mansion, about two miles from the College.

The date is April 1, the time three o'clock. Already Griffis has reached an important conclusion: in this hierarchical society, real change will occur only when the rulers themselves have become Christians and republicans. This invitation provides a first good chance to influence the course of Japanese development at the highest level, and Willie does not fail to make the most of it: *We rode out and met him there, with four of his head officers, and found a gorgeous dinner spread out, cooked by our trained cook, served by the pages and in thorough style. And eaten properly, chairs, table, plates, knives and forks were of the best, the courses numbered 10, the wine and beer of course were there; and, finding the officers and Prince Matsudaira in good humor, I told him of our glorious country with its free schools, free institutions, where labor with the hands was not a disgrace, where our chief magistrate came from the people, where we educated our women as highly as ourselves. We told them that Japan could never be a great country until they honored labor, made the privileged classes work, educated their women, and elevated and cared for the common people. Think of it: in a despotic country, and in a Daimio's presence, promulging such revolutionary ideas ... As soon as I found that we had said all that could well be remembered, we took our leave, not wishing to dissipate their minds by other ideas. A swift gallop brought us back to the city. A glorious moon swept the heavens and flooded the land with transfiguring glory, as I rode under the tall pines that shade my yard.*

‹›

Always a gap between experience and what he commits to paper. Journal notations, letters, the neatly formed paragraphs of articles never fully capture those daily encounters that nudge Griffis toward new feelings, new perspectives. In the margin of the diary he notes, *Reproduce some of our Jap. conversations*, then never follows through. This loss to the biographer may be serious but not crucial. Learning here does not take place through a clash of ideas. It would be out of character for priests, samurai, even the *daimyo* himself, to take issue with opinions. More likely Griffis's views on everything, including Japanese institutions and customs, are greeted with silent respect or seconded as unimpeachable wisdom.

Protection from argument is not the same as protection from explanation. Everyone is willing to tell him about local history, customs, legends, superstitions, but words seem to have less effect than the impact of his surroundings. Things always taken for granted assume importance in this strange environment. Rarely in many years of journals has he commented on the shape or texture of a countryside or bothered to describe the parade of seasons. Here the climate, the cycle of the year, the winds and hills and trees seem laden with meanings unimaginable at home. To describe them lovingly seems at once a necessity, a duty, and a joy. The jutting mountains surrounding Fukui are a source of constant wonder. Lovingly he charts their changes: March's pure white shapes turn to brown, to blue, to *living green*, grow *glorious with autumn tints*, and by December are white *stainless masses* once again. The river that bisects the city goes from stream to flood and back again. Spring arrives in a glory of blossoming trees. The rainy season brings ceaseless torrents—mold grows in shoes and stains the pages of open books. Summer is the purple droop of wisteria, wildflowers in the woods, frogs croaking in wet fields, the singing of birds, battles with clouds of hungry insects.

Rice becomes a symbol of something that eludes the conscious mind. The muddy countryside of March prepared by *ploughs as old as Job*; the square flats of tender shoots, carefully transferred by the hands of girls and women into the earth; the thickening green of summer that carpets valley and hillside; the yellow of October and the *reaping hook in the style of 2,000 years ago* that lays the world bare once again. Not to forget the bearded wheat, harvested in June; tea leaves and tobacco, spread on the ground to dry before thatched country houses; thick stands of sugar cane and familiar fields of cotton and corn; white streaks of buckwheat glowing in the *dusky gold of October*. The geese that cry south return; the fishermen of summer vanish when the trees shoot yellow and red. Every change is marked with festival days— women in kimono dance in fields and on bridges, Shinto priests intone the solemn chants: all is part of an unchanging round of harvests, thanks to ancestors, rice cakes offered to the gods.

The contours of Fukui soften into familiarity, but the original impression remains: no magnificence here, but instead, the homey rhythm of eighty-five thousand lives. How Griffis comes to love it all: the solemn castle quarter north of the river, where streets are plotted at right angles, houses with blue tile roofs hide behind neat fences of bamboo or wattle, and foot traffic is limited to *the dignified samurai, the well-dressed young lady, or the pretty children and their maids*. The bustle of shops and workplaces of Gofuku-cho, Dry Goods Street, with its clothing stores, Chinese pharmacies, booksellers, carpenters, watchmakers, tiny restaurants. The area south of the river, where buildings give way to temples, orchards, theaters, storehouses for rice, crematoria, the prison. The hill named Atagoyama, where 160 stone steps lead to picnic sites, miniature archery galleries where one may fire six-inch arrows at thirty-foot targets, and teahouses with banquet rooms graced by *the prettiest of the 200 or more singing girls in Fukui*.

To come to know the town, its places of work and entertainment, the movement of its seasons and festivals, is to internalize rhythms that throb with new knowledge. By the end of April Griffis claims, *I am beginning to enter into and understand Japanese life quite well*, a conceit supported by a variety of evidence: he handles chopsticks *very nimbly*, finds the *temperate* native diet of rice and fish good for the health, has come to enjoy the *insights* into local life gathered on evenings that feature *genuine Japanese entertainment*, geisha who sing, dance, and engage in repartee which must surely leave him baffled but charmed. In June he can meet a newlywed *blushing piece of maidenly beauty* without minding that her teeth are, as custom demands, stained black. When his guard marries a girl of just fifteen, Griffis is ready with an excuse for sister Maggie: *It must be remembered that Japanese girls develope at least two years sooner than American or European girls.*

Hints here, small indications that a certain weight of history and length of tradition are having an effect; no better example of this can be found than in Griffis's attitude toward his residence. Proud reports to Maggie about plans and ground-clearing for the new European-style house cannot ward off the spell of the old mansion. Two hundred years of history have consecrated the building—the sloping roof and shaggy eaves, the spacious rooms and wide corridors, the neglected gardens and overgrown fish pond. Generations have been born and educated here, have married, gone off to war, returned to die. *Pagan, heathen, Asiatic* they may have been, but their laughter, tears, and lives have *sanctified* the dwelling, have made it—that most sacred of nineteenth-century American words—*a home.*

This notion both comforts and disturbs. Sometimes Griffis feels like an intruder. He can sympathize with local conservatives who object to a foreigner living on *classic soil.* He comes to see the *vulgarity* of having as his dining room the former family chapel, *where ancestral tablets once stood, and the sacred lights and incense burned.* He preserves an ancient amulet designed to protect the house, not out of faith in its efficacy but because *everything human is sacred.* At night he strolls in the garden, *shut in from all but the stars and the faint murmur of the city, and the few glimmering lights on the mountain across the river,* and wonders over his own role in Fukui. The educator who is bringing a *new civilization that must destroy the old* has difficulty answering the question, *Why not leave these people alone?*

An acceptance of Japan's integrity begins to permeate Willie's remarks. You can hear the reverence when, after joining street crowds for a performance by an itinerant group of musicians, jugglers, and clowns, he exclaims: *So in this ancient land, men ate, drank, played for thousands of years.* And when he asserts that productions at the rude local theater *are perhaps as good as Shakespeare or Sophocles attended.* And when he compares the local practice of cremation to burial: *How much better is the method of returning to the earth by pure, quick fire, than by hideous, slow decay.* Inevitably, such comparisons sometimes make it difficult to justify his own actions; sometimes he is forced to wonder whether the lessons he brings are really for the good of this Asian land.

By summer, Griffis is well on the way toward idealizing Japan. The nation seems blessed, at once gloriously free of many *evils that disfigure our civilization* and *full of the happiest people in the world.* This happiness is based on virtues familiar—at least in theory—to any Christian: a willingness to live in simplicity, to forgo ambition and all the material desires *which make us feverish and unhappy.* Such thoughts have to raise worries over the process that he is helping to initiate: *It gives one solemn pause to think that along with the many luxuries and unnecessary extravagances that attend the solid blessings of the Christian civilization, there must also come fearful evils and sorrows that these simple people never before knew.*

In such words lurk a challenge, not so much to Western civilization as to Griffis himself. Doubts and questions now claim part of a consciousness once wholly given over to plans for change. The challenge concerns notions of right and wrong, the fit between expressed ideals and behavior. Griffis neither explores these issues directly nor relates them systematically to the self. He tends to vent them in the kind of exasperated outburst that follows a delightful weekend at the home of a small-town merchant: *I don't know that I am pure Jap yet, yet to think of our American shoddy . . . beside this quiet and gentlemanly and cultured 'savage and heathen,' as the Japs are often supposed to be.* The thought may be incomplete, but the emotional meaning is clear. For Willie, words, categories, definitions have begun to slip, blend, and overlap in unexpected ways.

<>

Three months after arriving in Fukui, Griffis is split. Some divisions in him are obvious, others subtle. All oscillate between poles of contradiction, between broad categories like feudalism and democracy, or intimate ones like loneliness and fulfillment. For the biographer this provides an opportunity. The great temptation is to deny the splits, to collapse them together, to bridge intellectual and emotional chasms with theories that satisfy a sense of intellectual neatness, completion. It makes us much more uneasy to leave the splits alone, to admit that a person can believe something and also its opposite, act in one way and then another and still retain a solid sense of self. We are not trained to see that integrity may lie in contradiction rather than consistency.

Griffis lives this issue every day. His consciousness is ours; he, too, wants consistency and finds it impossible to obtain. Japan is the reason, though he never fixes blame, never admits there is blame to fix. The mechanism of his denial is obscure but powerful. Take the issue of public baths. No American can avoid curiosity about this ubiquitous institution, for often the baths are open to the street and one is confronted with both sexes and all ages happily washing, soaking, dressing, talking with an *utter unconsciousness of impropriety*. Rare is the foreigner, however religious or puritanical, who does not succumb to the pull that Griffis admits in his journal on May 3: *Stepped inside a washhouse, while waiting for Iwabouchi* [his guard], *who was in the bookshop. Two young girls shrinking from the To-Jin, rushed into the bath-house full of naked men and women.*

Months later the incident surfaces in an article. The aim is to show Americans that, despite all the recent advances, Japan still retains much evidence of *beast-like innocence* or *barbarism*, and to affirm that change in such attitudes will come only with the adoption of Christianity. Yet in making this point, a slight but significant alteration is necessary. Willie's published story also has two young ladies fleeing from him to take refuge in a bathhouse, *afraid of a foreign face, yet unstartled by a dozen forms of masculine nudity*. But it also contains a fiction. In this version Griffis makes no move toward a washhouse himself, but remains the passive innocent: *We were sitting in a book-shop, looking at some Japanese illustrated histories*—how specific a detail!—*when two girls in passing caught sight of the foreigner, probably never having seen one before . . .*

Natural enough, one may think, for a religious young man to make such a modification in a piece of writing for a hometown newspaper. How many in Philadelphia would understand that, in Fukui, the impulse to step into a bathhouse might be impossible to resist and yet be no sign of prurience or sin? More important is what Griffis may think of such an act, or how he weighs it against altering facts, telling a small lie in order to make an argument for the necessity of Christian morals. On this question there is no answer but the silence that envelops other disjunctures between behavior and words. To Maggie he has boasted that the locals have altered their normal practice of holding *entertainments* on Sunday because *I have told them, I cannot come on that day*. In mid-April the diary records the first of several occasions on which he attends a Sunday party—in this case from 4:00 to 11:30 p.m.—that features *singing girls, dancing*. Another claim is that although the Japanese love to indulge a taste for liquor—*sake*, beer, wine, brandy, whiskey—he never lets a drop touch his lips. Why then, after a late party, this journal entry: *headache after last night's folly*. Or on another occasion, this: *Felt, as usual, after a wine dinner, very stupid*.

Easy it is to view these contradictions as no more than self-protection, the desire of a slightly errant soul to maintain a decent public image. But this cannot account for similar alterations that have nothing to do with personal behavior. The happiness of the Japanese extolled in letters to Maggie can change, in an article for public consumption, into a *happiness akin to that of the ox*. The licentiousness of the people may be admitted, even insisted upon, but then Griffis can calmly state, *In all the city there is not a house of prostitution*. Truth or falsity here is not the issue. Even if Griffis believes Fukui to be free of such houses—as in theory castle towns are—he certainly is aware that they have, at best, been moved off only a little way, in this case to the nearby seaside village of Mikuni.

Any explanation that makes a choice of the real Griffis is beside the point. For him life in Japan entails at least a dual consciousness. Division can be neither shaken nor ignored. One cannot even claim it blunts his moral judgments. These remain unaltered. The Japanese taste for *obscene* pictures, the selling of young women into prostitution, the practice of having more than one wife—all such practices are *disgusting*. At the same time there are virtues which must be recognized, acts of kindness that must be acknowledged, a *strong ethical sense* and *doctrines of rigid mo-*

rality that must please the strictest Christian. No choice can be made between the two ways by one who must live, literally, in two cultures at the same time.

Duality is bound to show in the realm of religion. The animism of Shinto, with its panoply of *kami* at once too vast and too localized to be numbered, is perhaps too exotic to explain in detail to an American audience. Yet Griffis finds it fascinating. On rides into the country he seeks out rustic wayside shrines of weathered wood, where tiny cups of *sake*, flowers in rude jars, and rice cakes reveal reverence for the god of this spring or pond, grove of trees or hillock. It would be easy to make fun of Shinto's magical practices—the shrines hung with sandals to invoke aid for people with sore feet; the one with stones drilled with holes for those who suffer toothaches; the one with breastlike balls of cotton that are a plea for rich mother's milk. Such things Griffis notes without irony, expressing distaste only for those shrines adorned with phalluses large and small, in wood and stone, that ask the blessing of fertility.

Buddhism, with its claim to universality, is a more serious challenge. As a good Protestant, Griffis found the gorgeous temples of Tokyo and their elaborate rituals to be repulsive, too reminiscent of that *bastard religion*, Catholicism. Such antipathy vanishes in Fukui, where he develops something of a taste for pageantry as well as for the *simple ceremonies of people at prayer*. On the four days a month when local government offices close, he joins the crowds in *rich silks and gay colors* that throng busy temple grounds, and sometimes on an evening walk he is moved by the sight of *a family at prayers before a lighted shrine, bell, book, & candle.*

However profound and heartfelt, such simple faith is not enough. Honest, true, and decent the Japanese may be, but the budding minister still sees thirty million people dwelling in darkness, ignorant of the true way. To transform the nation, the *doctrines of Christ* are necessary. Yet it is possible to see the Japanese moving in that direction, possible to discern in the nation's history a pattern of religious progress from fetishism to shamanism to Buddhism that is upward, toward the light. For a long time the nation has been on the right road, which means that one must *Thank God for Buddha and* [his] *doctrines.* Ultimately the Lord is responsible for this evolution. He has created Buddhism, with its *humane creed of brotherly kindness and charity* and its *solid foundation of immutable morals.* Christianity comes not to destroy Japanese ideas of right and wrong, but to fulfill them with a doctrine that is *higher and purer.*

Ultimately, Protestantism bends from the collective back to the self. Do not anticipate much change in a believer like Griffis, twice born these many years. What occurs is a slight psychic shift that only a sensitive instrument can record. You can feel a tremor when he reports to Maggie that he has traveled too much and knows *faiths and history too well to be a bigot.* Stronger is the movement heralded by the statement, *Away off in this land, the inner life becomes more intense, the narrow vision, once circumscribed by the blinders of custom and cant, opens out into a sunny breadth* . . . One can hear a veritable rumble when he moves to the third person in an attempt to distance himself from new and unaccustomed feelings: *My mother's son cares less & less each day for* . . . *humanly constructed ideals and theologies and clings closer each day to the dear Saviour of us all* . . . *peers into caverns of thought, daring to question all his creeds and traditions* . . . *learns to think lightly of, and to be amused with local* . . . *expressions of enthusiasm* . . . His return to the first person comes with a sentiment so strongly voiced it must represent a powerful new resolve: *I hope to stand firm in the everlasting right and teach these people the pure doctrines of primitive and not local or sectarian Christianity.*

How much this religious shift enters into consciousness is not apparent. In the autumn Griffis has a confrontation with Edward Warren Clark, who is a kind of double, an image of himself prior to leaving home. Ever since landing here, Griffis has been attempting to secure a good position for his Rutgers classmate and close friend. In October a job turns up in Shizuoka. Everything goes smoothly until the contract is brought to Fukui and Griffis finds a clause stating that Clark *must teach nothing concerning religion.* This is both annoying and redundant. Japanese law against teaching Christianity is quite clear, and Griffis's own contract contains no such provision. Yet he neither rejects the document nor attempts to negotiate a revision: were he to bargain, Clark could be taken for a missionary, the offer withdrawn, a *libertine* be hired instead, and *Our Master's cause suffer harm*. To this practical explanation Griffis adds sentiments that spring only from experience. One must understand the Japanese point of view, realize that *They look on Christianity with the same feelings that we look on heathenism*. Besides, words are not all that important: *I know well that if a man by God's grace can live a pure, Christian life here, [it] is worth more to Christianity than many sermons or even missionaries.*

What seems perfectly reasonable to Griffis sounds like heresy to his friend. Clark is inclined neither to sympathize with the sensitivities of heathens nor to accept the notion that a *model life* is nearly as important as *the truth* expressed in words. His response indicates a difference between the Griffis he knew in America and the one now living in Fukui: *Oh my poor boy!!! . . . for 'once in my life,' I must beg to disagree with you . . . Is it possible that Wm. E. Griffis . . . could so far forget himself as to give me the advice he did . . . that 'he' could advise a Christian man to bind himself to go for 'three years' among a heathen people, & yet hold his tongue on the Christian religion! I know that this can hardly be what you really intended to say, & yet I must say it seems difficult to put any other construction on your words.*

There is no way to know how Griffis reacts to this condescension. Neither the journal nor later communications ever mention the disagreement. But we may imagine his surprise, annoyance, and perhaps bewilderment, followed by a gleam of recognition. Might he not have written in similar tones not so long ago? Now he can understand that gulf between youth and age, innocence and experience. No need for anger or even for a response. Irreconcilable points of view have become familiar. It is easier to think: Clarkie sees the world through books and words, I understand it through the test of life. When he has been here for a while he will understand the difference between the two. Like me, he will learn from living here, even if the content of the lessons will never be quite clear. Anyway, disagreements over doctrine are truly beside the point, given all the work awaiting us in Japan.

<>

Montage. That's what is needed. The image of pages on a desk calendar turning while incidents fade into one another, overlap, the long and the short reduced to the same size frame. Views of construction. The European-style house is going up; a platform is built in the classroom; the laboratory next to it is completed with a skylight, large windows, workbenches, a furnace with a hood, a pump, closets for chemicals and apparatus. Students study, take exams. Classes grow smaller as many drop chemistry. Shots of the *daimyo* and his entourage of advisers, spending a morning at the lab watching experiments, visiting Griffis for a six-course dinner, listening to more advice on modernizing Japan. The sight of Alfred Lucy, his contract unrenewed, riding out of town, Griffis beside him for three miles, waving goodbye, then riding home with shoulders slumped. Images of home life. Griffis plants a garden: cantaloupe, eggplant, tomatoes, corn; a storm roars through Fukui, destroying most of his crops. Half a dozen young students arrive from far-off Higo, in Kyushu. Willie takes them into his house, along with some local students, until eight young men sleep in a back room, live on rice and pickles, gather after dinner for English conversation and informal lectures. On summer afternoons they troop down to the river to splash and swim together, a large family at play. Vacation. Griffis floats down the river on a boat, spends the weekend in Mikuni, where he watches women dive nude for pearls. With guards and servants he rides off to Mount Hakusan, that distant peak seen all year, climbs to the summit alone, carries a tube of mercury to measure the height, and finds it to be less than that of Fuji. A local conceit deflated by modern science. And the pages turn slowly into autumn.

<>

Temptation—that's the title of a story that has been building to a climax all year long. The word occurs only in letters to Maggie, not often, but always so laden with emotion as to suggest something more frequently felt than named. Worries over falling *into the slime* or yielding to *human weaknesses* never cease. Nor does the concurrent feeling, *I am very busy here. I must be.* Little doubt as to the nature of this temptation. Expressions of homesickness, complaints that family members do not write often enough, demands for the smallest details of Philadelphia life are linked to laments that he lacks *female society.* Confessions that he still *longs for Ellen* disappear, only to be replaced by desire that emerges in an oddly impersonal vocabulary: *My saddest and sorest need is for 'something' to love, 'something' to caress.*

Perhaps we should not be surprised—since the first moments in Japan, Griffis has been obsessed with native females. Recurrent images of the beauty and charms of the invariably dark-eyed *moosmies*—encountered at teahouses, restaurants, and rural inns, at picnics and temples, in city streets and remote hamlets—fill letters, the journal, and published articles. Perhaps such comments are a safety valve. To name the object is somehow to control it, to exorcise its power. Not that he entertains such ideas. His is a simpler mentality. Work and denial, surrounding oneself with people, teaching and more teaching, gardening, swimming, horseback riding, reading, writing—these are the ways to handle improper thoughts, unwanted desires, unnameable longings.

For a long time it works; by God, it works. But you cannot expect it to go on working, not if you know Japan. Not if you know the lure of summer, those warm nights along the river, stars powdering the skies above the hills, the soft air full of nameless invitations, subtle hints of pleasure. August is a season of celebration, a sensuous and happy time of continual *matsuri* (festivals). The banks of the Asawa and the bridges over it are lined with booths, strung with red lanterns; here you buy food and drink—sugar water, watermelon, candied seaweed, rice jelly, broiled eel, *sake.* The night streets are thronged with strollers, dancers, groups of musicians, itinerant comedians, storytellers, jugglers, buffoons, geisha dressed in the brightest of silks. To wander among them, to eat and drink and share the feelings of festivity, to judge the Japanese *a merry people* is simply not enough. That spectacle out there is too tempting. Inevitably, there come moments when you are pulled toward an unseen line, wish to cross it and merge wholly into the promise of something that can never be defined.

Griffis is too hampered and constrained by conscience to seek a woman, at least overtly. But he is less prepared to handle or understand unconscious acts, including—especially?—his own. Late August is the crucial period. Iwabuchi, his interpreter and constant companion, suddenly and unexpectedly marries *one of these rosy-cheeked and black-eyed charmers.* Apparent jealousy feeds feelings of loneliness just at the most trying of times. On August 17, school officials announce a three-week holiday. Certainly Griffis can use a break from teaching, but the real need is for relaxation, something dangerous to envision, impossible to allow.

A resolve to keep busy is difficult to fulfill on the following days, when the temperature hovers around 100 degrees and the humidity is oppressive. But Griffis does his best to maintain discipline: he visits the military school; studies facilities at the local hospital; measures the height of the castle walls and towers, and the breadth of the moats; spends time at the lab planning experiments and demonstrations; tutors several students; passes hours at his desk, pushing forward on the chemistry text. But it is a vacation after all, and the phrase *dolce far niente* enters the journal to describe naps, walks, rides, swims, strolls with the evening crowds. Something in all this does not agree with him. He falls ill, begins to run a fever. Massages, quinine, going to bed early— nothing seems to help. At night he sleeps poorly. We may blame the heat, or the free time, or perhaps see it as a reaction to a decision announced in a letter on the seventeenth: *I must take on a new servant . . . a girl of about 17, who will wait on the table, and take care of my room specially.*

The rest of the story is told in two diary entries and two letters. August 28: *Rose at 6. Breakfasted and waited on by my new servant.* September 4, to Maggie: *Nor can any, but they who suffer the fearful temptations of loneliness know how strong the feeling is, to abandon all true principle, and live the Epicurean life.* September 7, diary: *Consulted with Iwabouchi . . . relative to sending away the* _____. Two words fill the space, one on top of the other. He has first written *temptation*, then covered it over with *servant.* A full explanation two days later, to Maggie: *In my own household, I have made another change. The young girl of 18, whom I took for a servant to wait specially upon me proved to be very faithful, diligent and pleasant in every way, anticipated my every want, and made my house as comfortable as a home. I liked her very much. All of which to a sometimes weary and home-sick young man must necessarily be a strong temptation in his lonely hours. I found after two weeks, that she made too much comfort for me, and was too attractive herself. After having her 11 days, I sent her away before temptation turned into sin . . . and now, though with less comfort and a more lonely house, I can let all my inner life be known to you without shame.*

There it is, the whole story. Or at least all the available evidence. We are at the mercy of a single firsthand report from a witness who can hardly be neutral, one who has already bent evidence on similar sensitive issues—drinking, Sunday parties, prostitution. How we wish for more. Not just to clear up details and discrepancies: is she seventeen or eighteen, does she work for eleven days or two weeks? No. What we want are those lost, secret moments between two human beings when emotion suddenly flows in unsuspected channels. What we want are pictures of them together, the pleasure he begins to feel as she moves in silken grace about his room, the arousal as she bends her head over a tea set and fills his cup, the trembling of his hand as it begins to reach toward the forbidden, the stab of ecstatic pain as she raises her head and for just a moment eyes full of wonder search another mirror of the self. Does he ever touch her hand, move lips toward the whiteness of her neck; does he reach out in pidgin Japanese in an attempt to find who lives within that lovely form; does he somehow cross that line in word or flesh, however innocent, or is it all for later, for those feverish moments alone in bed when nothing but the imagination stands between you and all the possibilities of love?

At the most crucial of moments we are locked outside, prevented by lack of evidence from knowing more than what our source chooses to tell. No doubt our prurience is disappointed, our modern sense that sexuality may be the key to some long-lost door of understanding is frustrated. We are left only with this: one young American named Griffis experienced temptation and succumbed or did not, crossed that line or did not. For him, if not for us, temptation was enough. To feel that power, that pull across lines that defined his sense of self, was enough. Whether he blended physically with the other is not the question. To act or not to act; either way, he ran up against the boundaries of who he was, learned that the world is more complicated, difficult, and serious than once he believed. Before this moment Griffis knew sin only as something that could happen to others. Now he understands that it is possible to become one of those others himself.

<>

After September it is never the same. Not Fukui, not Griffis, not Japan. A moment of realization has come and gone. The once *glowing aspirations* have dimmed. Life on the surface, the daily round, may appear unaltered, but the underlying spirit is different. Gone are the grandiose dreams and plans. No longer does Griffis brim over with personal faith in momentous social change. He is, instead, a man who labors out of a sense of duty, who plods on *day after day, sometimes home-sick, heart-sick and discouraged.* His aims have dwindled. He who wished to alter an entire social order is willing to settle for much more modest goals. To leave a hundred students with a *general conception of modern science,* or twenty *really well grounded,* or a couple of translations of scientific texts into Japanese—such will be enough to show his time has been well spent.

Autumn abounds with signs of change. *Dark eyed moosmies* vanish wholly from journal and letter alike. *Temptation* drops from his vocabulary. Local students, praised unceasingly for six months, are suddenly subject to criticism for their inability to engage in *close, hard, consecutive thought.* The attractions of Fukui dissipate: the town seems dull, its happy citizens alien. No longer is it amusing to be the only Westerner in Echizen. Willie is tired of stares from adults and frightened cries from children, sick of always being on display, viewed as *a stranger and a curiosity.* Things passed over in the excitement of discovery now return as painful: his mind is crowded with memories of friction with officials, disputes with servants, misunderstandings with storekeepers, tiring conversations with men educated *under other systems of morals and ideals.* For months he has been torn by the *sharp angles of an Asian civilization.* Now he longs for a familiar atmosphere, for people of his own mind-set, posture, humor, language.

To attribute all this change solely to the episode with the female servant would be an exaggeration. That is no more than a culmination, a turning point, a marker in time of the kind that a biographer must seize to make sense of the messy evidence that is a life. The encounter serves to coalesce a cluster of changing attitudes, drives home a lesson of fearful future possibilities. The result is a desire to flee this alien realm while the sense of self is still recognizable. By October, Griffis has contacted officials in Tokyo and suggested the establishment of a system of normal schools to help boost the supply of native teachers. Envisioning a role for himself far from Fukui, he reports to Maggie: *A higher position may be in store for me.*

External developments intensify the desire for flight. For months his best students have been off to Tokyo in search of better educational or economic opportunities, and during the summer cuts in the government payroll have trimmed the school staff from fourteen to four. This is a minor annoyance compared to the dramatic change that comes in late September, when the government announces the abolition of the feudal domains. On October 1, a *golden day in the golden autumn*, Willie attends a solemn ceremony in the halls of the old castle. The *fusuma* have been removed and in the immense open area, three thousand warriors kneel in silent ranks. Clad in ceremonial robes, swords perpendicular to the ground before them, hands clasped upon hilts, these samurai bow their heads as the *daimyo* passes among them in a final farewell. No emotion shows on those dark faces, nothing to indicate that this is *the solemn burial of the institutions under which their fathers had lived for seven hundred years.* The *quiet sadness* of the single foreign witness issues in an attempt at optimism: *It is a new era . . . destined to be the grandest of her history . . . hereafter Japan will live and act as a unit, and will realize the truth of that old maxim, in union, there is strength.* More personal feelings emerge only after the *daimyo* stops by the house for a half hour. When he rides away, Griffis confesses, *I shall be more lonely than ever.*

The abolition of feudalism—in a way, a dream come true, a goal toward which so much of his effort has tended. But the reality is different from the expectation. Not joy, but a shadow hovers over Griffis through the crisp days of fall while early snow dusts distant mountain peaks. Good times are not wholly absent. There is excitement in the move to the comfortable European house; in the color of festivals for the god of Atagoyama and for the birthdays of both the emperor and the Buddhist patriarch, Shinran. Willie has the pleasure of seeing the laboratory at last complete, and on Christmas he hosts a celebration that introduces the locals to hot chocolate. But a certain melancholy cannot be shaken. He takes to wandering at night through the old castle grounds, always so *lovely* in the moonlight, so conducive to *reveries* about feudal days now gone. Sadly he reports the leveling of the great walls, the filling in of the moats, the sale for almost nothing of treasures that once belonged to the family of the *daimyo*.

Low moods are tied up with the now desperate desire to escape Fukui. With the *talent and energy* of the nation flowing toward the big cities, Griffis more than ever feels like an exile too many hundreds of miles away from anyone of his own race. But these are hardly reasons to cite in letters to those officials in the capital who have the power to free him. To them he must stress his sense of duty to Dai Nippon, his desire to use all of his expertise and valuable experience to help educate those youngsters who will shape the future of the nation. During the autumn, letters from Verbeck are full of hints about positions in Tokyo. By December Willie is in a constant turmoil: *Fukui or Tokyo? School here or there.*

Not until January 10 does a formal offer arrive. The Ministry of Education asks Griffis to become the first professor of natural philosophy and chemistry at a new polytechnical school in Tokyo, with the same salary and benefits as he receives in Fukui. No question that he will accept, but shaking free of his current contract is not easy. Willie is startled when his request to leave is rejected by Murata Ujihisa, head of the Fukui schools, who retains the opinion that a three-year contract runs for thirty-six months, not ten. Suggestions that the national government should take precedence over local wishes only serve to make Murata obdurate and unbending through several uncomfortable face-to-face encounters. Understanding custom well enough to realize that he dare not lose his temper in public, Griffis pours all his frustration into a letter whose arguments are no doubt similar to those elaborated in person. They are a mixture of anger and pain, truth and falsehood, pleas for help and desperate stratagems. Willie claims that everyone has known for months he might be invited to the capital. He baldly lies by stating that to help Japan he left a position in America *with a salary nearly equal to what I receive now*. He hurls himself on Murata's mercy, begging to be treated as a son, or at least *as well as you would a servant*. Finally, he resorts to threat. No matter what, whether in honor or disgrace, he will depart, *whether I am lost in the snow, come good, come harm*. On January 18 Murata capitulates. In the journal, the simple phrase, *All right*. Four days later Griffis is on the road to Yokohama.

<>

Five days of ice and wind. During the day snow blows like *barbed arrows* into the eyes. Overnight it falls so heavily that in the morning all signs of mountain trails are gone. Guides must be hired to go ahead on snowshoes, punch through drifts to find solid footing, trample a path for the others to follow. This is no weather for horses. The journey must be taken on foot, step by slippery step through thick powder, ice, and slush. To combat the elements, Griffis has gone native. On his head, a straw hat like a huge inverted bowl; on his back a paper waterproof coat; on his feet, straw boots. These may keep him dry and comfortable, but nothing has prepared him for the immense exertion of the journey. Sometimes his strength fails and he must ride for a mile or two on the shoulders of a *coolie*. When they reach inns for the night, he collapses and sleeps *sound as a rock*.

Beauty and fear go together on this trek. When the storm lifts for a moment, the landscape looks like Switzerland: tiny villages sunk in snow to the eaves, a gleaming landscape quilted with the tracks of fox and hare, high crags marked with the dread sign of avalanches. When the group must travel after dark, the porters carry torches that light up *the awful mountain solitudes with lurid splendor*. At inns, meals of wild boar are flavored with stories of disaster—a priest has been found frozen to death; a mail carrier has been swept away by a snowslide.

How different a journey from that of last March. No armed samurai to serve as an honor guard, no barriers between ancient domains, no internal passports to be scrutinized by local officials. At tea houses, *moosmies* still serve hot drinks and food, but Griffis makes no comments on the beauty of dark eyes. His mind is elsewhere. Back it travels over the last ten months, smoothing away annoyances, problems, conflicts, as Fukui begins to sink into a haze of nostalgia. Even the final upset is forgotten, obliterated by the outpouring of emotion from students, friends, servants, and citizens on the days before departure. The well-wishers bringing presents, the lavish banquet in his honor given by colleagues, and the gift of a costly inlaid table from Murata himself have allowed Griffis to feel *I go away in honor, and regretted by all*.

The young man floundering through the snow is a different person from the one who crossed the same landscape ten months before. A missionary temperament has encountered a tradition both strong and appealing, suffered more than a few self-doubts, and been left with a distinct admiration for the alien. With *not a little sorrow*, Griffis has bid farewell to Fukui, *the scene of a year's severe toil, deep thought, bitter loneliness, occasional temptation, wondrous experience and calm joy*. What he fails to see are the deeper shifts in himself that will become apparent later. Griffis will never comment on them directly, but the teacher will come to recognize an old lesson: in the process of teaching, one also learns. Four years later, in the first of many books on Japan, he will remember that the young samurai who at first sight seemed *barbarians* soon proved to be full of *pride and dignity of character . . . diligence, courage, gentlemanly conduct, refinement and affection, truth and honesty, good morals*. Proudly he will claim that *they were quite able to instruct me in many things*. Ever after he will see Fukui as a place where he *found some truth*.

Ruminations give way to thoughts of the future on Friday, January 26. A weary Griffis rides in a *kago* carried by two men as the party descends from the highlands to the plains, from snow to silk country, where mulberry trees grow in rich, loamy soil. Lake Biwa lies in the distance, a streak of blue framed by massive mountains. Past the broad battlefield of Sekigahara, where in 1600 Ieyasu won the victory that established the Tokugawa regime which has just come to an end, lies the Tokaido. What a surprise: that new row of telegraph poles lining the ancient highway fills a Western heart *with thrills of home-like joy* and points to a glorious future for the *New Japan.* Feudal lords may no longer pass this way in *gorgeous procession,* but something better has taken their place, *silent flashes of electric current* [that] *will tell tales of progress.* An excited Griffis dismounts and walks along the rutted highway past these poles *to the native so mysterious, to me so eloquent.*

8

Enoshima Weeks, Tokyo Years

Little drama on this journey. A touch of the exotic, to be sure, but nothing to fill the screen with hints of action to come, to set the mind dreaming of romance and danger. More of a quiet trip, one that begins in the late afternoon. Instead of horses' hooves, rolling wheels; instead of armed samurai, ricksha men; instead of spring snow flurries, the leaf-wilting heat of mid-July. Plenty of holy and historic ground along the eighteen-mile road from Yokohama, but all that remains off camera. Down the tree-lined Tokaido fly the feet of Edward Morse's runners. No time to take the recommended tourist route, to view the pine tree at Nokendo, where the famed artist Kanaoka threw down a brush in despair at ever being able to capture the beauty of the landscape; the beach at Inamura Saki, where great battles were fought in the Middle Ages; the stream named Yukiai, where the Buddhist patriarch Nichiren was saved from beheading in the thirteenth century. No time for a short detour to Kamakura to visit the Hachiman shrine and see Shogun Yoritomo's swords in their silver and gold scabbards; to ring the great bell at Engakuji; to walk down the avenue of evergreens toward the monumental bronze Daibutsu.

Rice fields yellow in a low sun, wild pinks along the roadside, a long sandy hill, and suddenly the sea. Directly ahead, the green lump of Enoshima, linked to the mainland by a narrow bar of sand. North and south, beaches fringed with white breakers. Good it is to stretch the legs after the three-hour ride, to walk the sand

119

and pick up semitropical shells, known since boyhood only in museum collections; good to savor their names in Latin: *Cyprae, Conus, Dolium.* The village heaps upward along a street so narrow that sun rarely touches its damp surface, so steep that every so often the incline becomes a small flight of stairs. Three-story wooden teahouses crowd together; long bright banners hang from poles; shops burst with souvenirs. In shrill, insistent voices, innkeepers urge the traveler to rest, buy, drink, eat, sleep. Pilgrims push toward shrines on the wooded crest of the isle. From second-story windows come voices raised in song, giggles and bursts of hearty laughter.

Supper at a teahouse. Morse and Professor Yatabe, a graduate of Cornell, sit on the floor. The American is famished. Breakfast was long ago and lunch was skipped as part of a plan to become hungry enough to subsist on a native diet. Young girls enter and kneel to serve food; when they bow out, the contents of an aquarium seem to have been spilled onto the low table. Porcelain and lacquer dishes hold mountains of seafood—fried, broiled, in soup and raw. Tentacles wave and dead eyes stare with coldness of the sea. Morse grits his teeth, struggles to sit up straight, fidgets to keep his legs from cramping, fumbles with chopsticks, drops bits of food onto the clean mats, and, eventually, pronounces the raw fish *fairly good,* the fried fish *delicious* and his first Japanese meal, on the whole, *very agreeable.* But a nice slice of bread and butter would still be more than welcome.

The next day, the two men purposefully push through streets asurge with the rhythm of pilgrims who little distinguish between religious devotion and pleasure. Morse's face seems touched with the factual; he alone looks pressed, anxious, in a hurry. Only six weeks until school starts and so much to do before then—set up a laboratory, start collecting specimens for the museum, get his own research underway. To find a small waterfront building is not difficult, but how to get these people moving quickly, how to hurry Orientals who *give no value to time?* Exhortation, demands, emphatic words to the owner. No, next week is not soon enough to begin refitting the building. It must be done now, or not at all. Then the attempt to *hammer into the thick head of a country carpenter the idea of a long table against the wall, for they have*

*no tables; to get four stools made, for they have no such thing
. . . to get each sliding window and door locked, for they have
no locks on their houses.*

No need for Morse to worry—the Japanese are eager, *willing
to do anything.* He can jaunt off to Tokyo for a few days and
return to find the first zoological laboratory in the nation nearly
complete, shelves and tables piled with jars, kegs, sieves, ropes,
dredges, cans of alcohol. On July 30 all is ready. Time now for
the long-awaited moment; time to justify coming so far, spending
so much. Anticipation, fear, hope, doubt, yearning—all these are
carried into the intense morning sun on a small boat. Two men
lean into the sculls. Morse sits upright, blind to the beauties of
island, shoreline, mountains. Down goes the dredge to fifteen
fathoms and up comes little but mud and worthless debris, until
that moment of *astonishment and delight* when twenty tiny brachiopods spill into the boat and gleam in the sun like precious jewels.

The next four weeks vanish in a fury of activity. Morse dredges
in open waters and coves, scours pools at low tide, digs into the
muddy bottom of the tiny river that empties into the sea near the
sandbar. Each site yields so many treasures both familiar and new
that every surface in the small laboratory begins to overflow with
mollusks, urchins, starfish, crabs, worms, snails, shrimp, abalone,
clams. Three assistants sort, dry, prepare, bottle, and label specimens for the Tokyo collection, leaving Morse free to concentrate
on his specialty. So much time does he spend at the microscope
that his back begins to ache and a masseur must be summoned.
No matter. Pain is a small price to pay for the discovery of *a
number of new organs never before seen in Brachiopods*, for
proving this species is not exactly the same as that in North
America. By mid-August he has learned more than enough to
justify the journey to Japan.

<>

Now the difficulties begin. Not for Morse, but for his biographer.
The problem is sources—the journal he kept in Japan, the letters
written home. Neither reveal what you really want to know;
neither give enough detail, or the right kind of detail, to fill out
the story that lies behind the words, the story that the biographer

wishes to tell, of how and why Japan caused this American scientist to switch from a lifelong interest in the natural world to a passionate interest in the artifacts and customs of the human world. Easy enough to speculate on causes. Just point to his age: thirty-nine. Time for a midlife crisis, a reassessment of values brought on by the lengthening shadows of mortality. Toss in the professional: natural history is dividing into narrower disciplines and moving toward the experimental, and the gap between popular and research science is growing too wide to straddle. Add the economic: Japan is a hot topic for lectures and articles. Surely in these factors you have explanation enough.

Maybe yes; maybe no. Evidence for each explanation is available, but the material by Morse eludes easy categorization. The contents of the journal and letters are much the same—details, incidents, disconnected events, customs, habits, artifacts, all described with a kind of clinical dispassion. Judgments and emotional reactions are so toned down, so distanced that they can seem those of a person other than the writer. What makes Morse a superb observer also makes him a poor subject for biography. Something in the last fifteen years has changed the young man whose diary brimmed with ambition, self-doubt, rage at his father, love for his mother, desire for Nellie, worship and then contempt for Agassiz. He has made peace with the world, which in this case is another way of saying he has disappeared into his profession.

How, then, to give movement and shape to his time in Japan? For Morse of the journal, life is always one thing after another, with no highlights, climaxes, momentous turning points. Things go down in the journal as he sees and hears them; forty years later they are published the same way. Order, development, change, any motion toward understanding must be imposed by a later mind. No plan, no conscious categories structure what he sees, sketches, records in words. His propensity is for the simple, the common, the humble gesture or artifact that tends to escape foreign eyes and can remain hidden from natives by patterns of familiarity and routine. Observation, not surprisingly, is what he likes and does best. Action is usually a way of getting somewhere to observe something. Now try to make a story out of that.

Okay. But don't expect too much from the period in Enoshima.

Work is the central experience there; for Morse, that does not make it different from anywhere else. He is under pressure—so much to do in such a short time. But life cannot all be work. You cannot dredge or use a microscope at night; you must let assistants enjoy alcohol, games, local holidays. Outside the window of the lab lies a world that can tempt the eye away from the research table. In the streets and teahouses, at the inn where he stays, the behavior of the people, their customs and artifacts—the simple things that define the rounds of life—seem interesting. Not perhaps as important as brachiopods; not as significant as naming a new species or producing a first-class scientific paper; but often worthy of a note in the journal, a quick sketch, a memory filed away for some future time when the world will grow narrower and its colors begin to fade. Yet this *infernal journal* can also become a kind of work, one that begins to absorb so much time that future payoffs become part of its justification. Articles, lectures, books—surely useful things will spring from all this effort.

That's for later. First get down the routine, the simple events, the daily encounters, opportunities, and difficulties. Like the problem of sleeping. Often Morse's nights are restless, and not just because of the summer heat and thick humidity. On the first evening swarms of mosquitos drive him from the hammock to a futon beneath netting on the matted floor. Comfortable enough, except that the wooden headrest gives him a stiff neck, so three waistcoats and a pair of trousers rolled inside a shirt serve as a pillow. This leaves two problems unsolved—voracious fleas and persistent noise. Insect powder helps with one, but for the other there is no cure. After dark, these normally polite people have not the slightest touch of consideration for others. Through the thin walls of the inn, music, singing, and loud conversations, punctuated by the slamming of *shoji* and *fusuma*, are part of the nightly ritual. And after the parties finish, eager messengers with no sense of time are likely to shake him awake at any hour between midnight and dawn to deliver a letter, a newspaper, or a dredge and rope ordered from Tokyo.

Daylight makes it all worthwhile. The morning view from his room maybe *indescribable*, but he tries anyway: *beautiful cove . . . spacious bay, magnificent Fuji.* Each day he watches fishing boats, whose graceful lines repeatedly evade the skill of his pen, as he takes breakfast on some odd pieces of Western furniture—a table so tall and a chair so low that his head comes *conveniently level* with his plate. Thoughts of living on native food quickly vanish. A single morning meal—fish soup, rice, pickles—that looks suspiciously like dinner the night before, and he summons a cook from Yokohama. Soon he is getting a breakfast fit for a hardworking American: eggs on toast, ham, cheese, broiled fish, and—most important—coffee. No doubt it would save a lot of money and trouble if the *strange* local food would satisfy him. Living on it remains a good idea, but not now. Maybe later.

The inn, just below the shrines and groves of trees on the crest of the island, never elicits either a full description or a sketch. Overfamiliarity, perhaps, or the fact that this is a workplace. However lovely the room, its appointments are soon hidden by a jumble of his stuff. An eating table becomes a clutter of dishes, cutlery, glasses, tins of food; his round worktable holds books, paper, pens, ink bottles, tins of flea powder, jars full of insects. Corner shelves overflow with small items—pipes, tobacco pouches, boxes of matches, cans of alcohol, shells, glass sponges. The floor is a mess, too, and visitors must pick their way over dredges, binoculars, straw hats, pillows, and a huge open valise bursting with clothing. Such disorder may be lamentable, but Morse has neither time nor patience to keep things straight: *There is too much to do in this world to fuss about trifles.*

Just as well to leave things in a mess—it's another way of providing entertainment for the natives. Already they find Morse's belongings and behavior a source of endless fascination. From other windows at the inn, the eyes of guests follow his movements. Serving-women wander into his room and gape to see him write in a journal from left to right with a metal-tipped pen rather than vertically with a soft brush; they pick up unfamiliar items—his microscope, pith helmet, and meerschaum pipe; they giggle and ask questions he cannot understand. It is the same when he leaves the inn to stroll toward the lab. Heads turn his way; people approach to touch his clothing or hat; an itinerant barber calls out—but all such actions are full of deference and kindness. Such a sharp contrast to what he imagines would be the experience of a Japanese in kimono walking the streets of an American city—rude shouts, loud laughter, clods of dirt hurled by ragamuffins.

Comparisons are impossible to avoid. Daily, even hourly encounters turn the diary into an ongoing evaluation of *two civilizations*. The simplest of experiences can provoke a comment. Never does he cease to marvel at the politeness and good manners here that highlight the crude behavior of Americans at home. This is not just a matter of how a foreigner is treated. The routine greetings of townspeople can cause him to stop and stare with *vulgar curiosity*. There they are, two friends, bowing a formal hello in the street, then bowing again and again, each bow lower than the previous one. A few words are exchanged, then bows of departure begin and continue as the two back away along the street. To an *active American* all this is a terrible waste of time—but charming, most definitely charming.

Not far from the foot of the street is the lab, a square wooden building with windows that look along the shore of a small cove and over the sandbar to the mainland. Step inside the door. Three men work at tables amid a jumble of buckets, kegs, bottles, and wooden frames for drying starfish and urchins. Both assistants—Matsumura, paid by the university, and Professor Toyama, here at his own expense—are diligent and dedicated. So is the local man, hired originally to lug things, who shows such an unexpected ability to locate the tiniest of mollusks and the most microscopic sand shells that for Morse he comes to represent the *general intelligence of everybody in Japan*. This unnamed man is incredibly helpful, too, like everyone here. Many locals deliver huge buckets of specimens for the tiniest of payments, and some help with collecting for the sheer joy of the activity. There are even riksha men who, on trips into the countryside, throw themselves into impromptu searches for land shells. Just try to imagine *a hackman at home volunteering his services on such a quest*.

Afternoons in the August heat are the most difficult time. Too often in the lab the eyes grow heavy with drowsiness. Morse is capable of sneaking away for a nap or going off to sketch the nearby huts of fishermen. So much do their boats, nets, and techniques impress him that ever after he will refer to Enoshima as a *primitive fishing village* and ignore its main enterprise, reli-

gion. For eight hundred years the local shrine to Benten—tamer
of dragons and motherly goddess of the sea—has drawn pilgrims
from all over the empire. Morse never records her name, never
bothers to inquire into the legends that have made the island a
place of worship. Twice he sails to Benten's sacred cave, but
viewing its shrine and the dragon carvings on the wall interest
him far less than collecting *twilight* spiders, sow bugs, and crickets. Only once does he make time to visit the famous hilltop
shrines, and here his journals pass without a word over the relics
they contain—the armor, the bronze mirrors, the rare wooden
statue of the goddess nude.

So much interest do the locals show in his research that Morse
tends to assume that all Japanese accept the procedures, judgments, and worldview of Western science. During evenings in his
room this attitude is at first reinforced, then shaken. When Toyama and Matsumura drop in to enjoy the luxury of kerosene
lighting, it is difficult for the American not to hold forth on
science, and more difficult not to be impressed by the serious
attentiveness of his listeners. Yet something familiar is missing,
something he cannot at first name, something that only comes to
consciousness when, in reply to his perpetual questions about the
whys and wherefores of local customs, habits, and artifacts, his
Japanese companions smile with the embarrassment of people
who have never thought about something so familiar and obvious.
Three weeks into the stay, Morse is faced with a distinct oddity:
never has one of his assistants *asked a question as to how we did
such and such things at home, or about the various objects on
my table, in which, nevertheless, they take an interest.*

There is a pattern here. Willingness to learn, lack of bias against
new modes of thought and new techniques—so far as he can tell
these seem to be national traits, but ones which go along with a
kind of passivity, an acceptance of authority that makes Morse
slightly uneasy even if he is the authority. Not that he worries
this point. Noted in passing, it is unconsciously illustrated by
glimpses of the hours spent with four *laughing and pleasant*
premedical students, who reside in a nearby room. They teach
him difficult board games like Go and a native form of chess,
along with simple, lightning-fast hand contests like scissors, paper,

stone. Though bright and alert, these young men seem different from their American counterparts in their complete disinterest in the practical or public aspects of their future profession. Not one of them would find it of *interest or importance to learn the death-rate of a town or of what diseases people died.*

No reason to make too much of this, one of many hasty observations recorded during Enoshima weeks that pass *like a flash.* The round of days is hardly regular. Interruptions include two typhoons that bury the sandbar and make it necessary to evacuate the lab, three trips to Tokyo on university business, two visits from Westerners eager to see the progress of Morse's endeavors. We need not weight his generalizations with too heavy a burden of meaning, but this first exposure to Japan unmediated by other foreigners gives rise to judgments that will not much alter in coming years. Different these people are from Westerners, different too from whatever Morse had imagined. Not that he is one to claim that difference means worse—or better. And yet there is a pattern that he can see long before the end of his island stay. Like all foreigners, his initial impressions were that the Japanese do things *just the reverse from us*; like the others, his reaction was that *our way is undeniably right.* Now he is willing to entertain the notion that because they *are a much older civilized race, it may be possible that their way of doing some things is really the best way.*

An odd comment for a Westerner. A sign of changes undergone since landing in Yokohama, changes that have raised to consciousness things taken for granted at home and opened his mind to new possibilities. No, he does not say this, at least not directly. Perhaps he does not even know it yet, though all the hints and bits of evidence are there in his own words. For the first time in years, Morse puzzles—if only momentarily—over the goals, behavior, habits, and beliefs of human beings. Unused to grappling with such notions, unfamiliar with conceptual frameworks for such ideas, he is reduced to a kind of observational common sense. To live among people who seem so open, simple, curious, and friendly is to see them as *a set of overgrown, good-natured, kind-hearted, laughing children.* Yet, another image, equally strong, refuses to blend with this: in certain kinds of self-control, self-composure, reticence, and stoicism, the Japanese are very much adults indeed.

Morse is too much the observer to reconcile such contradictions, too far removed from social analysis to desire a theory to explain them. Only after returning to Tokyo is there even time to reflect on experiences in Enoshima, time to draw up a rough balance sheet on these important weeks. In his rambling reminiscence you feel his wonder that things on the island really were as they were, a growing dissatisfaction that things at home are as they are, and an indirect self-criticism that he, a scientist who has discarded a religious upbringing, should have until now accepted the notion that pagans must be uncivilized: *I have spent six weeks in that little crowded collection of houses, with people overworked and at it from four o'clock in the morning till midnight, with an overwhelming amount of work to do in providing for the crowds of pilgrims thronging in upon them . . . The visitors seem to demand four or five meals a day, and are constantly calling for tea, coals for their pipe, hot sake, etc. Children of all ages were swarming everywhere; yet, living among them in the closest proximity, I did not hear during my whole stay there a single cross word; babies cried, but mothers laughed at them, and when they were in actual distress sympathetically stroked their ventral region. A pleasant smile always greeted me from all, and though I chased their barking dogs through the single street and occasionally threw stones at them, they looked amiably upon my behavior as the eccentricities of a foreign barbarian and laughed! Now this is paganism—to be kind and obliging, courteous and hospitable, generous with their food and their time, sharing their last bowl of rice with you; and whatever you may be doing—collecting, pulling up a boat, or anything else—jinriksha men, or fishermen, always ready to lend, or rather to give in abundance, a helping hand.*

<>

Tokyo in the summer of 1877—as it has been for at least a century, the largest city in the world in area and perhaps in population. Nobody then or now knows the exact number of inhabitants, but eight hundred thousand is a good estimate. Twenty-five years earlier its name was Edo and the population close to a million and a quarter, then the great earthquake of 1855 destroyed half the city and a cholera epidemic further wasted the population. More significant for the inhabitants is the year 1856, when the foreign barbarians came to Japan to stay. In September, Townsend Harris took up residence as the American consul near the port town of Shimoda, isolated from the population centers of the empire by the wild terrain of the Izu Peninsula. Fifteen months later, after lengthy negotiations and scarcely veiled threats of action by the U. S. Navy, Harris arrived in the capital city to present a letter from President Franklin Pierce to the nation's military ruler, thirteenth in the Tokugawa line that dated back to 1603. No foreigner had ever before stood on his feet in the presence of the Shogun. For the dynasty, this was a fateful symbol. For the historian, the date presents one of those ironies of history that he cannot refrain from underlining: December 7, 1857.

Barbarians are ultimately more devastating than any earthquake. Political conflict, social strife, economic upheaval, the rising of clans in the south and west—and by 1868 the Tokugawa rule was at an end. The new regime governed in the name of the seventeen-year-old Meiji, who became the first emperor in eleven hundred years to move from Kyoto. When this youngster took up residence in the Shogun's former palace, Edo became Tokyo, or "Eastern Capital." Not that this was done directly. The Imperial edict stated: *Edo is the great bastion of the east country. Upon it converge the crowds, and from it one can personally oversee affairs of state. Accordingly the place known as Edo will henceforth be known as Tokyo.* Among the Japanese, arguments will rage for some time over whether this constitutes a legal change of capitals; among foreign diplomats and residents, the city will be called Edo for many years to come.

To Westerners, Tokyo in the eighties does not look like a real capital. *A collection of villages* is the usual description of this city nine miles long, eight miles wide, and interlaced by rivers and countless canals. Seen from a high point, it appears as a vast sprawl of trees, gardens, and dark roofs, with large open areas. Missing are the great public buildings, the squares, the monuments, the steeples, domes, and bell towers associated with European capitals. The emperor's palace itself is no more than a one-story wooden structure, hidden behind a series of huge stone walls and wide moats, the one feature of Tokyo that seems to speak the word *empire*. By the eighties, even these are vanishing. Since the restoration of 1868, many of the outer walls have been leveled, the moats filled, and the great wooden gates dismantled.

Changes like this do not much alter the shape of the city. From the expansive palace grounds at the center to the bay in the east and beyond the Sumida River to the north lie the miles of unpainted, weathered structures of the so-called Low City, home to the common people, to laborers, artisans, entertainers, and small merchants who reside in tiny houses that line narrow alleys and streets. By 1877 one can see here and there a foreign-style building, but the only parts of the city which can be called westernized are Tsukiji, the original foreign settlement, which now houses some two hundred merchants, missionaries, and teachers, and the Ginza, rebuilt after a serious fire in 1872 with shops of brick, its main thoroughfares illuminated with gas lighting. The Low City also houses the licensed quarters, the centers for geisha and prostitution. Best known, most elaborate and expensive is the Yoshiwara, set off behind high walls and canals, but in Tokyo pleasure spills across official boundaries. Commoners and country pilgrims flock to the most popular temple in the land, that of Kannon, goddess of mercy, at Asakusa, another region of music halls, wax museums, Kabuki theaters, and archery galleries where, on the second floor, you can buy a cup of tea or rent a young woman.

West and south of the palace lie the wooded hills of the High City. Here once lived the great *daimyo* and their retainers, whose sprawling *yashiki*—small palaces surrounded by barracks that housed thousands of samurai—are falling into ruin. Some have burned to the ground; others have been demolished to sell off the land for the homes of newly rich merchants; a few have been donated for national purposes. That of the Maeda family, rulers of the former Kaga domain, has been donated as the site for the highest school in the land—Nanko Daigaku, renamed Kaisei Gakko, renamed Tokyo Daigaku (Tokyo University) in April 1877. This huge, wildly overgrown estate, the longtime residence of foxes and flocks of crows, has now become the home of all foreign professors who teach at the university.

◇

August 29. Morse arrives at the Kaga Yashiki in a ricksha, weary with the effort of holding a basket full of delicate marine specimens in his lap, and sore from two bumpy days on the road. Palm trees, a banana plant, and blooming rose bushes front Number Five, his official residence, a large house built *in foreign style*. The chimney, broad veranda, sash windows, and swinging front door may speak of the West, but a massive tile roof, delicate carvings over the doorway, and matted floors all proclaim its hybrid nature. That night—those first few nights are lonely. Rats scurry along thin ceiling boards and changes of temperature make wooden walls and floors creak until he is *prepared to take an oath* that stealthy footsteps are sounding along the porch. But there is no real cause for alarm: *I am in a pagan country, where house-breaking, pocket-picking, etc., are unknown; in fact, I feel a great deal safer here than I should in my quiet town of Salem.*

With large rooms and fourteen-foot ceilings, the house is perfect. How delightful to *scatter things from one end to the other* and be able to give strict orders to the maid, hired for $3 a month, *not to touch a thing on the tables or on the floor.* Most of his time is spent in the huge parlor, where he has four tables—one for the journal and correspondence, one for shells, one for scientific notes, and one as a *catch-all, though somehow or other the other tables catch a good many things that do not belong on them.* In the evening he works here undisturbed, by the light of a single kerosene lamp. Outside, once the shrieking of crows dies with the twilight, absolute quiet reigns, save for the occasional distant high notes of some late drunken reveler staggering toward home—*these people, when in that condition, seem inclined to sing instead of to fight, as is the common impulse with the Anglo-Saxon or the Irish, and particularly the Irish.*

Two days after reaching Tokyo, Morse is down to the docks early to supervise the unloading of the specimens collected at Enoshima. By man-powered cart, the nucleus of Japan's first zoological museum rolls toward a large room on the ground floor of the main university building. On the second floor a science lecture hall is being prepared; nearby, a long low building has been set aside as a lab. These empty spaces waiting to be filled become a test of ambition. Nothing less than facilities comparable to those in America will satisfy him. Helped by student assistants, Morse begins to relive those glorious days in Cambridge seventeen years ago. This time he is an Agassiz, but one hampered by limitations unknown to his mentor. Here both theory and practice—the classification of living things, techniques of dissection, methods of preparing sections and slides for microscopic study, and the means for preserving and displaying specimens—must be taught to absolute beginners.

Regular work at the university commences on Tuesday morning, September 11. First a faculty meeting, then a reception for some fifty foreign professors—German, French, English, Chinese, and American—an affair featuring sandwiches, cake, fruit, and pyramids of ice cream that *would have done credit to the best caterers at home.* Classes begin the next day. Morse's hall has been fitted with a blackboard, a desk, and a case holding illustrative objects—shells, starfish, and papier-maché models of the digestive organs and nerve centers of animals. The contents of his courses are unrecorded, but one educational desire is clear enough: Morse desperately wants to exercise a freedom denied him at home by teaching Darwinism *pure and simple.* His first talk on evolution is so well received by students that he begins to plan an entire course on the subject. Even more *delightful* is his experience on Saturday, October 6, when he lectures to some six hundred faculty members and students on Darwin's theories *without running up against theological prejudice as I often did at home.*

The comment is premature. Protestant missionaries are appalled that this doctrine has followed them across the Pacific. As Morse addresses ever larger public audiences, the religious community moves into action: prayers implore that this sinner see the light and abandon his *peculiar socialistic views,* and the popular minister Henry Faulds, founder of the Western hospital in Tsukiji, begins a campaign of articles and lectures against evolution. Neither divine nor human effort has much effect. Native Protestants are quick to reconcile Darwinism and Christianity, and opposition raises Morse's antireligious ire. Soon he is collecting data to show that the expenses of missionaries are *entirely out of proportion to the good they accomplish*, and that the teaching of their *peculiar* views is a hindrance to the progress of Japan.

More important than what Morse teaches is whom, at least to judge by the journal, which says nothing about courses and plenty about students. Each of his two classes has an enrollment of forty-five, and every young man seems attentive and *greedy to learn*. How different from his own wayward school days. Memories of pranks played on teachers—blackboards greased, chalk stolen, tacks placed on seats—underlie his favorable reaction to young men who show a respect for professors and a deep seriousness about studies. He enjoys visiting their rooms; takes delight in learning the nicknames for his colleagues (*Cube*, *Cuttlefish*); spends long hours helping favorites in the lab; composes the epitaph for the gravestone of one who dies of beriberi; and oversees the formation of a biological society where research findings are presented and issues discussed just as in scientific meetings back home.

A few of the best students help with the beginning of another major project. On the first train ride to Tokyo in June, Morse caught sight of a heap of shells in a railway cut near Omori station. The words *kitchen midden* jumped to mind and teased him for the next three months. In Maine and Massachusetts he had visited with friends who were excavating such ancient refuse heaps, and now it is his turn to take a step toward archeology. Carrying a letter from the principal engineer of the railroad and accompanied by three students, he takes the train to Omori station on Sunday, September 16. On the half-mile hike back along the track, Morse explains what they will find: ancient pottery, worked bones, and some crude stone implements. For the young men, it is a good lesson in the predictive possibilities of science. Upon reaching the site, they begin to clamor that he must have been there before. Barely beneath the earth, there they are—bones, clay tablets, and heaps of pottery shards.

A week later Morse returns with Dr. Murray and two workmen for a two-hour dig, and on October 9 he leads two students, two professors—Yatabe and Toyama—six laborers, and General Le Gendre, an American adviser to the War Department, on a day-long excavation with shovels. Back to the university go more than three hundred pounds of material, which constitutes the beginnings of an archeological museum that quickly draws the attention of local newspapers and scholars. Fascinated by the *diversity of ornamentation*, Morse devotes a good deal of time to drawing fragments of pottery, then begins to prepare papers both scholarly and popular. His first public presentation, "Traces of Early Man in Japan," is delivered to the most mixed audience he has ever faced—Americans, Europeans, Britons, and Japanese—at a meeting of the Asiatic Society in Yokohama on October 13. Two years later a thirty-six-page monograph, *Shell Mounds of Omori*, becomes the first publication of Tokyo University Press. But long before that his accomplishment is acknowledged at the highest levels. In December 1877 the Emperor himself makes a visit to an exhibition of Omori antiquities. Ever after, the American hired as a zoologist is honored as the father of archeology in Japan.

<>

Wandering. He is wandering in the streets, floating from place to place. Not Edward S. Morse, the man who has no time to waste. Yes, the selfsame. Poking into shops; watching jugglers, acrobats, sand artists; feeding tame monkeys; buying candy from strolling salesmen and handing it out to street kids; sampling baked grasshoppers. Losing his sense of time, of space. Taking two hours for the one-mile walk to Asakusa; leaving the laboratory and purposefully turning the wrong way in order to lose himself in unknown areas of the city; waving away the ricksha and strolling home from school by the most circuitous of routes. What has gotten into the man? We know him too well to easily believe such reports, even written in his own hand. Difficult to remember a time when he lost himself even for ten minutes, let alone an hour or an afternoon. For recreation, he has purposefully tramped through the countryside, climbed mountains all over New England. Such activities can be justified as healthful, a way of offsetting too much food and too many cigars. But to wander and wonder?

Impossible to be precise about when it begins. Shortly after the return from Enoshima, hints first appear in the journal, phrases and sketches hidden among the reports of work. Only later does a pattern emerge. Something is changing, something has changed: his interests, his vision of the world—one is tempted to say his values, but that is more difficult to demonstrate. Some kind of turning point, some step in a new direction can been seen in his response to Japan's First National Industrial Exposition. Mounted in Ueno Park, just a mile from Kaga Yashiki, the expo is dedicated to all that is modern, forward-looking, progressive. Its temporary wooden buildings are in Western style, with separate structures devoted to machinery, farming, natural products, and art—a total of sixteen thousand exhibitors, one hundred thousand items on display, and masses of visitors from the opening in late August to the closing in November.

Seven times Morse is drawn to Ueno, down the long aisle of pines, past the booths vending food, under the imposing old gate and through turnstiles that remind him of the U. S. centennial celebration in Philadelphia just the year before. Only on the first day does he linger in the industrial pavilion, *astonished* at the progress in Japanese manufacturing, at the clocks, telegraphic instruments, microscopes, electrical machines, and air pumps. More compelling are the traditional crafts—the flower boxes made of worm-eaten wood, the panels of cedar decorated with metal birds and bamboo, the large lacquer screens with forests, fish, and birds—their images rendered with a startling *purity of design* and a remarkable *truthfulness to nature*. On the first visit, he is critical of a black lacquer table that depicts a silver moon reflecting gold on a dark sea—*It is such violations of truth in many forms of Japanese art which irritate us.* On the second he vows to visit the place twice a week *to make a study of its art treasures.* By the last, he can accept the distortion of objects as heightening a kind of artistic truth.

Similar attitudes carry into the wanderings. He never pens a word about the Bricktown area of Ginza, with its bright lamps; he no longer feels cheered by the sound of a sewing machine coming from a traditional home. Sweeter now to hear the chant of Chinese classics in schoolboy voices, or the sound of *samisen* or *koto*, or the cries of peddlers vending wares. Such traditional things help to slow him down, force him to acknowledge that at home people have little time for common pleasures. Americans hurry along *bent on business* or *ride in closed cars and see but little that is going on.* By contrast, the slow pace of this land allows you to experience things more deeply, to indulge the taste for crafts whetted by the expo, to find that the humble worker in shell, wood, stone, leather, bark, and wicker is, by American standards, a master whose skills of design and execution *beat us out and out.* Thoughts of a book devoted to these *household arts* come to Morse's mind; so does a wish for money and leisure enough to *collect every kind of an object of this nature.*

No time for that now. A growing desire to capture beauty must be expressed in other ways. Sketchbook in hand, Morse roams the streets in search of pleasing sights—wall hangings, baskets, the elaborate and curious signs for shops that sell *tabi*, rope, brushes, rice cakes, sugarplums, candies, wigs, combs, and umbrellas. As his eyes grow more sophisticated, he records moments that can be explained only on aesthetic grounds—the stark image of a girl set against a typical background of drab, dingy, unpainted buildings, *walking along dressed for company, her hair black and shining like . . . beautiful lacquer, her sash, or obi, strikingly brilliant in color, with face whitened with powder, bright red lips, and the whitest of stockings and cleanest of sandals.*

Unexpected sights like this make the streets a *never ending source of enjoyment,* an informal school, a way of learning more about this civilization and—nonverbally, to be sure—of losing and confronting the self. Proof of this can be seen only indirectly, in changes of language and style. Morse has always been a writer you might quote for information, but never for imagery. And yet something in Tokyo in the fall of 1877 can momentarily change his normally flat prose into a succession of sharp, compact images, a kind of poetic evocation, a celebration of the romance of the streets:

You are sure to see something new and you never tire of old: the low and queer-looking houses; the odd signs and fluttering awnings; children running across the path of your jinrikisha with their long sleeves flying; women with their highly dressed hair and always bareheaded, the older women waddling like ducks and the younger ones scuffing along; women nursing their children in the streets, in the shops, and even while riding in jinrikishas; peddlers of all kinds; traveling shows; restaurants; stationary and peripatetic hawkers of fish, of toys, of candy; pipe-repairers; shoe-menders; barbers with their ornamental box,—all with different street cries, some like the call of a strange bird; blind men and women strolling along the street blowing whistles; two old women and a girl, with cracked voices and a cracked guitar, singing; a bald-headed man with a bell who prays in front of your house for a tenth of a cent; another man reciting stories with a laughing group about him . . . Everybody walks in the streets, for there are no sidewalks—handsome-looking little boys are seen on their way to school, or a group of highly dressed little girls with pow-dered faces riding in jinrikishas bound for some gathering—and all the while such a clatter of wooden clogs on the hard roadway and a continual hum of voices. People profoundly bowing to one another; the interminable shops . . . all open from side to side and all the activities fully exposed; the umbrella-maker, lantern-maker, fan-painter, seal-cutter, every craft being practiced in open daylight, all seem like a grotesque dream . . .

<>

Fine. But don't overdo the artistic sense, the poetry, the wander-ing. And don't exaggerate his sense of leisure. Morse in Japan remains what he has been all his life—a man locked in a silent struggle with time, one whose days are filled with a pursuit of practical truths that can be shared with a world hungry to un-derstand itself. So wandering does not come easily and does not come often, and it may be followed by spasms of guilt over time wasted and a renewed dedication to his normal pursuits. At least that would explain the polar swings, the contradictory attitudes that mark his years in Japan. Admissions of the pleasure of a daylong sumo wrestling tournament, an afternoon sports meet, or an evening at Kabuki have to be balanced against complaints about precious moments lost while watching dancers at a restau-rant, or reports of an abrupt and early departure from several dinners on the grounds of having *a lot of work to do.*

Any confusion here is ours, not his. It springs from the desire to understand changes that he accepts silently, or perhaps does not notice at all. Not that he is wholly blind. Alterations in attitude—*My point of view in many things is repeatedly changed by my experiences here*—are easy enough to admit. But broader changes in the self go unmentioned. Lack of perspective may prevent him from seeing a pattern obvious to us, just as lack of vocabulary prevents us from clearly delineating this pattern. How, after all, does one talk sensibly about something that lacks weight, height, distance, and color, that is always in process and never complete? By analogy, perhaps. Take food. The pattern that begins at Enoshima continues. At the end as at the beginning of his three-year stay, he is always *getting accustomed* to native meals or *acquiring a taste for almost everything.* Trips to remote areas of the northern island of Yezo and the western island of Kyushu turn his stomach into a *dietetic laboratory.* He brags about being able to get along on all manner of food—sea urchin eggs, sea cucumber, marine worms, and other *things that I do not know and cannot even guess what they are.* Sometimes at specially prepared foreign dinners, he complains that a Japanese meal would have been preferable. Yet whenever he has to live for several weeks on seafood, fish, rice, and tea, a desire for the taste of bread and butter never fails to torture him.

To understand this we must accept Morse in all his complexity, as a bundle of beliefs that contains many contradictions. That he has acquired a taste for Japanese food is certainly true; that he prides himself on this acquisition, even more so. But this new set of tastes supplements rather than replaces lifelong pleasures of the table. Raw fish will never be quite as good as beefsteak; tea is ultimately no real substitute for coffee, or *sake* for beer. He can wander the streets and lose himself, but this hardly becomes habit enough to interfere with duties. He can greatly admire the manners of the people and learn to bow, without ever giving up a blunt manner of speaking that would be impossible to any Japanese. He can enjoy the spare simplicity of rooms, yet turn every space he occupies into a jumble of clutter. He can, one might say, begin to be Japanized, but this does not mean that Morse can or will ever cease to be a Yankee—which is only to state the obvious by saying that any story of change is also one of continuity.

<>

May 1, 1878. How strange it seems to begin the journal again and in the same house where I made most of the records before. Our trip across the continent was extremely pleasant, and on the plains I studied the groups of Indians at the stations and was interested to see among them certain resemblances to the Japanese: whether these resemblances betray any ethnic affinity with the Japanese can be learned only after long and careful study. There are certain superficial resemblances: their black hair, the depression of the nasals, and other similarities have led some to suggest a common origin.

Back at Kaga Yashiki after a six months' absence. The family is with him now. Through the thin walls he can no doubt hear eight-year-old John, thirteen-year-old Edith, and his wife Nellie moving around as they settle into what will be home for the next eighteen months. The Japanese government has done well for its professor of zoology—fresh paint on the walls, new paper on the sliding doors, clean tatami on the floors. But it is beyond the powers of any agency to make it easy for an American family to set up a household in Tokyo. For more than three weeks Morse has frantically combed the city for furniture, dishes, and all the other necessary goods so common at home, so impossible to find here. Now the job is done and at last there is time for work and the journal.

To turn to the written page is to escape from the world of family life. In the months to come, the children will be mentioned but rarely and his wife not at all. But Japan—how it glows with bright colors, present and past. Those of the countryside first claim his pen. Different now from June the year before. Today everything is fresh—black rice fields patched with the bright yellow of rape; the pink and white of cherry and plum; camellia trees crowded with blossoms; dwarf maples blazing with tiny red leaves. As he strolls the vast grounds of the estate, past tumbled bamboo fences and over mounds of gardens long gone to seed, the man who once claimed to be *too much absorbed in present things . . . to look backward* is caught by some wayward spirit of the past. Think of it: less than ten years ago the Shogun was in power, the *yashiki* filled with armed samurai, the gates locked at six o'clock every evening. No foreigner dwelt in Edo then, or even visited except as a high representative of some alien government—yet here he is, a boy from Maine, *roaming round the city unguarded and unmolested.*

Feelings of security briefly vanish two weeks later when Count

Okubo, a leading modernizer and father of one of Morse's students, is hacked to death by eight young ex-samurai not far from the college grounds. So swiftly is the matter settled that Morse has little time to wonder about the antiforeign implications of this action. The culprits give themselves up, are tried and executed immediately: *There was no plea of emotional insanity; no indictment under a wrong initial . . . no trial in a wrong court; no appeal to higher courts or disagreements among the jury with the result that the criminal finally goes free: all so different from the way they manage matters in our blessed country, which as a consequence has the highest murder rate in the world.*

Safety returns and the journal continues, but something is different this time around. Not necessarily for Morse, but for the reader—and yet, how to put it? The details are less interesting than before. In the published version you are at page 400 of the first volume. Behind him are five months in Japan and half a year away that certainly included some time for reflection, at least on those two long voyages back and forth across the Pacific. Yet once he settles into Kaga Yashiki with the family, the entries go on almost as if he has seen nothing, learned nothing, and thought nothing. No new levels of understanding or self-reflection; instead, observations of the sort we already know too well: the *wonderful* complexity of hill, plant, rock, and bridge that make up the 250-year-old garden at Shiba Rikyu; the pleasure of dining at the home of Professor Toyama, *who lives in true Japanese style*, or at a famous teahouse amid *the simple beauties and the cleanliness of the rooms*; the pride in delivering the first public lecture ever given to a general Japanese audience; the amazement at the willingness of people to help in the perpetual hunt for land and water shells.

Suddenly it is enough. You are tired of smiling, polite people with exquisite manners, tired of children who never fuss or cry, tired of honest merchants, helpful ricksha men, graceful waitresses, skillful carpenters, fearless firefighters, jolly vendors, smiling priests, elegant ladies; you are tired of street festivals, actors in masks, beautiful gardens, colorful kimonos, weathered shrines, elaborate coiffures, clever toys, immaculate rooms, artful shop signs, unique designs for umbrellas, baskets, pottery, tools, and flower holders done in bamboo, wicker, ceramic, and wood; tired above all of hearing that chopsticks are efficient and economical and should be used around the world. You begin to think about— no, positively to desire—anger, awkwardness, hostility, ugliness, cruelty, rudeness, racism, incompetence. From Morse you won't get them, even though he has watched criminals march through the streets, their ankles chained together; visited insane asylums; seen friends overcharged at an Enoshima inn; gone through sections of town where the Eta, former outcasts, still dwell in unofficial segregation. To ask why he does not make more of the darker side of this society is to ask him to be a different man. Morse has never been much interested in what might be wrong with Japan; by now he seems to care only what it might have to teach.

That is not the only thing about the diary that calls for explanation. Consider: twice as many pages in his journal are given to the initial five-month period as to the second one of eighteen months (and half of these pages are devoted to two short scientific trips). Remember: never in this year and a half does he describe the process of teaching; rarely does he mention students, the lab, the museum of archeology. When it comes to events, Morse describes only the extraordinary: visits to a newspaper office, or the famous Mitsui silk store, or the newly opened Shintomiza Kabuki theater in Kyobashi; or the wondrous events of his first Tokyo New Year's holiday, a time when girls play battledore and shuttlecock and boys fly kites, and house fronts are decorated with pine, bamboo, and plum, and there are banquets and *sake* parties that turn cheeks red and loosen tongues until everyone sings and laughs, and you realize *how staid and sober our New England method of celebration of New Year's appears in contrast to all this gayety.*

Routine clearly does not move Morse to words, and routine is what life becomes, in Tokyo as in Salem. Scientific journeys to Yezo in July of 1878 and Kyushu the following summer are full of new places, landscapes, people, customs and adventures, but the observations on Japan only reconfirm those already made. Detailed entries on these jaunts serve another purpose. By now the frivolous notion of writing a book has turned serious. To John

Gould go pages of the journal instead of letters, along with brief notes filled with a new kind of worry: Be careful with the manuscript. If it gets lost there will be no way to remember all the details and they are essential. You will find it interesting and so will the public, especially because it will be *chock full of sketches.* Brachiopods? Been finding them everywhere, as far north as Tsuruga Bay, off Hakodate, as far south as Kagoshima, with the volcano of Sakurajima smoking in the distance. And there's this one funny moment I must share with you: May 13, in Nagasaki harbor, a day of *great dredging.* Two men and a woman at the sculls and me in fine shape, pulling out *tropical shells, echinoderms, crustaceans* in all kinds of marvelous forms I had never seen before. But it is *difficult to concentrate on the work at hand . . . to bury my head in the mud of the dredge.* Blame it on that harbor, the *magnificent views—the long bay hemmed in by high hills, green with foliage from the water to the summits, and the little houses, temples, shrines, hidden in the trees, with flights of stone steps leading up to them.* There I am, looking at scenery rather than shells. You know something, John, that's never happened before.

<>

Now comes the temptation to do his many trips, with their landscapes, voyages, adventures, incidents, meals, mishaps, discoveries. He traverses large areas of the country—goodly sections of Yezo and the northeast region of Honshu, the ancient Yamato area of Kansai, the Inland Sea, the southern and western coasts of Kyushu. No family member goes along, but always an assistant from the university to guide, translate, and arrange for collecting specimens living, dead, and archeological. Enjoyable always to be the only foreigner; to meet with people noble and lowborn; to dine with fishermen and the governors of provinces; to take meals in the filthy huts of the *savage* Ainu, where the only decorations are animal skins, racks of poison-tipped arrows, and the purple tattoos around the mouths of the adult women; to journey by steamer, ricksha, and riverboat; to learn how to ride a horse in Otaru and, after being thrown twice, to cross the 150 miles to Sapporo in the saddle.

Not all his experiences are pleasant. Somewhere between

Aomori and Tokyo, an old woman startles him by scowling; somewhere else two ruffians attempt to crowd him off the road. In Nagasaki, the most international of Japanese cities, the natives are impolite; in Kagoshima, starting point of the final rebellion against the Meiji regime, he endures the glares of the defeated, their taunts, rude words, and overt hostility. How much sweeter are the old centers of culture—Osaka, with the ruins of Toyotomi Hideyoshi's great castle; Nara, with its grand temples and vast deer park; and Kyoto, smoothed by a thousand years of art and refinement.

Seeing, doing, and hearing so much in so many places is one way of changing what the eye sees and the ear hears and the mind feels to be natural, beautiful, and right. No wonder that somewhere, but in no particular place, and somehow, but for no particular reason, the feeling grows in Morse that this must really be part of him; then comes the day when it is true. At a Kyushu inn an officer arrives to invite him to dinner with the governor. This *delightful* gentleman bows so profoundly that Morse automatically responds in kind: *How natural it seemed to me to be kneeling on the floor and bowing again and again till my head repeatedly touched the mat.* Sometimes the body knows things better than the brain. Even when involved in this most solemn act of courtesy, Morse claims *I could not help laughing at myself.*

<><>

Collecting. He is collecting again, and with all the energy once devoted to shells. Collecting, but now something little known outside Japan and distinctly alien to foreign taste—pottery. Not the porcelain treasured in the West. What touches Morse is the stoneware that derives from *chanoyu*, the tea ceremony, developed in the sixteenth century. Simple, restrained, with minimal decoration, this ware exhibits an aesthetic of *wabi* and *sabi*—austerity, sobriety, and feelings of loneliness, like those that grow with the slow fade of a sunset. Little color, rough surfaces, blisters, crackle glazes, accidental lumps, and odd indentations—these are its treasured characteristics. So refined is this cult of the plain and simple that among the most highly valued items are common bowls made for daily use by unknown peasant potters of Korea.

This new taste calls for explanation. Any Westerner has to

wonder, as does Morse at first, *what there is to admire* about such work. His own appreciation grows slowly and—unusual word for him—*unconsciously.* The comment dates from February 1879, a first reference to what by summer will be a *passion,* inexplicable if familiar. Put it this way: there are *natural born* collectors and he knows himself to be one. This begs the historical question of when, why, and how the love affair began. The only attempt to supply an answer has been made by Morse's first biographer. Late in 1878, the story goes, his nerves and digestion are out of whack. Ten years of lecture tours, train rides, restaurant meals, and hotel beds, first in America and now in Japan, are the culprits. As a remedy, a doctor prescribes not medicine but a five-mile daily walk, and when Morse objects to the boredom involved, recommends he pursue a hobby at the same time. The result: one day he comes home with a small ceramic saucer that is an exact replica of a scallop shell. Picked up casually in a local shop, this crudely made item leads to all the rest.

Neat. Possible. Consonant with what we know of the man and his habits. Not, one must admit, documented with a footnote, but what does it matter? The consequences of this first piece of pottery are more important than the details of how it was acquired. Soon Morse is picking up many other pieces and pestering friends and colleagues to tell him all they know about pottery. Someone introduces him to Ninagawa Noritane, a wispy, bearded scholar who has published a book on the ceramic traditions of Japan. From him, the American learns how to identify different styles, clays, kilns, lineages, and the all-important potter's marks, and hears the history of native collectors and collections. For hundreds of years the Japanese have cherished pottery, porcelain, swords, coins, *kakemono* (scrolls), and roofing tiles. But they collect in a manner different from Westerners—they specialize less, make aesthetic qualities paramount, and are *never so systematic or scientific and generally not so curious nor so exact as to the age and locality of the objects.*

Here is an opening that lets desire move towards obsession. The child who once wished to make a complete collection of Maine land shells still lives. What in the winter months is called a *little collection* has by spring become an attempt to obtain *representative pieces* from every tradition and region of Japan. His guide in this endeavor is Ninagawa. Sunday afternoons at Kaga Yashiki the two men kneel on the floor to study the pieces that Morse has purchased during the week at Tokyo's secondhand stores. The scientist is a good student. An eye that can locate the genitals of a brachiopod, or identify thousands of species of mollusks and worms, can readily learn to recognize variations in clay, glaze, and potter's marks. That the aesthetic of the art is subtle does not daunt Morse, who soon enough begins to make value judgments and to lust after works he finds beautiful.

On a summer journey in 1879, Morse's love for pottery competes with that for shells. In Kyushu he makes special stops to spend many *charming* hours handling antique works in private collections. At an official dinner in Kagoshima, he succumbs to flattery and notes that the governor of the province *expressed his amazement several times that a foreigner, whose interests were supposed to be in other directions, had learned to distinguish so quickly the Chinese, Korean, and Japanese pottery.* Kyoto is the high point of the trip, the perfect place to indulge in ceramics. Unlike other tourists, Ned avoids the hundreds of historic temples nestled in the suburbs and spends his time visiting kilns. Most are family operations, with everyone from children to grandparents involved in the leisurely production of highly refined works. The few exceptions are instructive. Those kilns that have switched to *making stuff* for export, to answering orders for hundreds of thousand of cups and saucers in bright red and gold, are full of feverish workers *slapping it out by the gross*, splashing on decorations of flowers or butterflies *in sickening profusion*. Here the workmanship is terrible and the results wholly contrary to the *exquisite reserve* of objects used by the Japanese themselves. No wonder they believe foreigners to be people with *barbaric* taste!

Traditional kilns are where his real interest lies. And more than collecting is on his mind. Morse is doing research, and that takes more time than any working potter can afford to give. A slight payment in advance smooths the way. At each modest but lovely workshop home, the inevitable greeting from the aged head of the family over the inevitable tea and cakes. Then hours to watch potters throw, decorate, glaze, and fire; to sketch the hillside brick-

and-mortar ovens, built on Chinese models; to take an occasional turn at the wheel himself. The most important part of each visit is an interview with senior potters. Questions about the origins of each kiln, the history of the family, and styles of the past are followed by a detailed examination of works old and new, and by the exacting, precise labor of copying the markings, or signatures, of each generation. This is the tip-off that something grandiose is in the works. Morse leaves Kyoto satisfied with *a large addition to my pottery studies*. But if he has plans, if he knows where these studies are heading, he never confides them to the pages of his journal. No doubt it all remains at some unconscious level. Like us, he cannot foresee where this passion for pottery will lead.

<>

Separations and endings are never easy. Ambition, family duty, isolation—all are there in a letter to Gould, written in May 1879, four months before Morse's departure from Japan: *I want to get out my Japanese book while the vim is on me. I want to get out my Second Book of Zoology while I am young. I want to publish a popular work on Evolution while it is still remembered, for if I wait much longer it would be like working on a book trying to prove that the Earth revolves, etc. This, however, is all selfish; Edith is growing up, so is John. They are literally alone in having no playmates and they have no competition in their studies. They must have that stimulus. I need the same. The Boston Society of Natural History meetings I miss. So I come home and face starvation . . . with a courage only equalled by my paganism.*

Not much of note happens in those final months. Presumably he refuses a contract renewal. Without doubt he is feted at lavish banquets given by students, colleagues, friends, and government officials. Journal entries do not mention farewell lectures, final moments in the laboratory, last glimpses of the glass cases and displays at the archeological and zoological museums. When Ulysses S. Grant reaches Tokyo on the final leg of a worldwide tour in July and the American community gives a dinner reception in Ueno Park, Morse decides he has *no time for such affairs*. But after friends urge him to *do the proper thing*, he reluctantly attends. A longtime prejudice against the general vanishes as soon as they shake hands in the reception line. The man is quiet, dignified, soft-spoken, and at dinner he does not *touch a drop of wine of any kind.* So much for all those wartime stories and *the infernal slanders of our newspapers.*

Rainy season, muggy season—the days dribble away. The mind is suspended. Japan begins to recede but America draws no closer. Through an interpreter he has the honor of delivering four lectures to an audience of the highest nobility in the auditorium of the Nobles' School. His final public appearance is at the famed secondary school of Fukuzawa Yukichi, one of Japan's leading theorists of westernization. Evolution is the topic and the illustrated lecture easily understood because the Japanese are so *familiar with the plants and animals of their country.* But lecturing on Darwin is not the thrill it once was, and the best part of the day comes after the talk when the future leaders of the nation, dressed in thickly wadded armor, wearing helmets and holding long foils of bamboo, give a stunning demonstration of swordplay. Forty years later Morse lets the paragraphs on this traditional martial art remain the final ones in the published diary of his Japan teaching years. Perhaps he neither sees nor means anything symbolic, but we cannot refrain from noting that the man who has introduced three sciences to Japan—zoology, archeology, and anthropology—ends with admiration for the spirit of something past:

The class was divided into two groups of fifty, the leader of each class standing back with his retainers protecting him. The leaders had tied on top of the hood a disk of soft pottery, two and a half inches in diameter, with two holes for the string, and the object was to smash the disk of the opponent. The noise of the clash was terrific; the slats of bamboo made a resounding whack, though the blows did no damage. Mr. Fukuzawa called my attention to one of the boys who was the son of a famous fencing master. It was wonderful to see the dash with which he penetrated the crowd and smashed the pottery disk on the head of his opponent. This disk flew into many fragments, and one could instantly see the result of the combat. Though the boys wore long-sleeved gauntlets, many came out of the fray with bruises and bleeding scratches on their wrists.

9

Magic Matsue

Dear Professor Chamberlain, —
I went to Kobe by rail, and thence by jinrikisha across Japan over mountains and through valleys of rice-fields—a journey of four days; but the most delightful in some respects of all my travelling experiences. The scenery had this peculiar effect, that it repeated for me many of my tropical impressions—received in a country of similar volcanic configuration,—besides reviving for me all sorts of early memories of travel in Wales and England which I had forgotten. Nothing could be more beautiful than this mingling of the sensations of the tropics with those of Northern summers. And the people! My expectations were more than realized: it is among the country people Japanese character should be studied, and I could not give my opinion of them now without using what you would call enthusiastic language . . . in a mountain village I saw a dance unlike anything I ever saw before—some dance immemorially old, and full of weird grace. I watched it until midnight, and wish I could see it again. Nothing yet seen in Japan delighted me so much as this Bon-odori—in no wise resembling the same performance in the north. I found Buddhism gradually weaken toward the interior, while Shinto emblems surrounded the fields, and things suggesting the phallic worship of antiquity were being adored in remote groves.

148

‹›

Later, a single page becomes eighteen; the journey swells from a letter into a chapter entitled "Bon-Odori." But Hearn ignores the first part, does not describe the long train ride, the five hundred blurred miles of seacoast and tea plantation, tunnel and sprawling city—Nagoya, Kyoto, Osaka, Kobe. Better to leave behind train tracks, smoke, cities, newspapers, Western clothing and faces; better to begin with two ricksha, high in the mountains on the journey from the Pacific to the Sea of Japan, from the nineteenth century to Izumo, *the land of the Ancient Gods.* Slowly the vehicles cross from one high valley to another, move beneath rice paddies terraced upward like enormous green flights of stairs, disappear into shadowy forests of cedar and pine, emerge to pass small fields of barley, rice, indigo, and cotton, and an occasional thatched village tucked into a fold of hills.

The eyes seek unfamiliar shapes; the brain, words to render them enchanted. Always the stress is on the odd, the picturesque, the extreme. That sky, the *tenderest* blue, *loftier* than any other; those wispy clouds, *ghosts riding on the wind*; these forests, *night-black* as in Dore's etchings. Signs of two religions edge the miles and days—temples with blue tile roofs; weathered shrines with offerings of rice, flowers, and wine; *torii* in wood and stone, towering over courtyards or framing mossy stairways. Note too the tiny stone bodhisattva that line the roads, the boulders carved with ideographs, the icons smiling from leafy recesses, the statues of the three mystic apes that guard the high passes—Mizaru, See-No-Evil; Kikazaru, Hear-No-Evil; and Iwazaru, Speak-No-Evil.

Never does he forget the human landscape. Those young men who stare wonderingly from the roadside, those girls at teahouses who giggle and turn away—surely they have a message. So must the old men at each village stop. Out they come, a bit unsteady; bowing, smiling, gently reaching out to touch his jacket, posing questions in a dialect difficult for the interpreter to understand. No matter; good feelings need no translation. Each evening at a rustic inn, Hearn is pampered by hosts and serving-girls, treated with a kindness *unknown in any other country*. Little wonder that the rice each morning is flavored with regret. This is the place to linger, to enjoy Japan, to find out why they always seem so content, to discover what it is they know that we have forgotten or have never learned.

The most picturesque town, the kindest people, the most magic experience are saved for the final evening, a set piece in which the dance named Bon-Odori expands from three sentences to eight pages. It begins in a drab village directly *out of old Hiroshige's picture books*, where the local inn proves to be full of stunning art works. Imagine finding treasures in this remote hamlet. Touch them, bring them close: that exquisite lacquerware box for sweetmeats; the *sake* cups dashed with leaping shrimp in gold; the iron kettle figured with dragons; the bronze *hibachi* with lion-head handles; the scroll that shows Hotei, the roly-poly god of happiness, drifting *in a bark down some shadowy stream*. Now look through the heart-shaped window to a garden with pond, bridges, stone lanterns, and dwarf trees. No longer is it possible to stifle that insistent cliché: *Here I am in ancient Japan; probably no European eyes ever looked upon these things before.*

Dinner brings eggs, vegetables, rice, and apologies from the landlady. No fish because this is the first day of *Bon*, the festival of the dead. Tonight the ghosts of ancestors return to be honored by their descendants with a sacred dance. Wearing a cotton *yukata*, Hearn rushes into the street, disappears into the native throng. The night is—what else?—*divine*. So still, so clear, so mild—somehow *vaster than nights of Europe*. A full moon flings down shadows of tilted eaves, horned gables, and robed figures. At a great courtyard with a drum in the center, spectators wait in silence. A young girl beats the drum once, and out of the darkness floats a line of female dancers who look Greek or Etruscan in their high-girdled robes. Sandaled feet glide forward; hands wave and clap softly; long sleeves flit silently back and forth; supple bodies bow and sway as the procession circles the yard.

A dance—yes, it is that, and something more as well, something beyond the power of words. Later he will call it *phantasmal*, an evocation of spirits that belong to *the unrecorded beginnings of this Oriental life*, a performance full of meanings long forgotten. But at the moment what can there be but astonishment and wonder as the dancers begin to chant, as those massed female voices move through the weirdest melodies, the oddest intervals, the strangest tunes. Call it a dream, but no dream was ever like this; claim to feel haunted, but those weaving shapes are no ghosts; say time vanishes, but can we believe him? The dance goes on forever; the ending comes too soon. A temple bell sounds. The voices grow silent, the figures still, and then suddenly the lines break into clusters of noisy young ladies who laugh aloud, shout to friends, call farewells, shuffle off gracelessly on wooden clogs. Damn and double damn. These *visions of archaic grace*, these *delightful phantoms* are no more than *simple country girls.*

<>

He arrives by water, but never describes the trip on the small steamer from Yonago across Nakaumi Lagoon and up the short stretch of the Ohashi River, never mentions his first view of the low mass of gray buildings that is Matsue. The clamor of the docks; the unloading of bags and passengers; the shouts of porters and ricksha men; the bows and speeches of the greeting committee (if any); the short ride across the bridge to the Tomitaya Inn; the size and decor of the room where he will dwell for three months— none of these does he choose to write about. We know, or can make a good guess, at the view from his room. But the excitement or depression (if either or both) of those first hours and days, or his first reactions to the people, canals, and streets, or to the Black Castle on the hills, its broad moats draped with willows—none of these do we know.

The explanation is easy enough: Hearn is neither diarist nor journalist, but a writer. His sketches, articles, and personal note-books may be autobiographical, but they are never comprehensive. A journey, an arrival, a love affair, a marriage—anything can be ignored or sacrificed to achieve a dramatic effect. Chronology is unimportant; the world created by his words is specific about place, hazy about time. Like the stories that will run in magazines and later fill his books, Hearn's journals and letters are highly literary, full of paragraphs so carefully composed, contoured, and balanced that the original experience is at once revealed and hidden. Both his private and public writings make it almost impossible to know what he sees happening and what he wishes had happened; what he feels at any given moment and what later, pen in hand, he imagines it would have been nice or appropriate or interesting to feel. Equally difficult is knowing which impressions, sayings, and images in any given piece of writing may have been pulled in from some other place and time and put here because they feel right.

All this is to say that Hearn represents an extreme case of a problem common in biography and history, one made worse when the subject is a first-rate literary figure. How often does the desire for a good moment or story lead to a certain stretching or conflation of events, or toying ever so slightly with evidence to get an effect that may have its own larger, even symbolic truth? Aware of the power of unconscious behavior, the biographer has difficulty answering this question for himself, let alone for a subject skillful with words. All he can do is point out that with Hearn, the problem goes to the heart of who he is. Remember: he has come to Matsue to write. The teaching job that brings him here is no more than a means to the long-pursued end of literary recognition. His wager—made even before leaving America—is on a Japan that is changeless, eternal, weighted with a tradition too subtle and complex for Westerners to grasp easily, or at all. Such a land would suit his temperament; that its expectation shapes what he sees, describes, and leaves out of his writing must never be forgotten. Nor dare we neglect something equally important: the bulk of the evidence for his stay in Matsue comes from Hearn himself. From other sources there are only scraps—letters by friends, reminiscences of family members, fragmentary local records. But so prolific and convincing is Hearn that every biographer has to struggle to avoid being seduced by his prose, to escape from becoming a kind of mirror that does no more than reflect an image he wanted all readers to see.

This chapter is part of such a struggle. With less self-consciously artistic people like Griffis or Morse, the task is to build a biographical structure from bits and pieces of evidence; with Hearn, a well-designed edifice must somehow be demolished and rebuilt at the same time. And this must be done by a biographer well aware that the new structure is also an artifact to be demolished, that his task is not to find the truth, but to create one. So he begins with trepidation, begins with the notion of Hearn as a man who has been looking for something all his life. The evidence is there in the forty years behind him, in the journalism of Cincinnati days, the illegal marriage, the broken friendships and quarrels with editors; in the passion for the occult, the ancient, the primitive, the bizarre; in the flights southward to Latin New Orleans and tropical Martinique. All this may simply add up to a wish for esteem, recognition, and love; for the home he lost so young and the family he never had; for mother, that dimly remembered figure evoked indirectly in so many images of Creole, black, and Caribbean women. But this is our retrospective view. For Hearn the serious question is not past, but future: Will Matsue give me subjects worthy of my art?

An answer starts to come the first morning, with a dull, muffled pounding that brings him awake. Later he will learn that the noise comes from the *kometsuki*, a huge pestle used to clean rice. But now it is a small mystery, an annoyance that lasts no longer than the time it takes to get up, push open the *shoji*, and glance down at the silver rush of the Ohashi River, its banks tightly packed with two-story buildings and lined with docks where small steamers lie next to narrow fishing boats and shadowy figures move about in silence. The boom of a temple bell shakes the inn, seems to stir the town awake. Vendors stroll by to cry their wares. At the first rays of light, people in the streets and along that many-pillared wooden bridge off to the right come to a halt, clap their hands, and bow to the rising sun. Beyond the bridge Lake Shinji gleams in the dawn.

The scene is pure Hearn, made for—and by—his prose. He will describe this view from the window, cherish it, long to see it again in years when Japanese mornings have become like mornings anywhere. Now it is an invitation. Come out, explore, see what you have gotten into this time. He needs little urging. A writer belongs in the streets and these promise to be rich in images. Feudalism lives here. You can see it in the castle, rising from great stone foundations, *a vast and sinister shape* against the sky. You can sense it in the old divisions of the city—the district of merchant shops; the region of temples; the quarter of the samurai. You can feel it in the tales people are happy to relate, of the beautiful maiden, buried alive in the castle walls, who makes the town shudder if anyone dares to dance in the streets; of the poor soul named Gensuke, sacrificed to the gods of the river three centuries ago to ensure the stability of the long bridge; of the fox-god, Inari, who promised the *daimyo* that he would protect the town from fire in exchange for a suitable home.

Most of these stories he hears later. But as Lafcadio walks for the first time across the bridge; climbs the broad stairway to the tiny shrine where thousands of foxes, tiny and life-size, in terra-cotta and stone, jauntily raise their tails aloft; strolls beneath the shaggy pines of the castle hill and surveys the network of streets and canals below, he has to feel pleased. Matsue seems at once remote and manageable, strange and homey, a place where there is much to see, to do, to learn, and more than enough to keep his pen busy. His initial letters describing the town are cautiously optimistic: the climate is fine, the people friendly, the landscape magic. Hidden from friends—and himself?—are the difficulties of his situation. The only native speaker of English in this town of thirty-five thousand, Hearn has already given up on the Japanese language as too difficult and time-consuming to learn. Yet his reason for being here is to write a book about daily life, about what he calls the heart and soul of the common people. To attempt this without the language may be audacious or foolish. Whatever the judgment, it is bound to be a challenge, but in vain does one scan his letters for signs of worry over the artistic tasks ahead. Missing too is any sense of a major problem that seems so obvious to us a century later: that loving the ways of an alien people from a distance is one thing, and attempting to live among them distinctly another.

<>

Tuesday morning, September 2, 1890. Imagine Hearn nervous, full of questions and self-doubts. He is climbing the broad stairway to the second floor of the Kencho, prefectural headquarters, with the English teacher Nishida Sentaro by his side. Already he has toured the buildings, classrooms, and teachers' lounges, has met the faculties of the two schools where he will work. Time now to pay respects to the governor of Shimane Prefecture. Together he and Nishida enter an office where the half-dozen officials awaiting them are clad in ceremonial silks—wide trousers and *haori* with family crests—that make Lafcadio feel drab, ashamed of his *commonplace Western garb.* Such thoughts vanish when Governor Koteda Yasusada greets him with a hearty handshake, a cup of green tea, and a brief lecture—which Nishida translates—about local history and customs. So grateful is Hearn for this reception that after a few minutes in the presence of the governor's frank face and friendly voice, he is ready to pronounce Koteda the flower of the race, a man cast in the mold of *old Japanese heroes.*

The meeting ends with handshakes and bows, bows and more handshakes. Back in front of the Kencho, Hearn can see the most Westernized part of Matsue, a large, open square edged with wooden European-style buildings: the dark gray-blue middle school; the *much larger* and *much handsomer* snowy white normal school, its roof topped with a cupola; and the smaller elementary school. Raise the eyes just a bit and there is the castle, dating from the first decade of the seventeenth century. As always, it is tempting to make something out of the contrast between it and these school buildings, between the warriors who once peered from its lookouts and the smiling Nishida at his elbow. But today there is no time. Today it is necessary to hurry into the long corridors of the middle school. As the two men enter the classroom, the students rise and bow. Nishida calls the roll and remains beside Hearn during the first hours of teaching. But soon—too soon it seems—Lafcadio must stand alone in front of those blank, placid, still indistinguishable faces. He who is so painfully shy about his appearance and who has always avoided speaking in public must now begin to instruct them in English; he who cannot even pronounce the names of his students must begin to teach them grammar, reading, composition, and conversation.

We don't know what he does in the classroom, but he does it well enough to have his contract renewed at the end of the year. That's the only independent confirmation of his teaching ability, the only evidence not tainted by the I-was-a-pupil-of-the-famous-American-writer syndrome that affects Japanese memoirs. Hearn will spend fifteen to twenty hours a week with the middle school students and another five at the normal school, but nowhere does he leave any record of how he teaches. Evidently the process of education interests him less than the results, and from the first day these promise to be good. The boys, twelve to sixteen years old, are well prepared. Most have been studying English since childhood, and if some have difficulty understanding what he says, all can read what he writes on the blackboard. After a single day, he admits teaching is *a much more agreeable task than I had imagined*. After a few weeks he notes a development that seems symbolic of his acceptance: the students have stopped addressing him as Hearn-*sama* (sir) and have begun to call him *sensei*.

Success at school lets him enjoy the glories of the season—the clear, sunny September days; the mild, festive nights full of the off-key voices of men *whose hearts have been made merry with wine*. Life here is sweet. Officials, colleagues, merchants, and students all make him feel welcome and at home. Nishida soon changes from a congenial companion to friend; the governor invites Hearn to his house for dinner; the governor's daughter presents Lafcadio with a bird named the *uguisu*; the Educational Association asks him to deliver a speech, then has it translated and printed for general distribution; the local press carries articles on the doings and habits of the foreign teacher. All this is heady stuff, difficult to believe: *I am being for the moment perhaps much more highly considered than I ought to be.*

Fall weekends are a good time to explore the countryside. In short articles for the Yokohama *Weekly Mail*, a newspaper happy to print any scraps of information from the interior, Hearn chronicles his jaunts to hot springs, pottery villages, and seaside resorts. The most important of these trips—what he calls *my first really great Japanese experience*—takes him to Kizuki, site of Izumo Taisha, the oldest of all Shinto shrines and the one to which all eight million deities are supposed to return for a gathering each October. To get there takes more than half a day—a tiny afternoon steamer across Lake Shinji, then a ricksha over an open plain, dreamy and silent save for the *infinite bubbling* of frogs in twilight rice fields. At the best of Kizuki's inns, Hearn sleeps fitfully in anticipation of something special: a meeting with the *guji*, or head priest of the shrine, a figure once revered as a living deity.

The next day brings out the best and worst in Hearn, his remarkable ability to take seriously the rituals of a tradition that to most Westerners seems wholly alien and his striking inability to describe such a tradition, its representatives, artifacts, and his own experience of them, in any but heroic terms. So when, on a bright morning, he approaches the shrine flanked by his own interpreter and a young priest, the *torii* they pass under is *magnificent*, the path they stroll a *grand avenue*, the trees above them *astonishing* in their *majesty*, the surrounding groves *vast*, the gateway into the main compound *massive*, the buildings there *immense*, constructed of *colossal timbers*. (Go today and walk that same path through those same grounds. April is a perfect time; then the small groves of trees are stained white with cherry blossoms and the ponds reflect the clouds of the spring sky. When you pass the gate into the main compound and stand before those wooden structures gray with age, you think, *yes, for Shinto shrines these are rather large*.)

On the steps leading into the *haidan*, the hall of prayer, Hearn is met by a line of priests robed in purple and gold. Within the sanctuary, *a vast and lofty apartment*, awaits a white-clad *majestic, bearded figure*. Instinctively?—theatrically?—Lafcadio prostrates himself and is saluted in return with a gesture of courtesy that puts him at ease. Now they sit near each other on the matted floor, the *clumsy barbarian* and the dignified priest. Who knows how long they talk? The hours are out of a storybook, a tale told by a descendant of deities. For Hearn, the answer to his initial question is the most important: yes, he is the first Westerner ever to be admitted *into the dwelling of the god*, into the inner sanctum of a shrine whose origins lie in a period long before recorded history. The first to hear from the lips of the *guji* the name of each court, fence, holy grove, and temple pillar. The first to see the sacred relics—the prehistoric bronze mirrors and jewels; the hand drill for kindling the sacred flame; the swords presented to Izumo by emperors and shoguns. The first to watch a virgin priestess perform a dance of divination to the *sob and shrill* of *weird flutes*.

Back in Matsue his enthusiasm for Shinto knows no bounds. Here is a subject worthy of investigation and explanation. Every

writer on Japan has done Buddhism, but nobody has really tackled
Shinto. Not that Hearn knows exactly what it is—but then, who
does? Ancestor worship, emperor worship, an animism that makes
trees and mountains into gods—all are part of Shinto. Such practices may shock Westerners, but they are *delightfully natural*,
reminiscent of beliefs and rituals in the *antique world*. Surely
Shinto expresses just that heart and soul of Japan he wishes to
capture. Just look around and you can see that every house in
Matsue has a *kamidana*, or god shelf, for ancestors. And remember: long before Buddha woke up to his name, long before Buddhism arrived from Korea in the seventh century, Shinto was part
of the life of these islands. At that time it needed no name, but
was simply the way of the gods.

The passion for Shinto helps to structure Hearn's research and
travels. He begins to gather material on the local fox cult; regularly visits the shrine to Inari on the grounds of the castle; undertakes pilgrimages to nearby spots like Yaegaki Jinja, where men
and women go to pray for fulfillment in love, and where the
statues are too phallic and the *ofuda* (charms) too explicitly erotic
for him to describe in any detail. Time spent in these pursuits
draws him toward the culture, but it is at school that he comes
close to feeling Japanese. Between class hours he relaxes at his
desk in the teacher's room and imitates colleagues as they smoke
tiny metal pipes and sip tea in silence. When six thousand students
from all over the prefecture descend on Matsue in mid-October
for an athletic meet, he is among the cheering spectators. At the
formal public ceremony where Governor Koteda reads Emperor
Meiji's Rescript on Education, a document stressing the continuity
of modern subjects with traditional values, Hearn rises to sing the
national anthem. On the Emperor's birthday he joins with other
teachers as they march to the front of the assembly hall and bow
deeply to the portrait of *His Imperial Majesty*.

Moving into his own house is another way of feeling like a
native. Early in November, Hearn leaves the inn for a nearby
dwelling—*dainty as a bird cage*—that fronts the lake. Now, after
school hours, students come to visit. A servant brings tea and
cake while Lafcadio squats on a cushion and tries to draw out
his young visitors. Shyly they talk of their families and personal

dreams; show him heirlooms such as carvings and scrolls; or sit in that special full silence of the Japanese, who take simple plea- sure in being *comfortable with a friend*. These youngsters seem a plucky lot who work harder and live more frugally than students at home. To reach the middle school, they must spend seven full years mastering *kanji*, the Chinese ideographs, then tackle native history and literature along with all the subjects imported from the West—mathematics, science, history, and geography. Worse, they must study English, a language so different from their native tongue that the simplest phrase cannot be translated from one to the other without altering *the form of the thought*. And this they do clad in no more than thin cotton garments, even in the coldest of months, and eating only rice, vegetables, and bean curd, foods woefully inadequate for acquiring knowledge that was *discovered, developed, and synthesized by minds strengthened upon a costly diet of flesh.*

Admiration tends to obliterate any obvious shortcomings of either these young men or the system of education that shapes them. In and out of the classroom, the boys have a good deal to teach their foreign *sensei*. Their conversations are full of treasures for a writer—old sayings, folktales, family stories, legends, cus- toms, superstitions, the doings of local gods and heroes. Regularly they raise cultural comparisons large and small. Do European men really love their wives more than their parents? (We think that is immoral.) Why do Western women carry babies in their arms? (If they put children on their backs, like we do, their hands would be free for other things.) Why did our former teacher, a missionary, call us savages for revering the Emperor? (We think it a privilege to die for him!)

It does not take long to realize that such questions are not exactly a matter of personal curiosity. They are more an expres- sion of a conventionalized *national sentiment* that also pervades the students' weekly compositions. Ideas on almost any topic— fireflies, dragons, frogs, the moon, trees, the aim of life—seem less individual than collective; the language, comparisons, and moral lessons—the very images and metaphors—recur in many papers. Obviously, originality is not important here. The imagination of a Japanese *was made for him long centuries ago—partly in China, partly in his native land.* During boyhood a youngster learns to see nature through the eyes of great artists. In school he commits to memory *the most beautiful thoughts and comparisons* to be found in the native literature. So everyone knows Mount Fuji is a white, half-opened fan hanging in the sky, or that cherry trees in bloom look as if clouds were caught in their branches.

This lack of originality does not worry Hearn, but it is related to an elusive, *strangely pleasant* feeling he has had ever since the first days of standing before a class. The exact sensation takes a long time to identify, and longer still to render into words. Those placid faces before him always seem soft compared to Occidental faces; they are neither aggressive nor shy, neither curious nor indifferent. *Impersonal* is the only word that seems to describe them, just as it is the appropriate word for those student compositions. Call this a vague, imprecise, even meaningless concept, but to Hearn it is an important insight, a glimpse at the inner structure—what he likes to call the *race-soul*—of these people. To him the Japanese are pleasant precisely because they are impersonal. A classroom here, indeed any public gathering, large or small, lacks a kind of pressure that seems to pervade every situation at home. In Matsue, Lafcadio always is at ease, full of a rare *psychic comfort*, a feeling apparently born of an acceptance of who and what he is in his role. How difficult to explain—impossible, really, unless one is willing to use an analogy. He does: more than once he likens living in Japan to the sensation one has when, after a long time in a hot, stuffy room, you suddenly emerge outdoors into *clear, free, living air.*

<>

Life is not like that, not a matter of ceremonies and track meets, encounters with students and insights neatly brought together from October, February, May, and September. It is getting up in the morning, every morning, but you have shown that once already; it is walking to school, but you do not know the route he takes, or what bridges he crosses, or what shops he visits, what vendors he sees, and do they smile and does he nod hello? Later he will mention bands of pilgrims with straw hats and white leggings, but not whether he sees them once or often. He will describe Mount Daisen, the Fuji of Izumo, as a *stupendous ghost*, always covered with snow (of course). He will name the major thoroughfares, but not say when he walks them—the Street of New Lumber, where the nets of fishermen, strung on poles, seem like giant spiderwebs; Teramachi, with its row of temples from the different sects of Buddhism; Tenjinmachi, the Street of Rich Merchants, where the shop doors are draped in blue cloth and a line of white telegraph poles recedes into the distance. He watches wrestling matches in temple courtyards and sees companies of smartly clad soldiers marching behind buglers, but never does he say what he eats for lunch, or how he feels after a day of teaching, or where he walks on any particular afternoon, or when he writes, or whom—if anyone of either sex—he visits day or night.

So you cannot do the day exactly, but must imagine it, or each day, one by one, a feast of new sights that become routine; a stroll, an antique shop, a group of tots walking in pairs hand-in-hand; a special moment on a bridge where a young woman chants a prayer for a dead child, while dropping one by one into the current one hundred tiny papers with an image of Jizo, guardian deity of children. He likes to watch sunsets over the lake from a little *soba* shop at the south end of town, likes to attempt to capture the subtleties of the fading light in words. Strolling homeward at twilight, he likes to record the cries of vendors who sell noodles, sweet syrup, and *sake*, and of fortune-tellers who will improve your love life or bring you wealth. After dark, he likes to look out at the paper lanterns along the bridge and watch the reflections trembling in the dark waters, and while he waits to catch the silhouettes of women on the *shoji* of nearby houses he fervently prays that window glass will always remain foreign to Japan.

<>

There has to be a catch, and there is: the weather. Cold rain in late autumn, enormous amounts of snow after New Year's. Drifts four feet deep pile against the thin walls of Hearn's house; icy winds off the lake blow through the narrow rooms. Those Japanese heating devices, the *hibachi* and *kotatsu*, prove to be more charming in theory than useful in practice; together they provide *mere shadows of heat—ghosts, illusions.* Soon it becomes a struggle to keep up morale. Lafcadio attempts to believe what the natives say, that this is exceptional weather, the worst in fifteen years. He comforts himself with the beauty of the winter landscape. He boasts about his immunity from illness—prematurely. When snow turns to rain and sleet in mid-January, he comes down with a serious case of influenza, *touched where I thought myself strongest—in my lungs.* Weeks in bed leave him with a bad case of *the blues.* Friends and officials are *astonishingly kind*—colleagues visit, their wives send special food, his classes are taught by someone else. But nothing helps to make the future look cheery: *A few more winters of this kind will put me underground.* From late January to April, Hearn writes no letters (or none that survive), makes no significant entries in his journal, and pens but a single article for the *Weekly Mail.* Nowhere does he record, or even hint at, the major event of this period (if not his life). Even today it is impossible to name with any certainty the exact date, or even the month, of Lafcadio Hearn's marriage to Koizumi Setsuko.

The weather, illness, and loneliness, the natural need of a middle-aged bachelor for companionship and a mate—these are the usual explanations that biographers give for the marriage. All seem reasonable, but none begins to explain Hearn's long silence on the subject, one that lasts at least until midsummer. For a man who wishes to write about the heart of this civilization, a relationship with a native woman must surely be necessary. Sometime since landing—in Yokohama no doubt—Hearn enjoyed and suffered a brief, passionate fling, *a delusion of the senses.* Now he is ready for something deeper. But just a bit. It is important to be clear about this. Like many arrangements in treaty ports between local girls and Westerners, Hearn's marriage is originally meant to be temporary—or so the locals always think. During all his time there, the Matsue newspapers will refer to Setsuko by the word *aisho,* which means not wife but *beloved concubine.*

Like any marriage in Japan, temporary or permanent, this one is arranged by a *nakodo,* or go-between, and solemnized with the ritual exchange of sips of wine from the same cup. All biographers agree that Nishida plays this role, just as all agree that from the first Setsu lives in the house as a wife rather than some kind of playmate. This is tradition, too, and certainly the role for which she has been trained. Twenty-two and not especially attractive, Setsu is the well-bred daughter of a samurai family that, like so many of their class, has fallen on hard times in the postfeudal era. To the extent that the interracial marriage might make early biographers edgy, they are able to stress Setsu's aristocratic background and upbringing. What everyone ignores is the far more important and interesting issue—their early behavior as man and wife.

How to imagine those first hours and days together? The solitary report is hers, written fifteen years later: *When I went to him, I found only one table and a chair, a few books, one suit of clothes, and one set of Japanese kimono.* Nothing here about her expectations or his; nothing about those strange and awkward moments when they first face each other alone, across a *kotatsu* or on a futon. Remember, they can barely talk to one another. So they must be mostly silent—or is there amusement, tender laughter, a recognition of the oddity of their situation?—as she dishes out his rice, hands him a bowl of soup, lies down beside him in the dark. Their first knowledge of each other must be of eyes, hands, bodies, at rest and in motion, the kind of knowledge that will outlast words.

Never will they fully understand one another, but that is not just a matter of language and background. Years later Hearn will confess, *My little wife remains a mystery to me*, but what husband—or wife—has not said the same of a spouse? More important, they will come to accept each other, to love each other for the differences they share. But that will happen only after years of adjustments, large and small. Trained to obedience, Setsu will do the most overt yielding, accepting his foreign ways even when embarrassed by them. And Hearn's behavior can seem odd, especially in their early days together. He is too individualistic, too honest to follow Japanese social norms. In public he will openly insult a man he does not like (violating the idea of harmony), or insist that Setsu walk beside him in the streets (rather than behind, as is appropriate for a married woman), or praise her accomplishments (one must always denigrate one's wife to others). His oddities can be private as well. More than once Setsu awakens in the middle of the night to find him in a trancelike state at his desk. When she confesses to Nishida that she fears for her husband's sanity, Hearn's colleague brushes aside her worries: Lafcadio is not mad—just a writer.

One thing is certain: from the day Setsu enters the house, Lafcadio's life becomes easier and more pleasant. She takes care of everything practical—shops, cooks, cleans, sews, nurses him, manages his money, hands him clothing as he dresses in the morning, heats his bath in the evening, waits up for him when he is out with colleagues at a banquet. Now it is always a pleasure to return from school, to change from a suit into a kimono, sit on a *zabuton*, and smoke a pipeful of tobacco. Under Setsu's care Hearn flourishes and—in her words—draws *nearer and nearer to the Japanese style of living.* Indeed, he seems to love the old traditions more than any native. Long will she remember his repeated comment: *There are many beautiful things in Japan. Why do they imitate Western things?*

Spring is beautiful that year, and not just because of cherry blossoms. The newly married man grows expansive, insists on buying his wife many new kimono and taking her everywhere with him. On April 3 they attend the celebration that marks the opening of the first iron bridge over the Ohashi, enjoy along with one hundred thousand visitors a day of artillery salutes, fireworks, food, drink, and dance. Two weeks later they are at a local crafts exhibition, where Lafcadio sees so many treasures old and new that he comments, *How fine a sense of art we have even in this little country province.* At the beginning of June they follow custom and move from their tiny house to a much larger one that can also accommodate Setsu's parents, grandparents, and longtime servants.

Kitabori is the name of their new neighborhood. Hearn prefers the word in the original, for in English it simply means North Moat, an accurate—if too literal—description of what seems a most romantic part of the old samurai quarter. Across the street lies a wide section of Matsue's innermost waterway; above that, Castle Hill. Once this was the residence of a high retainer of the *daimyo*. The impressive gateway was designed to keep out intruders; those heavily barred lookout windows set into the thick, high wall were manned by armed guards, day and night. Not so long ago, elegant women graced the fourteen *lofty, spacious, and beautiful rooms*; sat on those broad *engawa* (verandas) to play the *koto* while their men dashed off *haiku* on the beauties of the September moon. Thoughts like these come with the establishment. So does a feeling of affluence. Uncharacteristically, Lafcadio brags to friends in America: *I am able to keep up nearly the nicest house in town,—outside of a very few rich men,—to have several servants, to give dinners, and to dress my little wife tolerably nicely* (to some he will say, *like a queen*).

Now and ever after the house at Kitabori will represent for Hearn the exquisite life of traditional Japan. He never describes its rooms, but you can visit them today and see them as they were in his time—spare, elegant, and simple. This is Hearn's domain, the realm where he is treated like a great lord. Every morning, his wife and servants line up by the door to bow him off to work; every evening, after his leisurely stroll back from school through the overgrown, tangled park that is the castle grounds, they bow him home again. Wearing a *yukata*, he relaxes on the *engawa* and enjoys the world of his gardens—the two cherry trees; the huge gnarled plum; the pond with water lily and lotus; the stone lantern; the raked pebbles; the forest of bamboo. Twilight is his favorite time of day. High walls shut out the murmur of city life and all he can hear are the calls of the crows, swallows, and wild doves; the persistent shrill of the cicada; the tiny splashes of frogs diving into pools. (Can it really be this way? Yes, really.)

For a writer on Japan, this has to be the perfect setting, the ideal way of life. All needs are taken care of—meals appear, rooms are cleaned, the garden is trimmed and raked, unwanted visitors are kept away. True, more energy than he cares to give must go into his job, especially during examination periods. But once at home on the matted floor of his study, notebooks, paper, and pens on the low table before him, Lafcadio is left alone to wrestle with the demons of his art. Now there is nothing to keep him from producing, except the traditional question: What shall I write? How to slice Japan up into manageable sections; how to handle the complexities of such enormous topics as Shinto,

Buddhism, the arts, history, and legend; how to blend personal adventures and insights with what he can glean from so many other sources—books in English; compositions of students; information conveyed by colleagues who accompany him on trips; translations of talks with priests, innkeepers, fishermen, gardeners, and woodcarvers; stories that Setsu has—in response to urging—begun to relate in what he calls the *Hearnian dialect*, a pidginlike mixture of childish Japanese and English.

To capture a nation in words, to make sense of it for oneself and shape it for a reader, is a formidable (impossible?) task. Hearn will write literally thousands of pages as he attempts to locate an approach and suitable form for the pieces that will make up *Glimpses of Unfamiliar Japan*, his first collection. And he does so laboring under an unusual pressure, one born out of self-consciousness. Despite his reputation, Hearn is no simpleminded antiquarian. Sitting in his study with the *shoji* thrown open, he understands that the garden before him is a relic of seventeenth-century life. Beyond the wall lies a less pleasant Japan of telegraph wires, newspapers, and steamships. The world he chooses to write about will soon vanish. Someday a railroad will reach Matsue and the city will grow larger and more *commonplace* and be touched by ugly industry. And this town is only a microcosm of the nation. The old civilization is *doomed to pass away*. One wonders if he ever senses that writing itself is a kind of paradoxical act, a vain bet cast against the certainty of chaos. Or if he has learned to take comfort in the underlying philosophy of this Buddhist culture: *Impermanency is the nature of all things.* Certainly he understands this simple truth: a writer is a man who must write, even if he thinks the world is about to vanish (as it someday must).

<>

(Come to a banquet, but don't ask where or when. It doesn't matter, really. After a while they are all the same. But this is a special one: this is Hearn's, the sum and substance of the many he attends; a window into the culture for him, his readers, and us; a way of linking present and past, a single evening and countless evenings; an exploration of all those others and ourselves.)

It begins—they all begin—in the silence of a private banquet house surrounded by gardens. Men in formal kimono kneel upon cushions. Serving girls noiselessly move about, placing small, individual lacquer tables before the guests. The host breaks the hush by bidding his guests to eat. Everyone bows, takes up *hashi*, and begins. Few words are spoken until the *fusuma* slides open and in comes a group of women whose gorgeous kimono and elaborate coiffures, decked with mock flowers, wonderful combs, and jeweled pins, mark them as geisha. They begin to pour *sake*; to jest, laugh, offer toasts, and utter *funny little cries*. They play *samisen* and hand drum; they dance and posture; they pour more *sake*. Soon the banquet livens up. Everyone talks, laughs, shouts. Men move around the room, form small groups; some sing old songs, or recite poems, or tuck up their robes and dance across the tatami; some engage in drinking contests, play children's games, happily chase the girls. The music grows faster, the guests louder, the actions more disjointed until the room is *a merry tumult*. But as the hour grows toward midnight, the guests begin to slip away, the din dies down, the music stops, and, finally, the geisha stand at the door and cry *sayonara* to the last of the revellers. Only then do these girls sit down to rest and eat a meal in the deserted hall.

(That's a banquet—every banquet—all right, but not yet an article or story, not if you are Hearn. Too much surface here; too much present tense. It lacks thickness; it needs more layers. Any writer could do a banquet like this, but he is after something more. So come along again. Let's go from guests to geisha; let's get her away from the circle of banquet lights, away from judgments made under the influence of wine. Let's get the real story, the one beneath the surface.)

To some she may seem the most desirable of creatures, but the geisha is no more than what she has been made, a result of the human (read male) desire for *love mixed with youth and grace, but without regrets or responsibilities*. The cost of this *illusion*, of beauty, smiles, and perpetual merriment, is high—the geisha is essentially a slave. As a pretty child, she is bought from poor parents under a contract that can last up to twenty-five years. She is fed, clothed, and housed in a building run by older geisha; she is trained and disciplined, given rigorous lessons in dance, song, polite speech, grace, and etiquette, in drum and *samisen*. At the age of eight or nine she begins to serve wine at banquets; at thirteen she sings and dances; at seventeen she is in full bloom, an artist with a reputation, though she does not even own the clothes she wears. Hers is a world of darkness and artificial light. Every night she drinks wine without ever losing her head, never swallows a morsel during the longest feasts, never permits a cross word to reach her lips or a negative feeling to show. She has rich and powerful lovers who give her expensive gifts, but her dream is of freedom, not wealth, and her greatest wish that someone will buy up her contract. When this happens, a geisha becomes respectable. But more often . . . Oh, better leave her young and attractive, when she can still charm us. For the rest of her story too often involves degradation, humiliation, and lonely death.

(That's closer, but still not there. Hearn likes a certain kind of balance, a certain kind of moral. No joy without sorrow, life without death, art without pain. And no article, if he can help it, without something from the past—history, legend, folktale, it matters not, as long as one can summon up the richness of those centuries gone by. So wait—here comes the story of an early geisha who lived before the social role of her kind was fixed and regulated.)

Once upon a time, a poor young artist was following the old custom of traveling about the country on foot to sketch famous scenery. Long after sunset one evening in a mountainous region with neither inn nor temple in sight, he stops to ask for shelter at a lonely house. A beautiful woman makes him welcome in the humble but clean cottage; she feeds him a meager supper and gives him a bed behind a screen. In the middle of the night he is startled awake by the sound of moving feet. Peering around the edge of the screen, he sees the woman, now magnificently dressed, dancing with her back to him before an altar like a creature possessed, dancing so wonderfully that he can neither talk nor take his eyes off her. Suddenly she turns and sees him, and after he profusely apologizes for watching, she tells the story of her life.

Once she was a famous dancer, the darling of Kyoto. But she

fell in love with a poor youth and the only way they could be together was to flee to the country. Together they built this house, and lived their days wholly for each other. Every evening it was her great pleasure to dance for him, but such happiness as theirs could not last. One cold winter he fell sick and died. Ever since, she has lived only for his memory. Daily she places offerings before his funerary tablet, and nightly she dances before the *butsudan* to please him, as of old.

Deeply moved by her gentleness, devotion, and beauty, the young man wishes to help somehow, but he realizes there is nothing that can be done for such a profound sorrow. Nor will she even let him pay for the hospitality when he departs the next morning, on his way down from the mountain and into a brilliant career. Many years later, when he is rich and famous and the incident long forgotten, an old woman in rags comes to his house and asks to have her portrait painted. She can pay him only with some quaint garments of silk that he immediately recognizes. Yes, it is she and these are the robes she wore for that marvelous dance. Now she explains that years ago she lost her money and her house, and had to return to Kyoto to live as a beggar. Each night she continued to dance for her beloved, but, now too old to move very well, she wants a picture of herself to hang before the *butsudan*. Happy to repay his debt and to honor such devotion, the artist uses all his powers to depict her as he saw her years before—young, beautiful, full of the dance of life. Once again he offers her money and, just as years before, she refuses. Not to be denied this time, he has a servant follow her home, and the next day, bearing gifts, the painter goes to the hovel where she lives. He finds the old woman dead, a sweet, unearthly smile on her lips. In the dim light of a tiny oil lamp, his painting glows before the altar. The flesh is gone, but the work of art remains. (There now, that's complete.)

<>

Summer vacation. July and August blessedly free of classes. Days often so hot and humid that, during the haze of an afternoon nap, you can imagine yourself in the tropics. Lizards and snakes slip in from the garden to visit; spiders spin webs in the high corners

of rooms; huge moths hover near kerosene lamps; mosquitoes sit
hungrily all night long on the netting over the futon. Plenty of
time to write now; plenty of time to travel. The two activities are
connected. Each jaunt involves a search for topics, but not every
trip is productive or pleasant. Tamatsukuri, renowned for its hot
springs and agate jewelry, does not stir the imagination, so all
that comes out are a few descriptive paragraphs for the *Weekly
Mail*. Some spots are so awful that Hearn mentions his reactions
to them only in the privacy of letters. The worst is Otsuka, a
primitive, stony village, where an ill-tempered crowd begins to
jeer and to pelt the outsider with mud and sand: *It gave me the
first decidedly unpleasant sense of being an alien that I have ever
had in Japan.*

Remote religious sites and the seaside are his real loves. Hearn
savors *little drowsy sea villages—sleeping, eating, drinking sake,
and bathing.* He is a good swimmer who likes to venture out far
beyond the breakers while natives stand on the shore to watch; a
bit of a show-off who is disappointed when local boys upstage
him by hauling boards out to the high surf and riding in on the
crests of waves *after the fashion of Polynesian Islanders.* One of
his deepest, most persistent desires is to find a spot never before
visited by Westerners, but in 1891 this is not easy to do. From
Ichibata on the far shore of Lake Shinji, he struggles up a long
mountain trail, then climbs 640 stone steps to reach the windy
shrine of Yakushi Nyorai, where the magnificent view of far-off
peaks dims when the local priest explains that a group of German
naval officers once made the same trek. In midsummer when he
enters a quiet village with a superb beach that appears in no travel
guides, Lafcadio dashes off a note to Chamberlain: *I have discovered Yabase. No European seems to have ever been here before.*
Alas, this proves to be untrue, as the letter's postscript shows:
*Some detestable missionary was here before me—for one hour
only, it is true, but he was here!*

The place with the strongest pull is Kizuki. He spends the first
weeks of the holiday swimming in Inasa Bay and exploring the
extensive grounds and numerous shrines—tiny and large—of
Izumo Taisha. Late in July, the Guji welcomes Lafcadio to a
private pavilion to view Honen-odori, a nightlong harvest dance

at the festival of Tenjin, god of calligraphy and scholarship. Questions about things Hearn sees, and things he cannot, go to an assistant priest, a man full of stories that blend history and legend, who describes the choice and training of priestesses and the practices of divination; recounts ancient tales of carved dragons that come to life and bronze horses that can be ridden only by the gods; relates the adventures of O-Kuni, the sixteenth-century *miko* (temple maiden) who fled to Kyoto with a lover, became a popular dancer and the founder of Kabuki, and later—after the lover's death—returned to Kizuki to live in a small temple as a poet and nun.

Details like these go first into notebooks, then into articles and sketches. By now Hearn has found a good Japanese word for his literary aims, one that cannot be translated into English without linking two concepts usually kept distinct in the Western tradition. The word is *kokoro* and it means both mind and heart. His wish is to *get at the Kokoro of the common people*, to render their *religious and emotional home life*. If to do that he must focus on Shinto, this is no act of personal preference. Buddhism is more to his taste: its doctrines of acceptance, its reverence for all forms of life, its apparent ability to foster calmness and quiet lead him to exclaim he would be a Buddhist *if it were possible for me to adopt a faith*.

But Shinto is Japan. Not the recent variety, the nationalistic Emperor worship being fostered by Meiji leaders. No, he is interested in the local traditions and manifestations of this *vast, extraordinary* force that even experts cannot pin down: *It is not at all a belief, nor all a religion; it is a thing as formless as a magnetism and as indefinable as an ancestral impulse. It is part of the Soul of the Race. It means all the loyalty of the nation to its sovereigns, the devotion of retainers to princes, the respect to sacred things, the conservation of principles, the whole of what an Englishman would call his sense of duty.* Shinto, he believes, makes people willing to sacrifice their lives for loyalty, duty, and honor; Shinto, he hopes, will help to preserve tradition and keep the nation culturally intact; Shinto, he thinks, is *the irrefragable obstacle to the Christianization of Japan (for which reason I am wicked enough to love it)*.

On the last summer trip, Setsu is with him (though you would never know it from what he writes) as companion, interpreter, and caretaker. By now she is growing used to his ways. When he storms out of an inn he dislikes, she is embarrassed but forgiving; when he leaves silver coins and bank notes strewn about a hotel room, she is amused that he has *no mind for so common a thing*; when he sulks for two days after she prevails upon him not to swim in a sacred cave where there may be sharks, she has to remind herself how childlike he can be.

Bon-Odori is the aim of this mid-August jaunt. He wants to relive the year before, to have once again that *ghostly* experience at *a Dance of Souls*. The search takes them east, along blanched roads to towns by the shore and towns in the mountains; to villages with enormous cemeteries whose silent populations far outnumber *the folks of the Hamlets to which they belong*; to fishing settlements with rows of neat gravestones for men lost at sea. Almost everywhere the dance has been banned by the police, either through fear of spreading cholera (as Hearn says in his first book) or because the ritual is not suited for the modern world (as Setsu suggests years later in her memoir). He either accepts this understandingly (his book) or blames the police for destroying old customs—*they cast aside all the Japanese ways, and try to imitate Western things* (her version). Either way, he is dreadfully disappointed. Perhaps he senses that never again will he see a Bon-Odori as exciting as the one the year before. Perhaps he knows that no Bon-Odori could possibly be as thrilling as the one still dancing in his mind.

<>

By now you know it too: there are many Lafcadio Hearns; perhaps too many for a single book. There are the feeling Hearn and the thinking Hearn, the Hearn who loves and the one who hates, the settled Hearn and the one who is ready to flee all obligations. There are the pessimist and the optimist, the realist and the dreamer; the Hearn who writes stories and sketches aimed at the *Atlantic Monthly* and publishers in Boston; the one who reports on Matsue life for the *Weekly Mail*; the one who writes long and detailed letters to friends. There are the modest Hearn of the sketches and the more confident Hearn of the letters; the storyteller who explains and the theorist who asks questions; the evolutionist who knows that progress is inevitable and the antiquarian who wants to hold it back. One Hearn hopes to be a great writer, another doubts that will happen, and a third says go on and try. And all these Hearns can claim to be the real one; all demand our attention and want to have their say.

So does Hearn the thinker. But how to make sense of his ideas? To do this you normally bring together disparate comments from letters written in different seasons, moods, settings, times of day, and states of sobriety, and you make them say, *Here is what the man thinks! This is how he feels about Japan, its people, himself, the future.* This method turns a chaotic jumble of impressions into something systematic and coherent. But to really express how he feels and thinks, you have to do the reverse—jam the incompatible elements together and admit the contradictions can never be smoothed away. So you must say he loves the Japanese and hates them, finds them pleasant to be with but often oh so boring, because most of them *have nothing to say.* No doubt about it, he is always positive about the females. Ad nauseum he repeats, *How sweet the Japanese woman is!* But the men—you never get to know them. You cannot clap them on the back, or chuck them under the ribs, or call them "old boy," or even really feel close. After all these months they still smile and bow and keep their distance. How lonely one gets for the touch of another male, for a good cigar and your feet up on the desk and your vest unbuttoned. And your mind, too, for that matter—your mind, too.

Hearn's ideas are hardly his alone. Like anyone, he takes notions in through the eye and ear for so many years that it is impossible to say where they come from. It is difficult to trace what he has read, but you can give the names of scientists, historians, philosophers, and anthropologists who are mentioned in his letters: Schopenhauer, Darwin, Huxley, Renan, Fustel de Coulanges, E. B. Tylor. The thinker he turns to again and again is Herbert Spencer, that greatest of systematizers in an age of great systematizers, that exponent of evolution before the publication of *Origin of Species.* Spencer has managed to fit all phenomena into a grand spectacle of cosmic evolution. One-celled creatures, human beings, and entire civilizations all follow the same laws of behavior, the same patterns of growth and decay.

The science, the drama, the very reach and scope of Spencer are equally important to Hearn. He has not called himself a Christian since the age of fifteen, but for five years now cosmic evolution has been a kind of faith, one with no promise of individual salvation but long-range hope for the progress of the species. Spencer shows everything to be part of a pattern: the social problems of Cincinnati and New Orleans, the movement of Western countries into Asia, the trials of a Greek-Anglo-Irish-American writer with one eye—all are connected and explicable. How dismaying, then, to find that his theories do not apply to Japan. According to Spencer, Japan is an example of how a passive phenomenon disintegrates when it meets an active one. Under the impact of European civilization—its arms, commercial demands, and superior ideas—long-static Japan is in the process of dissolution. But Hearn sees quite the contrary: a nation growing stronger and more vital. In this conflict between theory and belief, Lafcadio turns against his own philosophy and predicts that Japan will be a *magnificent exception* to Spencer's general law. As it did with Chinese culture a thousand years before, the nation will absorb the lessons of the West and create a vital, new civilization that will somehow retain its traditional values.

Spencer is not the only example of theory gone awry. Hearn is beginning to see that Japan has a way of eluding theories—or turning them upside down. Take those of Percival Lowell. His book *The Soul of the Far East* was a factor in Lafcadio's decision to come here. To the Boston Brahmin Lowell (his brother is president of Harvard), the key to Japan—the *Soul* of his title—is the *impersonality* of the Japanese, their lack of *individuality* as it is manifest in the West. Charming, polite, moral, and artistic, they are wholly lacking in personal quirks (or genius, or imagination). But, says Lowell the Darwinist, individuality is a late stage of evolution, a measurement of the place of a people in *the great march of the mind*. By this standard, the Japanese are distinctly backward. Unless they become more individualistic, more like Europeans and Americans, their country will be unable to meet the challenge of modern scientific civilizations (which depend on the creativity of individuals), and will *disappear before the advancing nations of the West.*

Nonsense. That's what Hearn can say after a year in Matsue. He accepts the idea of *impersonality*, uses it to describe his students and their work, their weaknesses and strengths. But his inclination is to turn the argument around. For him the absence of individuality is a social plus. Because people here are less pushy and aggressive than Westerners, they are more civilized and more pleasant to be with. Yet the deeper question raised by living here is whether *individualism*—that glory of the West—is at all a *desirable tendency.* The view from Japan suggests not. Rather than judge this nation by Occidental standards, Hearn is prepared to do the reverse. He likes to quote an article by a Meiji politician who has denounced Western civilization for cultivating the individual at the expense of the mass, with results that are are negative in the extreme—*unbounded opportunities* [for] *human selfishness, unrestrained by religious sentiment, law, or emotional feeling.*

A Japan-based critique of the West is easy for a man like Hearn, so long at odds with Anglo-Saxon culture. For him to witness the carefree eroticism of a people who lack notions of guilt or original sin is to fuel longtime doubts about sexual morality at home. To dwell among a people who peacefully follow two religions and have *never hated any faith* is to highlight the schisms, wars, and inquisitions so characteristic of Christianity, that *religion of love.* (Yes, he can be ironic.) To know Japanese women is to question that *oppression* (for they are both oppressed and suppressed) is bad—how much sweeter and more giving are these females than those *objects of idolatry*, those *diamond hard* American women. To live here is to rethink major goals both personal and cultural: *What is really the main object of life? or what should be one's main purpose in life? To succeed in money-making by imposing on others, or to waste one's existence to win empty praise when one gets old, or to simply cultivate one's self as far as possible for the better, and enjoy all one can? The last seems to me much the more rational and moral, and it seems to be somewhat Japanese.*

Judgments, insights, perceptions—that's all. Hearn is no systematic theorist. Never does he attempt a detailed critique of the West, and not for another decade will he try a systematic approach to Japan. Love and admiration tend to flavor everything he writes for publication about this land, while all criticisms are confined to private letters. Partly this is self-interest: he has chosen a role as explicator and celebrator of this civilization. Partly it is humility: one-and-a-half years here are just enough to let him glimpse all the things he does not—sometimes fears he cannot—ever know. Most important: his discontents are so vague and inchoate that words can do no more than hint at them. How to explain the gnawing feeling that people here are less interesting and profound than people at home? He can say *Depth . . . does not exist in the Japanese soul-stream*; he can complain that they are essentially *unspeculative*, that they do not seem to find pleasure in *the suggestions of philosophy* or in studying the *relations of things*. Even such notions are difficult to hold onto, let alone prove. In truth, his moods and judgments are in a state of perpetual *oscillation*. This means plenty of self-contradiction: *There are times when they seem so small! And then again, although they never seem large, there is a vastness behind them,—a past of indefinite complexity and marvel,—an amazing power of absorbing and assimilating,—which forces one to suspect some power in the race so different from our own that one cannot understand that power.*

Only one idea remains constant through the mood swings of the passing months: *the Japanese are the happiest people in the world.* Self-restraint, the willingness to live within well-prescribed social limits, the ability to enjoy fully the simple things of life— these are the reasons he gives for such a blessed condition. Social and economic life here lacks the clash and struggle to the death— literal and figurative—that seem so marked at home. Or so he naively thinks. Like most of his judgments, this says much more about Hearn than about Japan. Repeatedly he uses the image of this land as a refuge, a place of escape from the high pressures of Western life. Whenever doubts and vexations trouble him, he retreats to this comforting notion: the Japanese are *the best people to live with.* But nowhere does he acknowledge what seems so obvious to us—that only an outsider could make such a statement.

‹›

Maybe on the first day of class he already knows that something is coming to an end. The faces before him on September 4 seem familiar. Did he not see them last year?—fresh, soft, placid, sweet. But many of the names are different and many of his favorites are missing; some have graduated or moved, others are sick with cholera; a couple have died. So it's the same but different. He knows the routine now, needs no help finding classrooms, calling roll, or getting started. He suffers no fears of failing and also harbors no expectations. Maybe that's the problem—he already knows too much. When Hearn asks a question in class, there is little doubt what the answer will be; when he assigns an essay topic . . . Yes, that's it. He can go on living as a teacher here, but by now he has to be aware that Matsue has nothing more to teach him. Except the possible lesson of what it is to go on. And on. Something he may not yet be ready to learn.

School now means less time to write than during the summer, but he has more than at the beginning of last year. Setsu has the house so well under control. He owes her so much, but gratitude cannot keep fantasies away. The tropics still tug at him; the old dreams return. Sometimes he aches with the old desire to steam up the Amazon and Orinoco, to haunt those crumbling cities with Spanish and Portuguese names, to spend his time pursuing *romances nobody else could find*. Yes, he thinks, the Latin countries were his real field. He could have done it; he could do it still. But perhaps it's all for the best. Last year an enormous earthquake in Martinique flattened St. Pierre and no doubt killed everyone he knows. He might have been caught in that. And besides, there are tropics on this side of the world. Not so far away, when you come to think of it; not so far to the Philippines, the Straits settlements. When will he get to them? *When I get rich!*

This is a season of doubt. Sometimes he worries over the *impertinence* of writing on a people whose language he does not know, fears the subject of Japan is too broad to master. But he will do it, by God. No one else has tried to tackle the common people; no one else has lived upon the floor, eaten the food, enjoyed (and suffered) the ritual courtesies of daily life. He will succeed, but when? There is so much work ahead and it goes so slowly. Once, long ago, in the tropics, he had a *pen of fire*. But not now: *I've lost it. Well, the fact is, it is no use here.* Japan is wrapped in fog and smoke, a place with no sharp lines between things or people: *It is all soft, dreamy, quiet, pale, faint, gentle, hazy, vapory, visionary.* Here people really do eat lotuses; here the seasons are feeble and ghostly. No fine inspirations move him; no profound joys or pains trouble his days. Writing is no fun, but *dry, bony, hard, dead work.* To make a decent book will require years of steady effort devoid of excitement, flash, ecstasy. So complex is the culture, so vastly different from the West, that each piece he writes must be burdened with explanation. The result is deadly: *I must try another method—but some stimulus is wanting, the stimulus of strong emotion.*

Perhaps. Or perhaps strong emotions get in the way of good writing. To judge by results, Hearn does better when it is necessary to reach for emotion, to create it rather than have it overwhelm him. Remember his difficulties working in Martinique. For all the complaints and worries, Lafcadio in the early fall mails a fifteen-hundred-page manuscript to Houghton Mifflin in Boston—not bad for a year devoid of inspiration. Of course even if the publishing house takes it (and eventually it will), rewrites will be necessary. Far too many books on Japan are full of first impressions, and you cannot trust first impressions here. They are misleading, *for nothing in Japan is exactly what it appears.* To finish his own volume will take at least two more years. So he has to prolong his stay. His art, his desired reputation, and his understanding all demand it.

This is not the only reason he cannot leave Japan. For the first time in life—if you ignore those weeks with Mattie Foley—Hearn has an obligation to someone other than himself. Marriage is a burden, but oddly fulfilling too. Say it simply: Setsu makes him happy. She lets him—helps him—write. The cost is this: what once seemed temporary has begun *to take the shape of something unbreakable and to bind me very fast here at the very time when I was beginning to feel like going away.* Nor can he think of taking Setsu with him to another country; clearly she would be unhappy away from her gods and her people. So it is necessary to face a truth at once unpleasant and comforting: *It does not now seem possible for me ever to go away . . . And to separate from her would be equally out of the question.* Indeed, maybe he will do the reverse. For her sake and the sake of any future children, Lafcadio has begun to think of becoming a Japanese citizen. One potential problem makes him hesitate. He fears the government might *try to take advantage and cut down my salary,* might pay him as a Japanese rather than as a foreigner.

If one has an itch to move, there are places not so far away, plenty of other cities in Japan that would like to have foreign teachers. We do not know exactly when Hearn first asks Professor Chamberlain to help him find another job, but by early October he has in hand an offer from the Government College in Kumamoto, on the island of Kyushu, at $200 a month. Weather and health are the official reasons given for the change (and Hearn's biographers find them convincing enough). Kumamoto, far to the south, is reported to have a milder climate and almost no snowfall, and sometimes Hearn can sound as if he thinks Kyushu is a tropic isle. But this is fantasy; this is too simple; this cannot be the whole story. Search a little for other clues to this decision and you find a letter from Hearn to Chamberlain, who is leaving for a long stay in England: *About 'seeing Japan from a distance'—I envy you your coming chance. I could not finish my book on the West Indies until I saw the magical island again through regret, as through a summer haze . . . I should not be surprised should the experience result in the creation of something which would please your own feelings as an author better than any other work you have made.*

The man who had to leave Martinique to write about it, who could complete his manuscript about the West Indies only while living in Philadelphia, and who knows that this was his first—so far his only—successful book, is doing more here than wishing godspeed to a friend. Hearn is not one to use words lightly. Maybe they rise unknowingly out of the unconscious; maybe he does not apply them to himself; maybe he never connects them to his own decision. But there they are for all to see, and interpret. Ultimately, emotion and its opposite can only be recollected in tranquillity. Does it seem an exaggeration to insist upon this point? To turn

Matsue—his Japan, after all—into a work of art, Hearn knows he must be living somewhere else.

◇

Later he will do the departure, will use it as the final chapter of his first book on Japan, will entitle it *Sayonara!* He will do the doubts, will admit that he refuses to dwell upon the thought of never again seeing *the quaint old city*, will try to believe that he will someday return to his house in Kitabori. He will describe the gift from the teachers, two huge antique vases, and the one from the students, a feudal sword with silver and gold inlay. He will quote the speech of the students to him, and his reply, full of advice that they revere their ancestors and honor their government. He will do the banquets, and the farewell addresses in English, and the poems in Japanese, and the singing of "Auld Lang Syne." And he will do the last morning, when two hundred students and teachers assemble before his gate and escort him to the wharf near the long white bridge. He looks at the crowds and remembers all the kindness and courtesy extended to him, and recalls that nobody has ever addressed to him *a single ungenerous word*, and he asks (then or later) a question that can have only one answer: *Could I have lived in the exercise of the same profession for the same length of time in any other country, and have enjoyed a similar unbroken experience of human goodness?*

The steamer shrieks for its passengers. Lafcadio shakes hands with the directors of the schools, the teachers, his favorite students. It is November 15, a gray morning, sharp with the first chill of winter. From the deck he can see bridges, the *peaked host of queer dear old houses*, the sails of junks tinted in the early sun. Mist rises from the lake, hangs in bands before the mountains— *sky and earth so strangely intermingle that what is reality may not be distinguished from what is illusion*. It is a magic land— how many times has he thought that, written it? The steamer shrieks again, puffs black smoke, backs into midstream, moves away from the wharves while students wave caps and shout *Banzai, Banzai*—ten thousand years to you, ten thousand years! Out on the river they go and into the lake, and the faces, the voices, the wharves, the bridges are suddenly part of the past. For a while longer he can see the crest of the castle, the shaggy pines, the long blue roofs of the school buildings. And then they too are gone, replaced by memories—the smiles of colleagues, the dog that waits by the gate every evening, the garden with its blooming lotus and cooing doves, the songs of children at play, the afternoon shadows on streets, the long glowing lines of festival lanterns, the sound of *geta* on a windy bridge—all are part of him as the steamer picks up speed and bears Hearn *more and more swiftly, ever farther and farther from the province of the Gods.*

Four

LEARNING

A Japanese artist was commissioned by an American to do a painting. The completed work had, in a lower corner, the branch of a cherry tree with a few blossoms and a bird perched upon it. The entire upper half of the painting was white. Unhappy, the American asked the artist to put something else in the painting because it looked, well, so bare. The Japanese refused the request. When pressed for an explanation, the artist said that if he did fill up the painting, there would be no space for the bird to fly.

—TRADITIONAL STORY

10

To Be a Literary Man

Huge, thrusting noses. Jutting chins. Blue eyes that stare ferociously. Hair, so much of it and such odd colors—blond and red and a hundred shades of brown. Beards swallow features, mustaches droop into scowls. Skin so white, so deathly pale, so unnatural. Repulsive creatures, and their clothing only makes it worse. A riot of outrageous colors. Odd-shaped hats. No harmony, no familiar patterns to soothe the eye. Jerky movements. Through the streets they lurch and swagger. No grace when they reach for something, no delicacy when they gesture. Voices too loud, insistent, the tones of language oddly harsh. No manners at all. In laughter, they do not bother to cover naked mouths with a hand. In greeting, they neglect to return your bows.

February 2, 1872. Yokohama. Eyes and ears expect the familiar, learn the familiar is not what it used to be. A shock to encounter such change. A greater one to recognize the change is not out there but in the self. So that's what it means to be in the interior for ten months. The very sense organs alter. You return with the *ken of a native.* You expect smooth faces, indirect glances, contained movements, dark colors, simple robes, cheery greetings. Instead you enter the jarring realm of an alien race, boisterous invaders of a land that is suddenly your own. For a moment you have to wonder if returning has been a terrible mistake.

No, it does not last. Cannot last. You would not want it to last. Not if you are William Griffis and you have traveled thirteen days to get here; not if you have covered three hundred miles by foot, litter, and boat; not if you are *blistered, weary and sore and faint* from pushing too hard, sleeping too little, and living on a sparse, meatless diet. The odd vision slips away as you call on friends, visit the tailor to order a new suit of clothes, spend an evening with the Reverend Ballagh and his family. Grace before dinner; familiar foods on the table; the *dear old music* of "Dixieland" and "Home Sweet Home" on the piano; prayers of thanks; and then the comfort of a bed. Here the vision may momentarily return. Sleep will drown it as daily life banishes it later. But never for good. It is part of him now, that odd sight from somewhere outside the self. Ever after, at odd moments he will be able to *see as the Japanese see.*

Dense fog the next morning. Griffis catches the 8:30 steamer for the capital, gorges himself on luncheon delicacies at the French hotel in Tsukiji, takes a stroll. Only eleven months have passed, but everywhere *great changes and improvements.* Streets are crowded with horse-drawn carriages, buggies, and traps, and swarms of *jinrikisha.* He sees houses of brick; glass set into the once-paper windows of older structures; butcher stalls; barbershops with candy-striped poles; and many stores selling Western goods. Startling are the alterations in male attire: thousands have cut their topknots; few carry two swords; large numbers wear hats, coats, trousers and boots, *the more serviceable, but not so becoming dress of the civilized world.*

Back from exile, from a year of dwelling in the wilderness. That's the feeling as he settles once more into the home of Guido Verbeck. Nothing can be sweeter than to hear English spoken as a mother tongue, to browse through newspapers and journals from home, to dwell again among people of his own beliefs. On February 11 in Yokohama, Willie's appetite for religious companionship can at last be fully satisfied. In the morning he has *the pleasure of worshipping God with a congregation* at Japan's first Protestant church; in the afternoon attends services for Japanese in the Reverend Ballagh's chapel; in the evening drops by a prayer meeting at a home on the Bluff.

Rest, reading, and relaxation soon give way to duty. On bleached winter days when snow piles onto roofs and muddies unpaved streets, he visits the site of the new Polytechnic School, the Shizuoka *yashiki*; meets with the Minister of Education and agrees to teach both chemistry and physics; drops into a government godown to examine available chemicals and apparatus. When the opening of the new school is postponed, he begins to feel restless, worried, useless. No wonder he seizes so eagerly on a suggestion made by a visiting San Francisco publisher that he partake in a project to get the *best teachers in Japan* to create a special series of schoolbooks just for native students. He will begin with a primer, then go on to geography and chemistry texts. His cut is to be 5 percent of the cost of the volumes, but so deeply does Griffis desire to be usefully employed that perhaps one can believe the comment, *I should be willing almost to do it for nothing.*

By mid-March the pleasure of return has definitely vanished. Clear days may bring stunning views of Fuji, but Willie is bored. Once he has noted the changes in Tokyo, and visited the palace, and driven the new road that winds down from the Bluff and along Mississippi Bay, and endlessly discussed with missionaries the hopeful prospects for Christianity here, and witnessed the baptism of several Japanese, and dropped in to meet the twenty-seven young ladies of Mrs. Veeder's first public school for girls, and seen the experimental farm of the American agricultural mission headed by General Horace Capron, there is little to do but start the round over again. Letters home are short because there is *nothing special to write about my own quiet life.* Only to Maggie can he admit a truth that will color all his Tokyo days: *Much of the charm and novelty of Japanese life is worn off.*

◇

Settling Griffis in Tokyo is no problem, but his two and a half years there present real difficulties for the biographer. The period in the capital seems shapeless. Emotional ups and downs are common enough. So are bursts of energy, passion, hard work, enthusiasm. But missing are the elements of drama found in Fukui. Here is no tale of a young man's growth, temptation, and flight, no story neatly bounded by a horseback entrance and a snowy retreat on foot. Tokyo is a series of disconnected episodes with no movement toward a climax, no resolution, no achievement of personal insight. For this you do not have to take the biographer's word. Griffis implicitly agrees. Much as he likes to dramatize his own experience, he is never able to turn the Tokyo years into the kind of narrative that in *The Mikado's Empire* can portray his time in Fukui as a dramatic period of growing insight into both Japanese civilization and the self. In the capital, political, social, and economic change always overwhelms the personal.

Anticlimax is the prevailing mood, with Griffis no longer the center of anyone's attention but his own and ours. The stage here is far too crowded with similar characters. Some three hundred Westerners—British, French, Prussians, Americans—currently serve the central government as teachers and engineers, agricultural, legal, and military experts, and no single individual can claim much personal impact on social change. For two and a half years, Willie's world will be that of the twenty-five hundred foreigners who live in Tokyo and Yokohama, bounded by the institutions of the European community—the church, the social clubs, the Asiatic Society, the English-language newspapers. In the capital, he will socialize more with Western professors, merchants, missionaries, diplomats, and naval officers than with Japanese.

The situation cannot make him happy. Continually he strains against boundaries, endeavors to portray himself as a shaper of history. Contemporary evidence, including that from his own pen, denies this view. Great change will mark his stay in the capital, but Griffis relates to it largely as a witness or chronicler of events. Denial of this secondary role takes more than one form. When Tokyo seems *too much like home and too little like Japan*, he flees to rural areas in search of *something more primitive, more purely Japanese*; when at home, he elaborates fantasies of self-importance. His letters are full of extravagant claims: he has the ear of high officials; his advice will shape the future of the nation. For the rest of his life, the same grandiosity will color his biographical and historical writings. Repeatedly Griffis will step forward in his own pages to take a place among those he depicts as major figures in the creation of the *New Japan*—Westerners like Perry, Townsend Harris, and Verbeck; leaders like Mori Arinori, Iwakura Tomomi, Fukuzawa Yukichi, and even the Emperor Meiji.

The need to see himself as an agent of social change is in part a legacy of Fukui. There social progress and personal ambition were linked; there Griffis could to some extent be accepted on his own terms, as a mover in a story of momentous change. Here such a notion is impossible to maintain. The bouts of anger and depression, quarrels with officials, expressions of cynicism and disgust toward the government that mark the Tokyo years seem to issue from the gap between personal desire and the realities of daily life. Were Griffis really an important actor, the years in the capital might produce drama. Instead, the journal, letters, articles, and later books provide incidents, opinions, feelings, moods. To capture the period, we must settle for quick takes, short sequences, individual scenes, moments of insight, and resist the impulse toward a smooth flow of narrative that neither subject nor biographer can find amid the sprawl of thirty months.

<>

Loneliness—that is the unexpected companion. Griffis thought it would remain behind in Fukui. He is wrong. Amid the crowds of Tokyo it persists and deepens. The first letter home from the capital poses a poignant question to Maggie: wouldn't she, or either of his other sisters, Mary or Martha, like to work in Japan? Here they could have *all the comforts of home*, the benefit of *good society and good physicians*, and the company of their loving brother. Long before receiving a reply, Willie makes an official suggestion that the government establish a seminary for young women, obviously hoping positions will open for one or all of his sisters. For female companionship, he regularly visits Yokohama to see Mary Pruyn, a missionary woman of such intellect, sweetness, energy, fervor, and piety that he confesses *my love and admiration for her is intense*. So intense that he wishes his mother could meet her.

She never will. On March 26, this simple diary entry: *American mail in, and read of mother's death*. Words cannot carry the burden of his feelings. A great chasm has opened; a void has replaced continuity, understanding, acceptance, *changeless* love. In the next few weeks, memories of mother gather and multiply, become strangely intertwined with *the untold and secret sorrow* that sent him to Japan—Ellen Johnson. Sharp images of that young lady once troubled him *amid the grand silences of the mountains of Echizen.* Now pain over both losses grows until he is weighted with a cross *too heavy to bear* and his letters fairly shriek, *I must have company. I can't stand it alone.*

Death as enlightenment. It raises to a conscious level his strong need for a woman. Knowing the odds to be *one in a million,* he writes Ellen *asking her to come to me.* Easy for him to say that this only proves that he is *a fool,* but Griffis is canny enough to hedge his bets. Requests that a sister join him now become demands. Little surprise that Maggie is the one he wants and Maggie he shall have. Indirectly—shall we say unconsciously?—he applies financial pressure, withdraws the rent subsidy on their Philadelphia home. The household must break up, and his father and brothers shift for themselves; the unspoken price of continued financial support for Mary and Martha is Maggie.

She lands in August, a month later than expected. The delay is his fault. Griffis has failed to inform Maggie that he is sending passage money not to the shipping company, but to a friend in San Francisco, and she cannot board the July steamer. This act calls for explanation. So do revealing phrases in letters home, those expressions of need voiced in the long months between the decision and her arrival: *I want someone to love, to be with me and we can keep house together . . . if I can't have a wife, I shall do the best I can with a sister.* No proof of anything, just the suggestion that the confusion of roles—sister, wife, companion, and, yes, mother—connect to the *mistake.* You may notice a strange ambivalence, the coupling of desire and fear in his wish to live with a woman. Perhaps Ellen Johnson also senses this. In the letter that once again refuses his marriage offer, she begs forgiveness for having *wronged* Griffis, but insists with God as a witness, *I could do no otherwise than I did, in justice either to you or myself.*

<>

He is a professor again, but not quite as expected. One week after news of his mother's death, on April 2, 1872, the government cancels plans for the Polytechnic School. Any upset Griffis may feel is brushed aside by alternative offers: a position either as an instructor in the Department of Public Works or as a professor in Daigaku Nanko. No surprise that he takes the latter. The faculty of this highest school in the realm includes seventeen foreign instructors, yet immediately Griffis claims *to occupy a position second only to that of Mr. Verbeck, the president.* What this may mean he never bothers to explain, but at faculty meetings and at the mess where teachers gather, he assumes toward others an attitude of *polite deference rather than familiarity.*

With students he is more relaxed—*Began teaching Nanko today, & enjoyed it fully.* His subjects are chemistry, physiology, comparative philology and moral science; his pupils the *most advanced* of the five hundred who attend this seven-year program that combines high school and college. At first it is a repeat of Fukui. The young men are *bright, eager and industrious,* and he glories in work as *my chief joy in life.* Genuine the sentiment may be, but there is no reason to apply it solely to teaching. The routine of the classroom is better suggested in the recurrent diary entries: *Usual day at school.*

<>

He is a preacher once again as well. Half a dozen times between March and June, Willie steps into the pulpit in Yokohama, and once he proudly writes to Maggie that *several sources* see him as the future pastor of that church. This idea vanishes, as does his consuming passion for religious services. With the onset of teaching duties, Griffis occasionally forsakes the Sunday trip to Yokohama to remain at home for a quiet day of rest. All the more reason, then, for him to subscribe $100 to the building fund of a church in Tsukiji. When it opens in September 1872, he issues a written call to both *professing Christians* and those *who have not yet publicly professed Christ* to join the congregation. Late in January of the next year, he conducts services there for the first time.

The press is another kind of pulpit. In local English-language newspapers—the *Gazette,* the *Herald,* the *Weekly Mail*—Griffis manages the difficult task of identifying with both the missionary community and the Meiji government on religious issues; he de-

fends the former against attacks as despoilers of native tradition
and the latter against charges of persecuting Christians. Faith does
not prevent him from reporting that no more than a quarter of
the more than one hundred English-speaking residents of the
capital ever bother to attend services at the white frame church.
Indeed, Willie himself is not there every week, and during his last
eighteen months in Japan he does no preaching. On April 27,
1873, he notes for the first time in years of journal keeping: *church
as usual.*

<>

Enter Maggie. Until now she has been in the wings, the recipient
of Willie's letters, the confidante to whom he confesses secret
aspirations and sorrows. She appears before us in photographs,
as the author of a two-hundred-page journal, and as the writer
of a score of letters home. The face is plain, that of a thirty-four-
year-old spinster—fiftyish by modern standards—who will come
to feel, amid the powdered young ladies of Japan, that she is *old
and ugly.* The journal and letters reveal the attitudes, desires, and
pains beneath the homely surface, show clearly that Willie is the
chief man in her life, reveal how she comforts and protects him,
manipulates him when possible, nags him when necessary, accepts
in short that role of wife, mother, sister, housekeeper, secretary.
Her realm will always be narrower than his, and her view of him
hardly disinterested. But for the two years they live together in
Tokyo, her portrait of Griffis is the only one we have that does
not issue from his own words.

Griffis has changed. That she sees at once. He is *not our old
Willie at all.* She remembers a brother who was jolly, talkative,
open; finds instead a man who seldom smiles; who seems alternately closed, severe, cynical, irritable, and impatient; who feels
superior to all who are not up to his level of thought, remains
independent of everybody's opinion, cares little whether people
like him or not, and is too *uncivilized* to disguise such antisocial
attitudes. The cause, for Maggie, is easy to pinpoint: Ellen. The
cure is equally apparent: Willie *needs to get married to soften
him.* Since none of the young ladies in Yokohama strike his fancy,
it falls upon her to cheer him up. By late October she claims

success: *He has grown quite gay, and is just as loving as anyone could possibly be.*

Missing here is the word *generous*. With good reason. Between brother and sister money has been both a bond and a source of division. The family's financial demands upon Griffis have always been heavy, and Maggie has always been the one to urge him to greater efforts. For all his large income, Willie in Fukui felt so burdened by money matters that finances occupy almost as much space in his letters as descriptions of Japanese life. Part of this is self-imposed: tired of debt, Griffis dreams of standing free and clear before the world. Over half of his first year's salary went home to pay off personal loans and to help the family. Now he has volunteered to cover his mother's medical and funeral expenses and *do all he can* to help both sisters at home. But that is the limit.

Brother and sister close ranks. Maggie takes up the task of handling the family, warns her sisters away from troubling Willie, and insists they understand that he deserves a respite because he works so hard, lives so frugally. No question that this is true enough, yet in such words one may also sense a conspiracy between siblings. Or perhaps we merely confront once more the fact that in life, as in history, point of view is all. In Fukui there was always a gap between his claims of a spartan life—announced regularly by boasts of living on rice and fish—and the reality of a diet rich in meat and fowl, of tinned foods imported from Yokohama, liquor served to friends, a grand house with four servants. Now the pattern of exaggerating poverty continues, with Maggie as accomplice. Now she is the one to claim a *modest* lifestyle while describing a round of activities in which food, travel, and recreation seem plentiful.

They live in a compound for foreign professors near the moat surrounding old Edo castle, in a house large enough to allow Maggie to preside as *Queen*, with Griffis *first interpreter to her Majesty*. The realm consists of eight rooms; the subjects are three—a male cook, a female maid, a man to tend the garden and serve as *horse* for their ricksha. Housekeeping is very different from at home; here there is *no work, only management*. Each evening Maggie hands the cook *a certain sum* to buy provisions.

She may fuss over the lack of silver and good linen for the table, but food is never in short supply. Breakfast includes tea or coffee, toast (spread with butter imported from San Francisco), omelette, sausages, fried potatoes and rice-batter cakes with syrup. Dinner consists of soup, fish and potatoes, meat and vegetables, boiled rice and curry, and dessert. To Maggie this diet does not seem unusual: *Everybody lives in this manner and some have as high as seven courses.*

Food may be a welcome diversion. Not until March 1873 does she land a job as an English teacher at the newly opened Tokyo Jogakko, the first government school for girls. For her, and no doubt for Willie as well, this is a difficult six months. She suffers several bouts of illness—her face swells with lacquer poisoning from a new piece of furniture; she endures heart palpitations, fevers, indigestion, and severe pains in the uterus. Routine provides another kind of pain: *monotonous day* and *another dull day* appear regularly in her diary. To make things worse, Willie is not easy to live with. Often he is busy, teaching or writing. At home, he speaks little and the house feels empty.

Work brings the pleasure of a salary and occupies three hours a day, but neither classroom nor pupils are much mentioned in her writings. Over the months she grows *accustomed to life here* but never comes to love it. Ambivalence is perpetual, and Maggie is equally likely to claim to be *much happier than I was at first* or to say *Japan does not agree with me.* Sheltered as a woman, she is doubly so as a foreigner. But this condition can lead to rare insight. She is the one to voice a truth that applies to both of them, to all Westerners in the capital: *I see . . . very little of real Japanese life.* Students and government officials may sometimes come to dinner, but all the natives *whom we know wear foreign dress, speak English and are entirely like ourselves.*

To report that Maggie endures is to tell but part of her story. She loves those festive occasions when Japanese life *in its glory* of costumes, banners, lanterns, food, and games spills through Tokyo—cherry blossom season at Mukojima; the opening of the Sumida River with boats full of flowers and musicians; the inauguration of the railroad when the Emperor startles her into an instant of ecstasy by bowing in her direction. More important are the social activities of the European community, the monthly meetings of the cultural society, the diplomatic and military receptions, the musicals on the Bluff, the social whirl of Yokohama. Sponsored by the wife of a wealthy merchant, Maggie for a time moves among the most *high flung* people, mingles with British, French, Spanish, Italian, Greek, and Dutch *Lords & Ladies* at parties like those *often read of in books.* Such social occasions seem the pinnacle of her Japan experience, what she fears missing most after returning home: *It will be very hard to go back to the old life after two years here of . . . perfect equality in society and even superiority to many.*

<>

They live together, but with different dreams. Maggie is passive, Griffis active; she a spinster bypassed by life; he a young man bursting with potential. Her aim is to care for him; his is to create some sort of future. Her presence keeps temptation at bay, provides a center for him, a refuge from the world, a base from which to launch a career. He is good to her within the limits of his own problems, takes her on journeys, allows himself to be dragged to more social affairs in Yokohama than are to his taste. But his mind is often elsewhere. Between the lines of letters, in petulant actions and outbursts of impatience, one senses an internal struggle, catches a glimpse of a Griffis aching toward a new direction. *He will not be a 'minister' . . . he wants to be a literary man.* This startling announcement comes in one of Maggie's first letters home. She excuses the statement as perhaps premature, swears her sisters to secrecy, never again repeats it. But she is not wrong. Eyes fresh from America catch the deepest of changes in Willie. Temptation is once again the proper word, but now with no sensual overtones and only so much of the erotic as may be contained in the lust for success. For a decade Griffis has looked forward to a career in the ministry. Teaching, lecturing, and writing have only been ways to earn a living until a pulpit is his. Japan has severely shaken this once firm life plan. In July 1873, Willie admits that whatever his future may be—as minister, professor, or writer—only to the press does he feel *committed for life.*

How to explain this to others; how to justify it to oneself? Griffis never tries. His decline of interest in teaching and religion may be seen largely in gaps and omissions, less in what is committed to paper than in what is left out. Entries on these topics are increasingly infrequent and routine, while letters home suggest rising excitement over the possibilities of learning the *magazine game*. Often he tests ideas in the local English-language press or in lectures to the Asiatic Society, then mails articles off to mass-circulation newspapers or prestigious journals at home. Success is quick to come. *Overland Monthly, Appleton's Journal,* and *Lippincott's* all accept pieces, and soon he has enough of a reputation for the *Chicago Tribune* to suggest an article and the *American Encyclopedia* to commission an entry on Japan. This *fine feather . . . in my cap* is more important than any monetary reward, for it brings a dream closer to reality. On September 25, 1873, he takes the plunge: *Made plan for my book tonight.* By the end of the next month, he is looking beyond a single volume: *I shall make Japanese subjects a study for life, and shall work the mine as long as it pays.*

No necessity to dig very deep. Suitable topics are everywhere at hand for someone willing to utilize his own eyes and the language abilities of his students. His articles deal with the humble and the highborn, the cultural and the political, the religious and the secular. The main theme is easy to anticipate—the glories of Westernization. Griffis likes to personalize abstract issues by focusing on the Emperor as a symbol of everything progressive. Day by day, that young man is abandoning traditions that would keep him a divine figure, and has begun to humanize his position—he rides in an open carriage; makes official visits to arsenals, dockyards, schools; shakes hands with the American ambassador and other diplomats; receives with grace the first Japanese translation of the Bible. Meanwhile the government strives to bring Japanese practices into line with those of Western nations. The growth in public education, the promises of representative government, the beginnings of a native-language press, the shift from the Chinese to the Gregorian calendar and the installation of public urinals in Tokyo—all are greeted as important examples of advances *in true civilization.*

The *extraordinary progress* of Japan includes the moral and spiritual as well. New proclamations compel workers to cover their bodies with clothing, forbid the sale of phallic symbols, abolish the selling of girls into prostitution, and require that bathhouses be divided into separate sections for men and women. That Christianity is ready to march through the land may be seen in portents large and small—the baptisms of Japanese, the formation of a native church in Yokohama, the placement of a Brussels carpet and a gilt-edged Western mirror in a state Shinto shrine. Best of all, in 1872 the government ends the 250-year-old ban on Western religion, a major step toward *that modern cosmopolitan civilization which is stamping its character on the entire world.*

Bells chiming, cannons firing in salute, cheers and waving hats—that's what you expect right now, since all he wants and hopes for Japan seems to be coming true. But no, that is only part of the picture in his articles, the desire in his heart. Muffle the bells and cannon, quiet the cheers and listen to the other part, to the man who has come to fear the cost of progress, the man who wishes to hold onto the past. You can sense him in the subjects of articles—*Fox Myths, The Festival of Dolls, Games and Sports of Children, Japanese Proverbs, Mythical Zoology, A Daimio's Life, Shintoism, Call on a Bonze.* You can find him in loving descriptions of the great temples of the capital, *honorable with age and history*, in praise for Buddhists as belonging to a faith *that was old when our Master's doctrine was new.* You can hear him in the strong objections voiced to proposals that English be made the national language, in laments over the demolition of the great gates of the Shogun's castle, in horror at plans to fill the moats to make room for housing or to cut and sell the sacred groves of Shiba Temple to raise revenue.

Once again Griffis is a man divided, torn between old and new. Documents can do little to let us understand the irreconcilable tugging in opposite directions, the endless argument in his heart. To know Griffis, the historian must look within, must recognize that his condition is not so different from our own, situated as we are between a future where hope and fear balance on a shaky tightrope and a past that slips through our words and categories even as we attempt to define it. His may seem a simpler world, a less fearsome choice, but the internal tension is the same. Yes, Griffis shares much with us, but there is a major difference—his future is our history. This provides the vantage point, the perspective that lets us see his problems better than our own, that lets us judge his love for Japan as a kind of luxury of the victorious, of someone so confident that history is on his side that he can afford to indulge in nostalgia for what is passing away. He is not conscious of this, any more than he is conscious of the tension that runs through his life and work. But we can see this tension as creative, can understand that in the struggle between love for traditional Japan and hope for change, William E. Griffis the professional writer is born.

<>

Friday, July 18, 1873. Precisely at 5 p.m. the narrow-gauge train pulls out of Shinagawa station. Nice to see the Japanese finally learning *the priceless value of time*. A conductor salutes, then punches tickets printed in English, French, German, Chinese, and Japanese. Thirty-five minutes to Kanagawa. Views of the great bay, crowded with warships and fishing boats, frigates and ironclads. Glimpses of the once busy highway to Yokohama, its hotels now deserted, teahouses overgrown. Just wait, Maggie. Beyond Kanagawa lies the past. Japan's. My own. You will see it for seven days from a lurching ricksha, the Tokaido almost as of old, winding through tea plantations on craggy hills, straightening through rice fields of the sea plain. You will recoil from it in the naked bodies of rural folk, the vicious fleas of the hotels, the *outrageous messes* served for dinner, the bleak poverty of farms and tiny towns. But maybe you will come to love it too.

For him it cannot be the same. The landscape too familiar now for that *freshness of surprise which greets you on your first jaunt*. His eyes are open to the disturbing evidence of *civilization*—no, better call it *foreignism*—that now tinges the interior. So many Westerners at Hakone, with its mountain lake, forests, and hot springs, that the landlords have become parasites, *bleeding their victims* by *extortion*. Beyond the mountains, people are more traditional, deferential, honest, but in stores you find foreign goods; in native inns, new petroleum lamps; on trash heaps, beer bottles.

Kyoto on July 26. Three days to absorb a thousand years of history. For him, it is the *Paris of Japan*. For her, an Asia of dreams at last made real. Throngs of refined-looking people in gorgeous silks laugh and chat as if on *perpetual holiday*. Streets are broad, clean, laid out in a familiar checkerboard. Houses tidy and elegant; shops full of exquisite crafts never seen in the capital. The past lives, breathes, swallows you in the rambling palace where for centuries the Mikado dwelt surrounded by *numerous wives*, the *sacred countenance* hidden from the gaze of the vulgar. Up on Higashiyama stands Kiyomizu-dera, with its tall Chinese pagoda, brooding over the city for eight hundred years; not far below, Sanjusangendo, where 33,000 images of Buddha return the gaze of the viewer with the blank stare of eternity.

Fukui lies three days beyond Kyoto. On the Lake Biwa steamer, he studies the landscape: *Fine views. Sat on deck. Storm of rain. Rock full of white herons.* Ashore, she charts the long, thatched villages, the naked children, the women spinning silk, the grand mountain views of *trees, rocks, & streams.* Homecoming is flavored with irony—the first to welcome them is Murata, now governor of the prefecture, *Willie's particular friend.* Then two hectic days of rooms crowded with former students and officials; of presents given and received; of *old scenes revisited*—the lecture room and lab, stores and homes, the teahouses of Atagoyama. Most things are familiar but much seems new: trousers and boots; postal boxes; horse-drawn wagons; gingham umbrellas; a girls' school; Western-style rooms in the homes of the wealthy; neat public water closets in the streets. *Great pleasure* is her phrase for his experience, for feelings he never bothers to record.

The week-long journey back to the capital is through an Asia far older than Kyoto. On the coast of the Japan Sea, no roads for rickshas, and danger enough for guards. Porters carry them along steep, narrow paths high above surf beating against cliffs, through regions so poor the houses are *mere sheds with mats spread on the earth.* Receptions here as in the old days—memories to him, revelations to her: town officers bow heads to the ground; guards shout carts and animals out of the way; peasants kneel silently as they pass. Up into the mountains, lush country with solid farm-houses, neat bamboo fences, well-tended gardens, then a fifteen-hour stage ride from Takasaki back to the capital. For her, no summation, just relief after *24 days in the wilds*, and the fine feeling that home *never looked so good, so comfortable, so invit-ing*. For him, no description, no summation. About this journey nothing but silence for the rest of his life.

<>

Action followed by reaction—the inevitable pattern leads to the end of Griffis in Japan. Tradition reasserts itself in mid-1873 with a revival of the custom of men wearing swords.́ At the same time many reforms turn out to be no more than *superficial*, or mere rhetoric aimed at placating foreign powers. Despite the edicts, prostitution continues to flourish openly and the government to draw *great revenue* from it. The separation of sexes in public baths proves to be symbolic, often no more than two different entrances to a common tub divided by an imaginary line. There is backsliding on religious matters, too. In Echizen, one hundred villages rise in revolt against the abolition of anti-Christian edicts; in Tokyo, the Mombusho, the Ministry of Education, issues a notice *forbidding students of the colleges to attend Christian churches.*

All this can be handled gracefully enough in print. Yes, things are not always what they seem; yes, progress can ebb as well as flow. That the great *advance* of 1872 has given way to *positive regression* is regrettable, but no doubt temporary. These senti-ments come from a man who is judicious, tolerant, understanding. But such a posture can last only until a fatal moment on July 15th: *Was notified today that my contract would not be renewed.* To say this changes his point of view, to say he is hurt, is to indulge in serious understatement. Twenty-five years later, rage will still color his description of events surrounding the termina-tion. The government may claim merely to be giving the six-month notice called for in his original contract (the three years will be up in January 1874), but he has another picture to show the world—a stark etching, black on white, of William Elliot Griffis nailed to a cross.

The problem begins in June, when the Mombusho decides to enforce the observation of Japanese holidays. For foreign teachers this will mean a day of rest every sixth day, and thus the necessity of teaching on most Sundays. Suggestions of a voluntary shift to this schedule by Westerners are underscored with a threat—in the future all new contracts will carry an anti-Sunday clause. Since Griffis is a self-professed *strict Sabbatarian*, this move alone should count him out. But that is to expect a rational response to an assertion of power which threatens his aspirations. Easier it is to fly into a rage and claim acts of *treachery* on the part of power-hungry officials; easier to organize a protest by all the English-speaking teachers against the changing of rest days; easier to see the dismissal as the government's way of getting rid of serious opposition.

The martyr can contradict himself. Later Griffis will claim a quick descent from the cross: *I dropped a note to Mr. Iwakura, the Junior Prime Minister, simply stating the case. The matter was very quickly settled to my satisfaction. Another position of equal honor and emolument for three years was offered me, which I declined with thanks.* Were this so, one might wonder at the rage. But the truth is different. For six months he struggles to stay on in Japan, wrangling with the Mombusho over legal technicalities, writing letters to the local press, complaining to the American minister, pestering influential friends and officials to intercede. When nothing seems to move the government, his moods vary from petulance (*I wouldn't stay in their service long if they begged me to do so*) to resignation (*The influences here are against me*) to fantasies of sweet revenge (*I shall return to my own country and tell everyone that a contract with Mombusho is worth nothing*).

Not until the turn of the New Year is the matter settled with a simple six-month extension of the contract. For a man who considers himself the second most important professor in the realm, this tiny victory must taste very much like defeat. So he begins to rationalize, to claim that he has at once defended high principles and enhanced his career opportunities. Proudly he says, *I would not work regularly on Sundays for any amount of money*; happily he predicts that going home to seek a book publisher in person has great advantages. But good reasons never banish pain. How wretched that his *life's best fruits and toil* have been repaid with *ingratitude and neglect.* The experience feels familiar. First Ellen, then Japan—he is the one to make the equation. Both are examples of *unrequited love*; both full of lessons impossible to learn. Once again he must divide that which should be indivisible, his deep feeling for this land and its people: *I don't want to say hard things of the Japanese . . . I love them, I love my students, but the petty-souled potentates in office in Japan—these men shall feel the lash of my pen for years to come.*

<>

Don't leave the wrong impression—rage and the desire for revenge are never all-consuming. Even during the wrangle with the Mombusho and the six-month teaching extension, life continues with the same duties, walks, visits, conversations, dinners, faces, colleagues, newspapers, lectures, and prayers. Tokyo remains the same city: stifling on ripe summer afternoons when the streets choke with dust and the foul odor of privies; lovable on hazy autumn mornings that can bring a biblical vision—crimson masses of maples that glow against white castle walls and seem *like bushes on Mount Horeb.* His moods are the same as always: annoyance when his sisters neglect to write, pride when articles appear in print, sadness when a favorite student grows ill and dies, impatience when Maggie longs too vocally for home, delight when Ed Clark comes to the capital and moves into their house. Money problems remain, and fear of arriving home penniless leads to new ventures—he prepares an annotated tourist map of the capital and writes guidebooks for Yokohama and Tokyo. Peace with the inevitable comes gradually. When a Kyoto college in September 1873 offers a post as Professor of Chemistry, it takes him three days to decline; when Horace Capron of the Agricultural Commission, in May of the following year, wants him to stay on as a private secretary, Willie refuses immediately.

Don't leave the impression that this is all, that you now know Griffis in Tokyo. Remember everything he sees, hears, smells and feels, but never commits to paper; remember all those other details you have no space to capture. And how about the experiences that don't quite fit in, those odd moments, those important images that can suggest more than words?

January 1, 1873. Midmorning. Griffis walks along Gojikken michi, past the shrine to Inari, the fox-god, through the great gate Omon and into the Yoshiwara. No girls in cages this day. The elegant brothels of Nakano-cho are hung with New Year decorations—bright green blinds, boiled red lobsters, branches of pine and bamboo, oranges and white rice cakes. A holiday crowd is here—young girls in bright silk, their parents and brothers in more subdued colors, all waiting to see the annual promenade of grand courtesans. That is Willie's aim as well, but he learns the procession will not begin until two o'clock, just when he must meet with other foreign faculty members at the Mombusho for special presentation to the Mikado. Does he follow native tradition and look wistfully at Mikaeri yanagi—*gazing back willow*— on his way out? All we have is the single word in his diary: *Disappointed*.

Tanned and bearded, Griffis blows into the house, blue eyes alight with a strange joy. A week alone, exploring the provinces of Kazusa and Awa, has cured a serious *fit of anti-Caucasianism*. He has encountered Nichiren pilgrims, stayed atop Mount Kanozan, enjoyed the *sweet simplicity* of several *ryokan*, thrived on the native diet: raw fish, radish, leeks, mushrooms, seaweed, tofu, foods that once tasted like *starch or sawdust*. The pride that once lined *his alimentary canal* is gone; to him *a Japanese meal tastes very much as it does to* [a] *native*.

Griffis walks inside the walls of the old castle. You can find him here often, in seasons of mud or snow, under sun, clouds, or the autumn moon. From the ramparts he gazes at the vast sprawl of black roofs that are the city. In overgrown courtyards he strolls in a *meditative* mood, never committing thoughts to paper. But one November day, at the height of the conflict with the Mombusho, the image of far-off Fuji, the twist of autumn trees and dying vines against a castle wall, and the sharp air pierce him with the fullness of the moment: *Glorious weather, fine health, high spirits.*

March 19, 1874. Four months left to go. Griffis at his desk just before bedtime, describing the day. Cool and clear. Breakfast in Yokohama. The train to Tokyo. Two hours of teaching. Two hours at a church meeting. An evening working on the book. Now his mind lingers on the fullness of sunrise, on the *golden flushed horizon and silver sparkling ocean* seen from that familiar train: *Lovely day, beautiful Japan.*

The end is like everything else: he refuses to reveal what you really want to know. Not whom he sees or what he does but how he feels. To read between these lines you must know him well. A good imagination helps.

Saturday, July 18, 1874. Up early, took 8:15 train to Yokohama. Busy all day, winding up affairs, etc. Evening, tea at Mrs. Pruyn's, calls on Mr. & Mrs. Stone, Miller, Hepburn, Syle, etc. Took sampan, and on Colorado at 10:15. Many friends on ship to see us off. Up till 12:45. Night dark, phosphorescence splendid, lights in harbor beautiful.

Sunday, July 19. Loading tea all night. Steam up and off at 6 A.M. Sky cloudy and Fuji not visible.

11

Chanoyu and Utai

Here you are again. So impossible. So simple. As if thirty-two months are so many breaths of air. Darkness, just like the first time. Once more the tall ships in the harbor, the stone piers, the huge shed that is customs, the officials in uniform, the brightly lit public rooms of the Grand Hotel. But that's not what you came back for. Go out into the rain. Wave away the ricksha men, cross the wooden bridge over the creek, and plunge along the narrow roadway through Homura. Close to midnight. Too late for any of the tiny shops to be open. No matter. People clatter along on high clogs, lanterns flicker behind *shoji*, the smell of tea and food cooked with soy sauce wafts from houses—that's what you have been missing.

Morning lets you play tour guide. Let's forget about the Bund, the Bluff, the Chinese quarter. Yokohama is a rotten town— reckless, indecent, full of *gouges* and *horse jockeys*, not to mention missionaries. Let's get away from here and into Japan. Board the train and point to the familiar fields and hills, rivers and bay. Omori station. Just there. Those are the shell heaps, or what's left of them. Shimbashi, the end of the line. The same brick building; the same crowds; the same rows of ricksha; the same sweet motion swaying through the streets. But the route has changed. Ginza and Nihonbashi are impassable, torn up to lay tracks for a horse railway. Up we go, over a moat and through the castle grounds to Hongo, where everything is just as you remember—the watch-repair man on the corner; the fish chopper tapping away; the gold beater pounding monotonously; the cooper; the straw maker; the dry goods shop. Dismount to smiles and hearty cries. Yes, they remember you; yes, they ask after your family—*Okusama*, John-san and Edie-san.

Those great wooden gates are familiar, but can that really be Kaga Yashiki? Dr. Murray's old house has a new wing, full of classrooms, and next to it the foundations of a large building have been laid. At the university, bows from clerks and warm handshakes from colleagues, fine tea in Kutani cups and excellent imported cigars. Toyama, Yatabe, Kikuchi, Hattori, and Kato—all are here, full of talk about their work and questions about yours. The lab looks much the same, but step across the street and into a new, two-story building: the zoological museum—your plans for construction carried out to the last detail. Next to the entrance in the main hall hangs a life-size portrait. Stop a moment and take a look. Your own eyes stare back with an unfamiliar gaze. Dare you call it immortality?

<>

June 1882. No family with Edward Morse this time, but he does have a companion: William Sturgis Bigelow, Harvard '71, an M.D. who prefers collecting objects to practicing medicine. Sword guards, Buddhism, landscapes—this Brahmin's interests run to anything that will keep him away from Boston. Morse is ready to collect as well. But no shells this time; nothing like spiders, crickets, or worms. Objects shaped by the touch of human hands are now his aim: pottery, and all those daily items described in such loving detail in his journals—tools, shop signs, baskets, candle holders, cooking utensils, dolls, hair ornaments, clogs, umbrellas, fishing poles, fans, marionettes, lacquer boxes, brushes, pieces of cloth and handmade paper. And also something else that cannot be crated. Something in the emptiness of rooms, the softness of tatami, the shadow of leaves on *shoji*, the upswept curve of temple roofs, the strange familiarity of gardens in moss and stone—these are the kind of things to be collected by pen strokes on paper.

Ask him, and Morse can explain why he's here in words that will sound reasonable enough. Pottery, my boy. Almost two thousand pieces at home, true, but that's no more than a good beginning. Two years of study and now I have a sense of what is missing. Let me do research for a few months, buy carefully in the right places, and my collection will be the largest, the most complete, the best in the world. Besides, as new director of the Peabody Academy of Science, I have an obligation. To the board, to the people of Salem, to posterity. Imagine the first ethnological collection of things Japanese. Nobody else is gathering such objects. Think of it. If I do this right, fifty, a hundred years from now people will have to come to Salem to get the feel, shape, and look of all these simple items that every Japanese sees or uses every day.

Other reasons fill the gaps between the words. To explain them is to look for meaning in things not done, in actions that remain forever incomplete. When Morse went home in 1879, it was as a kind of double missionary. On the lecture circuit he now had two major topics: natural history and Japan. At professional scientific meetings he could be asked questions about both. Even Darwin's letter, written to commend his Omori publication, slid easily from one realm to the other: *What a constant state of fluctuation the whole organic world seems to be in!* . . . *Of all the wonders of the world, the progress of Japan, in which you have been aiding, seems to me about the most wonderful.* The general public agreed. A Japan lecture series at the Lowell Institute became, according to the Boston press, the hit of the 1880 season: *No other of the several winter courses has been so thronged and no other has given such apparent delight.*

Popularity helped to keep Morse busy as ever. Lectures and articles, small research projects on wasps and bird behavior, trips to New England shell heaps, and the new position as director of the Peabody—all this should have meant that he was occupied and happy. Yet as the months went on something was amiss. Work was not working its usual charm. Hints of restlessness and dissatisfaction showed in one striking fact: the most important projects were not underway. That long-planned popular work on evolution, that second book on zoology—he now had little taste for either. Odder still: for all the notes and journal pages and pieces of pottery, he could not get started on a volume about Japan.

Blame nostalgia, a wordless longing for certain sights, smells,

tastes, and feelings that become so precious in memory. Then look
at a photo taken in the study of his Salem home. Morse sits at a
plain plank table heaped with pottery, shells, papers, ashtrays full
of cigar butts. Overhead, a gas chandelier with four opaque white
globes; on the floor, a torn strip of coconut-fiber matting. Wooden
folding chairs flank the table; shelves sagging along the wall are
heaped with pamphlets and books; cardboard filing cabinets are
piled in the corner. No curtains soften the windows and the only
decorations are a horseshoe crab mounted on a board, a photo
of son John, a small engraving of a European city scene. Now
picture the rooms in Japan, at inns and the homes of colleagues;
think of them as they appear in Morse's loving words. And think
of him in that Salem study thinking about those rooms. Then you
know that the desire to return to collect crafts and folk arts and
still more pottery is also an expression of something else.

<>

Call it the return of a hero. Those first weeks back in Tokyo,
everyone wants to see him, hear his opinions, show him things,
get his approval. So many dinners hosted by former associates;
so many public events that mix pleasure and duty. He delivers
lectures—on *changes in fauna* to the monthly meeting of the
Biological Society; on the *antiquity of man with a sketch of the
evidences of his lowly origin* to an audience of fifteen hundred in
a new, Western-style hall; on the work of their American and
European counterparts to the members of the Japan Fish Commission. He makes symbolic appearances—attends a concert given
by students of Western music; sits on the platform for the graduation exercises of the Tokyo Female Normal School.

   During this period Morse and Bigelow live in housing provided
by the university, a small two-room building set between the
astronomical observatory and a hospital for the insane, a pleasant
spot where one is *lulled to sleep by the songs of the maniacs.*
Within a few days the surfaces of Morse's bed, bureaus, bookshelves, washstand, and desk are heaped high with pottery, books,
and papers. Already he is collecting whatever he can find, and
finding that the capital city is not all that good for collectibles. A
visit to see the family treasures of a former *daimyo*, Prince Kik-

kawa of Iwakuni, serves to whet an appetite already keen. Time to get to work. Time to leave Tokyo, its modern schools and hospitals, its gaslit streets and brick buildings. Time to see *a little of the life of old Japan.*

Not so fast. Weeks go into preparations for the trip. Morse must gather advice on the best places for antiquities, secure letters of introduction to regional officials, obtain a passport valid *for at least a dozen provinces,* and make arrangements with his two travel companions, Bigelow and Ernest F. Fenollosa, a Harvard graduate who owes his appointment in 1878 as the first professor of philosophy at Tokyo University to Morse's recommendation. Four years in Japan have stimulated Fenollosa's aesthetic interests. Now his conversation is full of plans for explaining the great traditions of East Asian art to the West, and his rooms are full of a large collection of historic scrolls and paintings.

On the road in search of art—that's the title for the summer interlude. At the outset, Morse finds it easy to predict grandiose results for the summer's labors: *We shall have in the vicinity of Boston by far the greatest collection of Japanese art in the world.* These words, penned for his own consumption, swell with a pride that may seem strange for a man whose identity has always been involved with natural science. But Morse is after something new; clearly his aim is to become recognized as an expert on things Japanese. And not just pottery and folk art. Ned still expects to write that book about Japan, but now he plans to focus on something specific and tangible: architecture.

The choice is well foreshadowed. Since his first stroll through Yokohama, Morse has been charmed and fascinated by the universal cleanliness, refinement, and *Quaker-like simplicity* of Japanese homes and inns. Everywhere in the land you can rest on straw mats and let yourself be soothed by the subdued colors of walls and screens, and the natural wood of the ceilings; everywhere the eyes have the pleasure of lingering on the *tokonoma,* with its single scroll or rough bit of pottery and simple spray of flowers. How different from rooms at home, jammed with heavy furniture, stuffed like curiosity shops with *vases, pictures, plaques, bronzes, with shelves, brackets, cabinets, and tables loaded down with bric-a-brac.* In this great contrast lies a rare opportunity. By describing Japanese homes in detail, maybe Morse can help to improve American taste.

Let the long days begin to stretch out into heat, dense humidity, the thickening green of bush, tree, and rice field, the rasp of cicadas in the shade. But don't do the details of the two-month trip. Even Morse quickly wearies of recording each day's events. At first he carefully notes the departure from Tokyo on July 26; the stage ride to Sammaibashi; the eight miles he and Fenollosa do on foot up a steep mountain road while Bigelow rides in a *kago*. But soon the journey takes on the feeling of memory and details give way to summaries: *It was difficult to keep an itinerary of the journey overland. We lost the day of the week and even the month. We had grand rides and tiresome ones, saw beautiful scenery, crossed long bridges over wide and shallow streams, stopped at interesting tea houses; and at all times received that courteous attention which characterizes this people above all others.*

The search for booty makes this trip unique. Like warriors roving down the Tokaido, the Americans *make raids* upon unsuspecting towns, *ransack* the secondhand stores, and carry away all the local treasures. Sometimes Bigelow and Fenollosa tire of the game and spend a day relaxing on the tatami of a lovely inn. But not Morse. Each morning he bustles out and each afternoon returns accompanied by two or three storeowners, who carry piles of boxes and loose pots. With a gleeful look on his face, Morse spreads his new acquisitions on the floor, and then, as a finale, produces from his pocket, in Bigelow's words, *as a thing too precious to let the other men bring home, some particularly demoralized-looking piece of old coprolite.* Triumphantly he will shout: *A 'Koyashi,' by God!—650 years old—a genuine 'Unko Koyashi,' with a 'stamp!'—Never saw but two others & one of those Ninagawa asked 30 yen for, & I got this for 15 sen! And his stamp did not 'compare' with this!*

Real finds surface in the most unexpected spots. A town like Shizuoka proves rich enough in interesting objects to keep them for an extra day; a village like Toyohachi provides a startling number of good pieces. No surprise that cities detain them the longest. Nagoya has such a wealth of antiques that they manage only a rushed visit to its famed castle in the late afternoon of their fourth and final day. Here they pursue a strategy that proves useful in other large urban areas. Rather than stroll the streets looking for shops, they stay in the hotel to receive merchants: *Dealers were coming to our rooms all the time, sometimes eight or ten at a time, spreading out their stock in trade on the floor. Up to the last hour of our stay we were buying things . . .* First hours are important too. Early each morning Morse is up before the others to sketch the places where they stay. The eye that once scrutinized the tiniest of shelled creatures is not satisfied with the broad forms of rooms, hallways, roofs, balconies, gardens, and fences, but must seek out the smallest of details. Morse examines and describes *hikite*, the metal plates that fit into *fusuma* to serve as pulls; ornamental nailheads used in *tokonoma*; closets with swinging doors built under flights of stairs; shoe and towel racks, oil lamps, candlesticks, *hibachi* in wood and ceramic, and the blocklike pillows that once almost crippled his neck. He lingers in kitchens with their braziers and primitive ovens, bathrooms with deep wooden tubs that have built-in fireboxes, and privies with tiny flowerpots and hand-finished interiors.

The overland journey ends on August 10. Beyond Osaka, the waters of the Inland Sea carry the Americans into hazy reveries of ages past. In Hiroshima, steamer gives way to native junk, and when the wind dies, they are propelled by four men with long, clumsy oars. On the flat roof of the boat's cabin, Morse and Bigelow lean back against piles of straw matting, smoke Manila cigars, alternately dozing and opening their eyes to admire a visual feast—pine-covered islands, the jutting headlands of Shikoku, tiny orange shrines, sails bright against the sea. Something stirs within Morse. He wants words for the moment, words that will match the glory of the scene before him. But all he can produce are stock phrases: *The experience was unique, sailing . . . through one of the most picturesque and beautiful waterways in the world.*

Take such stirrings as a sign of change in the man who, five years before, never stopped at Kamakura on those trips from Enoshima to Tokyo. Now he can allow time for the historic and the sacred, for jaunts that have nothing to do with buying pottery—time to wander in the deer park at Nara, to climb the castle walls in Wakayama, to stay overnight on Miyajima, where tides run beneath the corridors of a great temple and a colossal *torii* rises from the sea. Descriptions of scenery, rare in his notes before this trip, become more common. Whether they are limited by perception or vocabulary is impossible to say. Often Morse seems to strain against the boundaries of his own words. Usually he settles for a well-worn image—the *crumbling* wayside shrine, the *charming* teahouse, the *picturesque* valley. But occasionally there comes a moment all his own—say, that special twilight moment riding in the country when he notes the *remarkable atmospheric effects* of *mists slowly rising from the meadows and rice fields* and sketches the sharply etched image of a village, its *dark thatched roofs silhouetted against the white mists and the range of mountains beyond.*

Such an image relates to *old Japan*, an exhausted phrase that Morse suddenly uses with regularity. Landscapes, buildings, people, customs—all help to energize the longings that brought him back. Once again cultural comparisons cannot be avoided; once again this nation highlights shortcomings at home. How clear this is on the night of a river festival when Bigelow hires a flat-bottomed boat complete with food, drink, dancing-girls, and fireworks. Out they go into a world sparkling with red and yellow lanterns, and one feels an air of innocent sensuality as *merry groups pass back and forth, with the sound of samisen and koto, singing and laughter* . . . Pleasure leads to rumination: *Nearly every town in our country has a river, bay, pond, or lake. Why can't our people indulge in similar holidays?* The answer—*such assemblies on the water are possible . . . only in countries of good manners*—leads to another question that he will never phrase. Better to forget questions altogether, to live this *old Japan* and not ask how it got that way.

Iwakuni is the place for that. They arrive on a balmy, mid-August night full of the spiky shapes of palms and the smell of the tropics. Crowds cluster around them. No foreigner, it seems, has been here for seven years. Everything the Americans do, every movement they make is watched with the kind of awestruck wonder that greeted the first Westerners in the empire: *One has a curious mixture of emotions at being deliberately stared at by a crowd; in a way, it is embarrassing . . . You feel how absurd or inexplicable some of your movements must be to the starers.* You try to affect indifference, and yet you are conscious of an added dignity and importance at being stared at. *You are guilty of performing acts specially to excite their attention, such as turning your pockets inside out,* for a pocket in Japanese clothing is unknown.

An invitation from Prince Kikkawa has brought them to this spot twenty-five miles west of Hiroshima. Just twelve years ago this was part of his domain. Feudalism may have ended, but you can hardly tell that here, where everyone is in traditional costume. The hospitality is traditional too. Not a sen are the Americans allowed to pay for the most royal treatment—they sleep in a hotel built to house the guests of the *daimyo,* eat specially prepared meals, receive presents of antique swords and ancient pieces of pottery, and undertake guided excursions day and night: to a once-famous kiln; to the local theater where they *afford a greater spectacle to the audience than the play itself;* to the recently established cotton mill, with rooms so immaculate and operatives so clean that one can scarcely recognize this as modern industry.

The fussing, the courtesy, the hospitality are *old Japan* incarnate. When they depart after two days while hundreds smile and bow their rickshas on, Morse feels *overwhelming gratitude and affection for the Japanese race, and particularly for the Prince of Kikkawa and his loyal subjects, who preserve, as of old, their fealty to their prince.* Elsewhere he puts it more simply. Except for the absence of swords, he has seen Japan *as it was in feudal times,* experienced the *manners, customs, and courtesies* of that bygone age. The good Yankee, democrat, and scientist has lived for a moment in a feudal social order and can sum up the experience in a single word: *Idyllic.*

◇

Tokyo in the fall. Visitors and natives alike find it lovely. Let the newspapers be your guide. You are off to Terajima for the *seven flowers of autumn;* Meguro and Asakusa for chrysanthemums; Konodai, Oji, and Tokaiji for maple leaves; the banks of the Sumida for *sweet singing insects.* And Fuji. It's always been there, but never so sharp as when the winds of autumn sweep the sky free of haze, never so beautiful as when the snowcap lengthens and the sun through clouds paints it with patches of white. But maybe it's not Fuji at all. Maybe it's this fresh autumn weather, and the summer behind you, the dozens of notebooks filled with barely legible scrawls, and the heaps of pots and artifacts. Maybe it's not Fuji. Maybe the change is in the eyes. Maybe it's you.

Not much to do these days, and yet you keep busy. No reason to stay, and yet you do not leave. Something is unfinished, but what? Surely it's not those empty pages. You could keep on filling them forever. More than a thousand are devoted to notes on customs, artifacts, names, implements, traditions, games. Who else has recorded the fact that the fishermen of Wakanoura boil pine bark to tan their nets but not their sails; or has sketched the difference between plows in the provinces of Yamashiro, Suo, Chikuzen, and Kii; or has noticed that brokers in the Osaka Rice Exchange fling their hands about and shout just like their counterparts on the Corn Exchange in Chicago? Who else has jotted down all those daily superstitions: that an itchy head means happiness, or that cutting fingernails at night shows that one is going crazy, or that tea leaves floating vertically in a cup are a sure sign that good fortune is on the way?

Pottery can't be the reason for staying. At the beginning of November, the packers are finishing their job. Daily they pick their way through the tangle of confusion that is your room, wrap cups, bowls, water jars, vases, and plates in handfuls of straw and place them carefully in large wooden boxes. Twenty-nine hundred pieces, more than double the original collection. You have taken such detailed notes in interviews with famed Kyoto potters, made so many impressions of the stamps of each lineage, copied down so many stories of great ancestors, that your pottery journal is now much longer than your daily diary. More than material for a single book, you have accumulated enough to last *a lifetime*.

How difficult it is to *leave this angelic country*. Life here seems so pleasant, so interesting, so full of some promise that cannot be defined. And the days are so easy to fill. At the laboratory and the museum, the professors welcome your suggestions, advice, and supervision. Private schools and public groups are eager to hear lectures on the animal kingdom, evolution, or the ancient inhabitants of Japan. Absorbing and time-consuming are some new passions that have sprung from older ones: the intricate patterns of thatched roofs have brought you to a serious study of roof tiles, old and new; the search for pottery in caves has led to detailed questions about ancient burial customs. The first mention of your interest in archery comes in August, when, at Sanjusangendo in Kyoto, you manage to hit a far-off target several times. Ever since then, you have been seeking experts—Japanese, Ainu, Korean—to learn about the bow-pulling techniques of their traditions. This is Darwinism applied to human history, an intuitive notion that the level of a civilization may be determined by the complexity of its methods of archery.

Curious what a natural scientist can get himself into if he's not careful. But hardly surprising. Shells lead to pots and pots to the world—the movement is from the hand of God to that of man. Not that you need to believe in either to slip from comparison toward social criticism. But there it is during your final months in Tokyo. You spend a pleasant afternoon at the crematory in Senju, find it a surprisingly efficient and inexpensive way of disposing of corpses, and wonder how long *prejudice* will stand in the way of *this sanitary process in our country.* You visit the poorest quarter of Tokyo and hear *no loud cries or shouting,* see *no bleary-eyed drunkards* or dirty children, encounter no hostility or fistfights as you would in the slums at home. You meet the government's chief statistician and learn that in a decade only eleven murders have been committed in Tokyo, then find a recent report from Michigan, where eighty-nine murders were committed in the single year of 1879. You finally get around to mentioning geisha as *good-natured, witty and sprightly girls . . . who earn their living by entertaining at dinners* and are far better company than *the usual run of girls and women* at home. You begin to think that Americans *have much to learn from Japanese life,* but are incapable of saying what you yourself can learn from it.

Some questions cannot be answered. That is the lesson of a glorious late-October afternoon when the Emperor's gardens are thrown open to university professors and high government officers. Hundreds of men, women, and children, dressed in formal kimono, wander through hills and valleys, rock ravines with plunging brooks, tiny lakes crossed by arched bridges, wooden summer houses. Words once again fail to contain experience: *I have neither the language nor the ability to describe the wonderful beauty of the grounds.* Never before have you been so conscious of some gnawing gap between what is and what you want. Maybe it is triggered by that new American professor, the *bull in the china shop* who stalks the gardens but sees no beauty, and whose comments are so *rude and ridiculous* that you must flee his presence. Yet his attitudes force you to face an unpleasant truth: that is what you are soon going home to; that is what you have to live with back in the United States. Take that one step further and face a simpler truth: at home you will also have to live with yourself.

<>

I have begun the study of the intricacies of the tea ceremony and have joined a class of Japanese. My teacher, Mr. Kohitsu, tells me I am the first foreigner to take lessons in the art. The fact that I was taking lessons got into the newspapers, and also the statement that I had astonished the old fellows at the school by rapidly identifying the pottery brought out for the occasion.

It's about time. That is one obvious response to this diary entry from early November, just a few days after the visit to the Emperor's gardens. For five years now Morse has collected pottery whose shape, purpose, and value derive largely from an aesthetic created by the great tea masters of the seventeenth century. Yet never has he shown the slightest interest in tea ceremony, or *chanoyu.* Not that such indifference is much of a mystery. This elaborate, highly formalized ritual is not something with much inherent appeal to Western taste. *Chanoyu* may be seen as a kind of exquisite performance with limited moves and virtually no room for individual expression, a complicated way of structuring, enjoying and—the impatient might assert—wasting time. For people from a tradition that honors meditation and an inward turn, it can be practical or therapeutic, an excuse to shut out the world and regain the silence of the self. But to someone from a culture that equates time with money, *chanoyu* is bound to seem a *grotesque performance* that is *uselessly absurd.*

Morse's first experience of tea ceremony is decisive. The time is early August; the place, a kiln on the edge of Nagoya; the host, a master potter who is never named. That he accepts an invitation to take off an afternoon right in the midst of the buying frenzy of the summer trip suggests that Morse is ready for something new—but what? There he is, pen and notebook in hand, translator on one side and local pottery dealer on the other, sitting on the verandah of the main dwelling, gazing at the tiny teahouse just ten feet away. When an unseen gong sounds, the three men slip their feet into wooden clogs and shuffle to a stone urn where the host pours water on their hands from a wooden dipper. Under a lattice screen they enter the teahouse on hands and knees, creep to the *tokonoma* to view the *kakemono* and flower arrangement, crawl back to the other side of the dainty room, adjust themselves in a row and remain silent.

Words won't do it, of course—won't catch the feeling. Morse must know that right away, but he does not stop taking notes. So it is possible to share the surfaces of that afternoon, the *simplicity and absolute cleanliness of the room*, with its sweet mats, brownish plaster walls, and unusual ceiling made of ribbons of dark wood, braided like straw. Not much happens really. Several times the daughter of the host formally enters the room through a sliding screen—from her knees to feet and back to knees—carrying tea bowls, jars, and utensils, and solemnly depositing them next to the sunken fireplace, where an iron kettle steams. In just a certain way, she unties a tea jar from a silken bag, washes and wipes the bowls, scoops the powdered tea with a slender bamboo spoon, adds hot water with a ladle, and stirs briskly with a whisk. The host takes a bowl, crawls towards Morse, and presents it with a deep bow. Up to the lips it goes for a swallow of *delicious* thick, green syrup, then he wipes the edge and hands it to his neighbor. After all three drink, the host finishes the tea, *kneeling upright as if in an attitude of prayer, with a most beatific countenance, smacking his lips with great gusto.* Bowls, utensils, and lacquer boxes made to hold them are then passed around and examined, and in soft voices the four men discuss their age and beauties.

So long, so full of detail is his initial account of a tea ceremony, that Morse's later decision to study the art should come as no surprise. Neither should a subsequent near-silence on the subject.

Only twice after beginning to take lessons does he mention *chan-oyu*, and then only to say that he has performed it once *after a fashion* for some Japanese friends and is still attending classes at the end of the year. Of the wordless experience itself he remains wordless, unwilling or unable to record thoughts that are his during training sessions. Later he will downplay the problems of learning tea ceremony, claim that what seems difficult or awkward to an untrained eye is simplicity itself. All the movements—the rising and kneeling, the proper placing of the utensils, the sequence in handling them, the making of the tea—are, with few exceptions, both *natural and easy*.

Perhaps. But it is hardly natural or easy to envision Morse performing them, to see this bulky American with a full beard bowing into a tea room on his knees, scooping and ladling and whisking with the delicacy he so regularly admires in the Japanese. Surely he must at times feel odd, foolish, out of place, caught in a strange dream. Surely he must wonder at the motivation under-lying the decision to do this, must see it as an act of either freedom or desperation. Surely he must understand that to study tea cer-emony is to cross some invisible but significant line, to move beyond the familiar solidity of objects and toward the spirit be-hind and in them, to let the outer world mate with an inner one unexpressed and inviolate for so many years.

No. Not yet. But soon enough he will come to understand these things in his own way, with his own words. The decision to study another art form, this one more esoteric than *chanoyu* and initially even less appealing, will bring on the revelation in mid-January. Like everything else, it enters the pages of Morse's diary in prose that gives little sense of carrying any emotional load. Listen: *I took my first lesson in Japanese singing this afternoon. With a letter of introduction, I, or rather my jinrikisha man, found the way to Mr. Umekawa, who lived at Asakusa Minami moto machi Kubanchi. He is a famous teacher of 'no' singing and acting, and has adjoining his house a stage for 'no' play. Takenaka accom-panied me as interpreter. We were presented and Mr. Umekawa was very hospitable and seemed pleased that a foreigner should wish to take lessons in singing.*

Surprised too, one should think. As the traditional theater of the high samurai, Noh is so recondite that even among Japanese it has never achieved popularity. For a Westerner to wish to learn Noh performance is startling enough; for that Westerner to be Edward S. Morse would seem to border on the absurd. Kabuki, yes: that crowd-pleasing theater of acrobatic movement and special effects is much to his taste, but Noh has to be another matter. Until now the word has never even entered his journals, though comments on music are so common that the most casual reader cannot fail to be struck by Morse's strong feelings on the subject. Indeed, from his first days here, Japanese music has elicited his wonder, distaste, and hostility.

These attitudes come from a man who, as a self-taught piano player, considers himself to have *a fair ear for music*. In Japan there is plenty to hear. Boatmen, laborers, carters, carpenters, fishermen—afloat or ashore, everyone seems to sing at work, only the sounds they make are so *odd, monotonous*, and *weird* that the nation can seem wholly devoid of musical sense. Trained performers only reinforce such a judgment. The *samisen* and *biwa* may be distant cousins to the guitar and banjo, but the singers using them in teahouse or street shows tend to create the most awful squeaks and grunts. Religious music is equally dismaying. At temples and shrines, ensembles of flutes and drums go on for hours, producing *one constant wail of the saddest sounds*. Sorely missing are all those elements he loves at home—catchy tunes, warm harmony, the power of a full chorus, the rich textures of an ensemble of strings, winds, and brass. No wonder this disappointed comment toward the end of his first stay: *I have as yet heard nothing in Japan that we could regard as music from our standpoint*.

A formal concert does nothing to change his mind. Shortly after returning with his family in May 1883, Morse joins a large audience in a hall at the old Chinese college to hear an ensemble of *koto*, flute, *sho*, and voice: *The performance began with the old man uttering a monotonous series of gruff howls. Had he been suffering from an overdose of cucumbers he could not have uttered more dismal sounds; it was really ludicrous and one found it difficult to preserve one's gravity. While he was making these sounds, another performer picked an accompaniment on the koto.*

This seemed to be a sort of prelude, for after a while one of the young men began to sing, and the old man played on the flute, and all the instruments started . . . Each piece, though widely different in title, sounded very much alike . . . The title of one of the selections was 'Moon on a Spring Night'; another was named after a certain general; still another was dedicated to a celebrated river; another, which I thought would never end, was appropriately called 'Time.'

Distaste can be fertile ground for the roots of understanding. After the concert, Morse keeps worrying: is this music in our sense of the word? Surely neither the stiff, sober performers nor the audience can feel any *inspiration or thrill*. And yet it has to be music, however *unlike ours*. Human beings pluck and blow those things, so they must be instruments; they raise their voices together, so it must be song. Perhaps the problem is ignorance. Remember: *We thought certain forms of Japanese pictorial art absurd . . . and yet these pictures command the admiration of our artists.* Consider: *It may be that their music will ultimately prove to have merits of which we get no hint at present.*

Within this comment lies a silent knowledge—that future is closer than he thinks. A few days later Morse has his first favorable reaction to Japanese music when the vocal accompaniment at a Kabuki performance helps to move him through a range of emotions from sadness to excitement to fear. Dredging off the coast of Yezo in July, he begins to hear the chanties of sailors as *musical and catchy*. At midwinter, he can enjoy, if not easily describe, the strong rhythms and sounds of a *koto* and *biwa* group. Thirty months of absence must make the ear grow fonder, for on the third trip his judgments are uniformly favorable. A solo flute recital by a court musician seems full of *delicious contrasts* and lengthy notes of *exquisite purity*. And the music of a full ensemble—*koto, biwa, sho,* and voice—is *impressive, sweet, distinguished*, even when compared with performances at home. Now he can admit *the power of music in a new direction*; now he can find merit here *that I had never heard before*.

Appreciation is one form of expression, the desire to perform distinctly another. With no hint in the diaries, it is impossible to explain exactly why Morse chooses to study *utai* singing. Status?

Certainly, like *chanoyu*, this form of music is a taste acquired only by the few. The difficulty? That is something he does not really begin to learn until the moment when Umekawa-sensei has him sit with legs bent directly under him and the first lesson begins: *He sang a line and I sang it after him; then he sang another; and so on through the eleven lines of the piece. After trying it twice in that way we sang together . . . I observed that, do what I would, my notes sounded flat and monotonous while his were full of inflections and accents, though all on one note. I felt awkward and embarrassed at the absurd failure I was making and perspired freely, though it was a cold day in January. Finally, in desperation, I threw off all reserve and entered into it with all my might, resolved, at any rate, to mimic his sounds. I inflated my abdomen tensely, sang through my nose, put the tremolo stop on when necessary, and attracted a number of attendants who peeked through the screens to look on, in despair, no doubt, at a foreigner desecrating the honored precincts with such infernal howls. Be that as it may, my teacher for the first time bowed approvingly at my efforts . . .*

Praise is nice, but several lessons later he is still not doing very well. To keep his abdomen distended in the proper fashion is *a constant strain*; to remember *two consecutive notes, or to recall any notes* seems impossible. No wonder. With no system of musical notation, the emphasis is on directly imitating the teacher, but Umekawa makes things difficult by slightly varying each rendition of a passage. Assurances that he will soon be able to sing in a Noh play cannot hide a simple truth: Morse will never come close to making those *rich and sonorous* sounds he has begun to love. Comfort comes from knowing that that is not the point. He is at last beginning to understand the music from the inside. And something else, something more important that breaks through into consciousness and the written page on the evening of the very first lesson: *It is by taking actual lessons in the tea ceremony and singing that I may learn many things from the Japanese standpoint.*

How long to get here and how good to be here at last, even if here is no location that can be pinpointed on a map. A century later the biographer and reader are implicated as much as—no, more than—Morse himself. Because we are at once more self-conscious and less hopeful than he, more interested in the experience of what it might be to become an other, more cognizant of such hopes and their failure in the years in between, more aware of the limitations of both language and reality. For him the insight is all; without much worry over implications, he returns to the stuff of daily life. Once he was like any foreigner, his reaction to Japanese music a mixture of bewilderment and laughter. Now he is suspended somewhere between that and a new identity, able at special moments to live in two worlds. Pleasure and pain mix closely here; not in general, but in specifics. When at a concert of classical music that brings tears to Japanese eyes, Englishmen in the audience burst into *contemptuous laughter*, Morse cannot—like the natives—withdraw into feelings of cultural superiority, but instead has an intensely *humiliating experience*. Which is to say he is learning, or showing, something we have to remember: It is far easier to step beyond the boundaries of one culture than to join another.

<>

Don't forget pottery—Morse never does. It has brought him back; it will send him away. Those large crates ready for shipment across the Pacific represent more than $5,000 in capital, borrowed through John Gould's banking connections. But money is hardly the issue; mastery of a subject is Morse's highest aim. During the final weeks he is still on the search for more information, still full of questions as he moves through widening circles of pottery experts. Disagreements, uncertainties, conflicts of judgment in the attribution of historic works become steadily more disturbing. Serious problems regularly arise: *Lately I have found a bowl with the mark of Fuji, which proves a great puzzle to the Japanese experts. Kohitsu called it Ninsei, Kiyomizu, two hundred years old, but he had never seen the stamp before; Kashiwagi identified it as old Akahata, Yamato; Ando said it was Hagi, Yamato; Masuda recognized it as old Satsuma; Maida thought it might be Naniwa, Settsu; and another expert, whose name I do not recall, pronounced it Shino, Owari.*
Such differences, such difficulties, such *puzzling pieces* suggest

a complexity that Morse tends to ignore, or to see as a problem of culture. The Japanese lack of interest in systematic knowledge can be corrected by a Westerner trained in taxonomy. Surely he is the one who will eventually do away with disagreements and bring order to a chaotic realm. Indeed, it is easy to see himself already well along on that path. Take that pottery *guessing party*, where he is the only foreigner among five longtime connoisseurs. Each person brings some specimens difficult to identify, which are numbered, listed by someone who does not take part in the contest, and then passed around a circle. While the others grunt, mumble softly, and worry their decisions, Morse makes the quickest of secret written judgments. When pieces are officially identified, he sometimes silently disagrees and confides to his diary, *I am pretty sound on that pottery.* At the end of the evening, he cannot restrain himself: *It may be interesting to record that I got the highest number of correct attributions.*

Arrogance—a modest arrogance to be sure—has to be the charge against Morse at this point. He has come a long way from shells; he is on a road that will take him much farther. He has learned a lot, but he has evidently not learned enough to know what he does not—cannot ever—know. Which is only to say he is no different from us all. Perfectly in character, he at the end sums up nothing, lingers sentimentally over nothing—at least not in print, and one suspects not in the flesh either. Late in February his mind is too full of the marvelous trip ahead. He is leaving for China, Java, and India, and then on to Europe for the first time. At the age of forty-six, Ned Morse, who once lingered with sailors on the docks of Portland, Maine, is going to circle the globe, meet with scientists and art curators of France, Germany, and England, and speak with them as an equal. Japan will go with him, will color the sights and tastes of every other land, and none will please him nearly as much. Perhaps that is why he does not have to write *Sayonara*, which he knows to mean *If it must be so.*

12

The Cost of Exile

No, it's not what he expected. The train, the brick station, the men in Western suits are bad enough. The town is infinitely worse. Kumamoto is an open sprawl of sheds, barracks, and low timber houses. In vain does the eye seek the contained, the quaint, the picturesque. But it can find no shadowy streets, no sweet temples or shrines, no shops full of lacquerware or porcelain. Gardens seem nonexistent and vegetation scarce—a stunted tree here and there, a *scraggy* line of them along Tojinmachi, that broad avenue with sidewalks that really belongs in Tokyo or Yokohama. Even the city's most famous sight is a disappointment. The great seventeenth-century castle, put to the torch during the siege of 1877, is no more than a charred hulk, rising darkly from a foundation of immense stones.

Dismal. Depressing. Those are the right words for both the city and its people, members of a race that has nothing in common with the sweet folks of Izumo. Charm, helpfulness, simple curiosity are all absent. On the streets, one meets with blank stares. In the hotel, the shops and restaurants, everyone is remote. The ricksha men are worse. *Oni!* That's what Setsu calls them. *Devils!* As rude and rapacious as residents of Tokyo. And difficult to understand. The Izumo dialect spoken by the servants is far different from the local tongue. So the cook, maid, and manservant from Matsue are in the same situation as Hearn—*fish out of water.*

224

A two-mile ride through a *wilderness* of flimsy structures leads to Dai Go Koto-Chugakko, the Fifth Higher Normal School. The scale of the campus is a surprise. So is its *magnificence*: enormous brick structures; a special building for science and another for *ju-jitsu*; large dormitories; a dining hall that seats four hundred; a bathhouse that can handle forty; and a small museum. But no decent library, not for foreign books. The few in English are much too difficult. Imagine trying to teach George Eliot or Dickens to young men who can barely speak the language! Blame the former teacher—a missionary. Or the Mombusho, for putting buildings ahead of books. And wonder how you will begin to teach.

Colleagues are not much help. Of twenty-eight, a dozen can speak French or English. But they don't. Or won't. Not beyond *Good morning, Good evening, Good day.* The students, mostly career-oriented men in their early twenties, are not much more promising. Clearly school here will be no joy, no source of articles or potential friendships. It will be a way of making a living, not a way of life. This means his home will be more important than ever. But at what cost? My god, everything in Kumamoto is *outrageously expensive.* Just as bad as Tokyo. Rent is eleven yen a month, three times what it was in Kitabori, and this for a house *not nearly so beautiful*, with a garden that is *horribly ugly.* It's a good thing his salary has doubled to two hundred yen. Even so, money will be a worry.

Don't dwell on it—that's the proper strategy. In print and private letters, emphasize your feelings of health, that you have a good appetite and are gaining weight. When the weather turns bad, joke about it. Say the afternoons are warm enough, and as for the frosty nights and icy winds—well, they are, of course, *extraordinary*, just like all the bad weather encountered anywhere and everywhere in the *last twenty years*. Write about the clear days when you can see smoke rising from the great volcano of Aso-san, but don't mention any fear of it as a portent of earthquakes. At the first faculty dinner, when no geisha arrive, hide your dismay and accept the explanation that to avoid criticism of the school this tradition has been abandoned. To friends far away explain things this way: *One must travel out of Izumo after a long residence to find out how utterly different the place is from other places.* But don't admit to any mistake. Not yet. And keep the growing terror to yourself.

<>

This is the sad part of the story. You can call it the return of the reality principle. You can say it is expected, that the honeymoon has been long enough (seventeen months since that first bright Yokohama day), that one cannot live in a dream forever. It is sad anyway. Something in us wants the magic to go on for Hearn, even though we know it cannot. And so there he is in late November 1891, this tiny man with one eye and a disfigured face; this feisty, insecure man with a wife, in-laws, and servants to support; this man who is fifteen hundred pages into a manuscript that represents no more than half of the book he wants to write; and suddenly the world is slipping out of the grasp of his words. *Kumamoto!* He hates it from the first moments; will go on hating it for three years while he begins to learn the cost of cutting himself off from his own civilization.

For a long time he will not (cannot?) face the truth. Better to locate the problem outside himself, in the city and in the people of Kyushu. *Kumamoto doesn't seem Japan to me at all,* he will say (just as sometimes he will insist that Tokyo is not Japan, and Kobe is not Japan, and Yokohama is surely not Japan). And why not? Because Kumamoto is *modernized*; because it is *too big, and has no temples and priests and curious customs*; because *it is ugly*; because he is *a stranger in it*; because *here the Gods are dead and buried.* Listen carefully and you can hear behind the written lines: Because I am lonely for the sound of English, and full of doubts about the future. Because I know that, apart from my family, nobody—neither my colleagues at school, nor my students, nor my neighbors, nor the local merchants, nor priests—really cares about me, cares whether I am here or not, cares whether they will ever see me again. And because I still need the illusion of Matsue and Izumo if I am to finish this book.

Such thoughts are not all voiced at one time. They begin as complaints in letters to friends, then spill over into articles for the *Yokohama Mail.* (Never do they reach the more formal pieces that go to the *Atlantic Monthly*, or are syndicated by the New Orleans *Times Democrat*, or wind up as chapters in books, because Hearn is too canny ever to forget that only a certain kind of Japan suits his literary talent and his audience.) They become increasingly bitter even as Hearn begins to know Kumamoto, to appreciate some of its virtues, and to realize that much of its ugliness stems from that devastating siege in 1877. Eventually he will move to a house with an excellent garden; find the splendid complex of shrines and temples at Akita-gun; and come to understand—even grudgingly admire—what he will call the Kyushu character, a blunt, practical, and conservative temperament far more willing to adopt Western technology than *Western manners and customs*. But never will he cease to think of Kumamoto as the *most unpleasant* city in Japan, *a prison in the bottom of hell*.

Such harsh judgments do not tell the whole story of Hearn in Kumamoto, even if they set its tone. His words provide a shifting sort of truth dependent on a complex mixture of elements present at the moment of writing—on the hour, the day, the season, the weather, the state of his health, the progress of an article, the reaction of an American publisher to a manuscript, the unrecorded chance meeting with a colleague, student, priest, or street musician. From his writings one could reconstruct his days in Kyushu as either pleasant or miserable. Because he makes no friends (which tells us something—but what?) and because Setsu ignores this period in her memoirs, Hearn remains for us the sole witness of his own behavior in Kumamoto. Even more than other periods of his life, his three years here are a study in indeterminacy, a kind of silent bet—like all history?—that behind his words lies a lost reality that we can locate, share, and understand. But only in fragments that will always add up to less than what we wish to know.

<>

What an education the Orient is.

The words come after two years, but the lessons begin immediately. Insecurity is one of them. Hearn is on an annual contract. Each year when the *beastly* Diet—Japan's parliament—debates the education budget, he worries over every speech suggesting that, as an economy measure, some of the higher schools be abolished or foreigners be dismissed from their jobs. Threats to resign—*I won't stay here after summer . . . It is too risky*—cannot amount to anything because of family obligations. But the uncertainty that hovers over the future, the feeling that he is a pawn in someone else's game, that any official future career here is built on quicksand, leads to a solemn vow: *If I once get out of Government employ, I will never go back to it.*

That's for the future. The greater problem is what to do right now. Those initial impressions of grandeur and magnificence quickly fade until the school seems *a sort of factory, to which we all go regularly to work at fixed hours and leave at fixed hours,—without feeling intimate either with each other or the students.* Even that might be bearable, were it not for the way Hearn is treated. The man who was honored in Matsue is now shunned and ignored. Or so he feels. Complaints that colleagues *never speak to me at all* begin when he arrives and never cease. Soon he refuses to attend faculty dinners, and after a year and a half has to confess: *I do not yet know the names of my fellow teachers.*

Making the daily pain worse is that he can find no reason for the ill-treatment other than one so ugly that for two years he hesitates to voice it: he is a foreigner. It's that simple. He is a foreigner at a time when Japanese nationalism is on the rise, when politicians are calling for the revision of the treaties forced upon Japan in the 1850s, when foreigners are no longer worshipped as bearers of enlightenment, but *despised as hirelings.* He is no more than an *intellectual machine*, a being whose moral notions, intuitions, and educational ideas are not trusted, for *every official* is convinced that no outsider can possibly understand Japanese students. From all indications, the students agree. How ironic. Hearn has always encouraged his charges to follow their traditions rather than blindly imitate foreign ways. Should he be happy or sad, then, that their indifference to him shows how well they take to such lessons?

Isolation is the killer. When Lafcadio complains that Kyushu students lack spontaneity, that they are *silent as death*, and that they seldom utter original ideas, he is only reiterating sentiments voiced in Matsue. But there each day brought new sensations and insights; there he had Nishida, and the students treated him as a *sensei*, and he was newly married, and still full of hope. Here he is starved for companionship, personal and intellectual; here he has *no mental company but books*. Here every noon, while others meet to dine, he leaves school and climbs a nearby hill to sit in a cemetery beside a mossy stone Buddha: *There is my only companion for you! but I like him better than those who look like him waiting for me in the classroom.*

Thank God he has a refuge—his home, a place with an atmosphere of obligations that seem a blessing: *There are nearly twelve here to whom I am Life and Food and other things. However intolerable anything else is, at home I enter into my little smiling world of old ways and thoughts and courtesies;—where all is soft and gentle as something seen in sleep. It is so soft, so intangibly gentle and lovable and artless, that sometimes it seems a dream only; and then a fear comes that it might vanish away. It has become Me. When I am pleased, it laughs; when I don't feel jolly, everything is silent. Thus, light and vapory as its force seems, it is a moral force, perpetually appealing to conscience. I cannot imagine what I should do away from it.*

Nor can we. Hearn in Kumamoto—indeed, in Japan—is Hearn *en famille*. Never could he have predicted how much marriage would suit him. It is a *haven from which you can see dangerous sea currents*, a blessed state that does away with the wayward longings, the *emotion and suffering* of bachelorhood. How he loves the daily round of a family life where he is the center of attention. After the 6 a.m. alarm clock, Lafcadio smokes, washes, dresses, and eats breakfast—eggs and toast, lemonade laced with whisky, and black coffee—attended by Setsu. Her parents, her grandfather, and a varying group of servants gather to see him off at 7:30 (when he violates local custom by kissing his wife's hand) and to welcome him home in the early afternoon. He is the first into the six o'clock bath, and after dinner joins the other members of the household around the table when they read the newspaper aloud, or tell stories, or play games with string, coins, cards, or blindfolds. Warm nights send them out for moonlight strolls, or to the theater, or into lamplit shops to rummage for *odd or pretty things*. Sometimes Lafcadio joins these excursions, but most of his evenings are spent sitting in a chair, writing at his specially built high table. When someone asks if he is not *working too hard*, this really means, *It is late, so please give us permission to go to bed*. He does. Then the servants spread the futon, replenish the *hibachi*, and prostrate themselves with an *Oyasumi nasai*; the older folk softly intone prayers; and the house grows silent. Each night Setsu begs his pardon for going to sleep first, while he remains awake to write. Like many of her wifely practices, this one is too humbling for his taste. But words to that effect upset her and so he must accept the *ancient custom* and concede, *After all, it is pretty*.

<>

Change is the story of Hearn in Kyushu, and change is what we want to measure—intellectual, psychological, attitudinal, even spiritual, could that word be used without a smile hovering about our lips. (He would understand; he is not so different from us: *I used to think I had no soul, but since coming here I think I have,—that if I try very hard, I could discover it.*) Any such measurement is, of course, impossible to do with precision. The model for Hearn is the pendulum. That oscillation of feeling toward Japan first mentioned in Matsue never ceases. Back and forth he swings over the months and years. I love this; I hate that; admire this; detest that; am attracted to this, and repulsed by that. And then suddenly—but not suddenly, in fact, for if you look through the letters you can find plenty of foreshadowing—some old belief is gone.

The two most dramatic changes come in his attitudes toward Japanese individualism and Japanese religion. Those ideas of Percival Lowell that Hearn once accepted, that *impersonality* and a corresponding lack of *individuality* are the basis of this civilization, simply cannot stand the test of experience. To live and work among the Japanese (which Lowell has not done) is to discover that people here are no different from people everywhere else. Anyone who can see beneath the surface of social life will find strong personalities, and eccentrics, and *millions of individualities,* and learn a lesson that all foreign commentators should take to heart: *There is nothing absent from Japanese life which we imagine to be absent; all we have is there,—only the colour is different.* That difference can be blinding, as it was for him with religion: *My first enthusiasm for Shinto, I fear, was wrong.* Why? Because what he saw as the *soul of Japan,* the source of its history, morality, and sense of beauty, has in Kumamoto come to seem more like a narrow appeal to *tradition and race feeling.* More than ever, he knows that Buddhism, with its universal comfort for *the human heart,* is the more appealing of Japan's faiths.

To chart his shifting views, to follow his hopes and dreams, his adjustments, his struggles with the meaning of East and West, past and future, primitive and modern, one need only follow him on trips away from home. Journeys have always been important to him—a mixture of the personal and professional, a good means of discovering hidden parts of the self and new topics for art. In Izumo he was regularly on the go, snatching an afternoon, a day, a weekend to discover the perfect pottery village, hot springs, or shrine. This pattern changes in Kumamoto. So rarely does he mention local spots that one might think Kyushu devoid of both history and beauty. Never does he bother to visit Mount Aso; or any of the craggy islands strewn across the bright water of the Amakusa Sea; or Yanagawa, its willow-draped canals swarming with eel; or Mount Unzen, famed for its frozen winter trees and sulfur baths; or Hara Castle at Shimabara, where, in 1638, thirty-seven thousand Catholics withstood the assault of the Shogun's troops for three months before being slaughtered for their faith.

Family obligations, the demands of school, and feelings of distaste for the crude country folk of the region—*Here the peasants and lower classes drink and fight and beat their wives*—are reason enough for curtailing local travel. But mostly it is the book that keeps him close to home. He must finish it soon, finish it before that first year in the country slips away, finish it before experiences here blot out those fresher ones that took place in sweeter surroundings. Yet when a succession of *infernally dull* days gets him down, or when *nervous lonesomeness* envelops him, or when despair over his future can bring him to write to his former editor in New Orleans about the possibility of a job in that city, it's time for Lafcadio to get on the road.

<>

April 1892. His first escape from Kumamoto. A feeling of excitement and a rare sense of liberation as the train rolls north through one of those unreal landscapes ablaze with the white fire of cherry blossoms. Seventy-five miles of track and here is Hakata, bright, busy, solid, and prosperous. He strolls through streets with clean plaster buildings and claims the scene to be *well worthy of an artist's sketch book*. Here even *modernizations* can seem agreeable. Lines of telegraph poles and four-story hotels somehow add to the *Oriental picturesqueness of the place*, and suggest the happy capacity of this nation *to assimilate Western ideas and still remain essentially Japan*.

That judgment is confirmed at Dazaifu, a few miles from Hakata, where Hearn visits the shrine to Tenjin, the eleventh-century Kyoto court official and scholar who, through deception and intrigue, was unjustly exiled to this remote spot. What luck!—a *matsuri* is in progress and suddenly it's as if he is back in Izumo. The feeling lingers long enough to flavor an article for the Yokohama *Mail*, one filled with his first words of excitement since Matsue; words that capture and hold against the growing pain of life in Kumamoto a series of sharp traditional images—arched stone bridges, bronze dragon fountains, ponds with *koi* that eat out of your hand, *booths glimmering with extraordinary toys*, and great crowds standing before shrines, clapping their hands to summon the ancient gods.

<>

July 1892. Summer holiday. A chance to forget school, to take a trip he has been wanting to make since before leaving Matsue. The final destination is the Oki Islands, a hundred miles off the coast of Izumo, a place so remote that *extraordinary stories* are told about it on the mainland, another of those spots supposedly unseen by European eyes. Not that Hearn will spend the summer here. Other places come first. The treaty port of Kobe, with its polyglot population, provides the *sharp, indescribable sensation* of meeting Englishmen and Scotchmen again after two years. While he stocks up on things unavailable in Kumamoto, Setsu touches Western objects with enthusiasm. Later she asks Hearn why, unlike other Westerners, he smiles even when doing business. Only then does he realize that Japan is changing him in ways he cannot notice, ways that must make him more than *a little odd to these serious Highlanders and growling Britons.*

Kyoto is next. What joy (laced with pain) to see, touch, and taste this leafy city, to walk its broad streets and visit such an astonishing array of temples, shrines, silk works, kilns, theaters, gardens, and parks, all of which—unfortunately—remind him of that awful town where he is condemned to live. He wants to linger here for five years; he wants to take up the study of Buddhism; he wants never to return to Kumamoto. Or so he feels at first. Then something happens. Or maybe lots of things. Perhaps it's that unpleasant encounter with an insolent college-trained clerk; or the sight of the church spire (in Kyoto!) at Doshisha College; or the rain—so much that for days he and Setsu are confined to the hotel. Whatever the cause, the result is a feeling of despondency—*I can't think; I can't enjoy anything.*

Three more days of sightseeing leave Hearn dissatisfied. Many things here are stunning, but something is missing, too. Maybe it's in him. His great passion for religious buildings and their treasures has begun to wane: *I have become too familiar with temples . . . [they] have lost their individuality for me. They resemble each other like the faces of Japanese students.* A jaunt to nearby Nara, the eighth-century capital, makes for a pleasant day. But neither the famed Deer Park; nor the enormous thousand-year-old bronze Buddha at Todaiji; nor the Kasuga shrine, where *miko* dance in the oldest of imperial rituals has the impact of Izumo Taisha. How odd. Only back in Kobe does he identify the problem. The old capitals may be filled with the most refined people and artworks in Japan, but he hankers after the *primitive west coast, where speech is ruder and ways simpler and nothing good can be had to eat,—but where the ancient Gods live still in the hearts, and the lamps of the Kami are kindled in every home.*

The second stay in Kobe is not so pleasant. Suddenly Hearn

seems in flight—from Westerners. They are everywhere, and much as he longs to get away from them, this proves impossible to do. The big steamer that carries him down the Inland Sea is full of Europeans with loud voices, bad manners, and impossible travel stories. His mood sinks. He begins to ruminate, to brood, to recall better days, to wonder if it can really be a whole year since he took a *thrill of pleasure* in anything Japanese? In Moji, a town at the tip of Kyushu with new docks, railroads, and factories, the obvious hits him with great force: *With what hideous rapidity Japan is modernizing, after all!—not in costume, architecture, or habit, but in heart and manner. The emotional nature of the race is changing. Will it ever become beautiful again?*

The Oki Islands help to dispel this gloom. They are just what he hoped for—great lumps of rock rising from the sea, stretching up through the summer mist into blue cliffs and wild mountains green with vegetation. *Primitive* is the word for them: here there are no telegraph lines or newspapers, no decent roads, no locks on doors, and virtually no crime. The inhabitants, some thirty thousand scattered through dozens of fishing villages, are a robust, healthy folk, *gentle* and *quaint*. But not undiscovered. In the port of Saigo, Hearn learns that Western sailors often drop anchor here. He gets plenty of attention anyway. Great silent crowds surround him in the streets; a physician takes him home, feeds him a sumptuous meal, and loads him down with gifts; a schoolteacher presents him with a collection of local insects and butterflies; a visitor to the hotel impulsively hands over his own precious carved black-coral pipe case.

Primitive life has its drawbacks. A few days in Saigo and Hearn is ready to move. He wants to flee the aroma of traditional industry, the pervasive, sweet, nauseating stench of squid decomposing into fertilizer. He wants to leave behind the atrocious roads that make it impossible to reach the interior of the island. He wants to forget the few spots flavored with history or legend that have proved to be so disappointing. So has the local folklore, or lack of it. Frankly, he heard more entertaining Oki Island stories in Matsue than anyone can tell him here. That's part of a larger problem he does not like to confront: the islands are changing too. As is happening everywhere else, the public school system here is beginning to undermine tradition. Youngsters laugh at ideas which their fathers held sacred, and tell him: *Oh, we used to believe those things when we were savages, but we are civilized now!* Statements like this underline what is apparent on the very first day at the hotel in Saigo, when Hearn is offered beefsteak and potatoes for dinner: *From a romantic point of view, this is a disappointment.* The same could be said of the islands, but for Lafcadio it is never easy to let go of a dream. Months later, as he finishes turning the three weeks there into the longest piece in his first book on Japan, he concludes with a burst of love for Oki, which allowed him to escape *the far-reaching influences of high-pressure civilization.* Even before sailing away late in August, he writes that he would rather live here every summer than in any other part of the nation. But for all such expressions, Hearn will never return to Oki. And after departing, he will never again mention a desire to be the first Westerner to find some undiscovered corner of Japan.

<>

July 21, 1893. At 5 a.m., Hearn sits in a rocker on the piazza of the Bellevue Hotel in Nagasaki, waiting for someone to wake up and unlock the door. Two hours off the late steamer, he is enjoying the rare stillness, the hint of night-blooming flowers, the silhouettes of ornamental plants and angular roofs and great looming hills etched ever more sharply against a graying sky. This is a moment to be savored, full of possibilities that need not be rendered into words. Let him enjoy it for as long as possible—for in his life as in ours, such peace is rare enough.

To tell the truth, so far it has been a rotten trip. He has come to this cosmopolitan city—the only one in Japan allowed foreign trade and foreign residents (Dutch and Chinese) during the 250 years of seclusion—to indulge in Western foods and luxuries unavailable in Kumamoto. Already this seems a mistake. Wearing a white duck suit—*as I was going to a European hotel, I dressed according to the code*—he spent a miserable twelve hours in the *steam-laundry* cabin of the small vessel that brought him here, seething with envy of his fellow passengers who seemed cool in their thin cotton *yukata*. Now, with the sun above the hills and the heat beginning to rise, he grows itchy once again. After the hotel opens, he hires a ricksha to ride up and down the hills, but the crushing heat soon drives him back to sit on the verandah and down iced drinks at twenty-five cents a glass. He should know better by now: comfort in Western clothing and buildings is impossible here in the summer, and yet it is equally impossible to defy *stupid convention* and take off your clothes.

By six o'clock, he can take no more. It's time to flee Nagasaki, but that's not so easy to do: *In a Japanese hotel, arrangements are made to take you anywhere . . . In a Japanese hotel, they buy your tickets for you and accompany you to the steamer . . . But in the beastly Western hotels, nobody will even answer a question.* Off he must go alone to the steamship company and beg them, in *bad Japanese*, to get him out of here as soon as possible. The first steamer does not sail until after midnight, so it's back to the hotel and heat *so atrocious that even the mosquitos had not the strength to bite.* After dark he attempts a stroll, but so many men in Western dress approach him with offers of a *nice girl* that he quickly returns to the terrace. This time tranquillity does not soften his view of the dark hills and quiet bay. When someone arrives to take him to the harbor, Hearn says a silent blessing and hurries away.

The next afternoon, comfortable in a *yukata*, he lounges about a hotel room filled with the glare of sea and sky. Below is the gray town of Misumi; above, enormous green cliffs; and beyond, *the blaze of summer to the horizon.* He has escaped; he is free now, like a soul *suddenly reborn.* No wonder the serving-girls appear to be goddesses, and the beautiful mistress of the hotel to move with the delicacy and grace of a *dragon-fly.* He wants it that way, just as he wants the hotel to be Japanese-style, with matted rooms, and futon, and lovely old vases and scrolls. But it isn't. It's a Western hotel, with beds, chairs, dressers, glass mirrors, and rugs. How inconvenient for someone who sees himself as a refugee from *the sorrows of the nineteenth century.* Yet he is a refugee with words that can improve reality, mold it closer to the heart's desire. So it is a Japanese inn after all—at least it is when, a few weeks later, he sits down to describe it in a piece entitled "The Dream of a Summer Day."

Part revery, part story, part memoir—this is one of those Hearn creations that eludes categories. But the starting point is clear enough. The name of the Misumi hotel, Urashimaya, leads him to recount one of the most popular of Japanese folk stories. In this tale a fisher boy named Urashima Taro is rewarded for a good deed—freeing a sacred tortoise from his line—by being brought to the island realm of the Dragon God of the Sea, wed to his beautiful daughter, and encouraged to live only for the pleasures of *that enchanted land where summer never dies.* For three years he does, but human obligations tug at him, and Taro wants to see his parents. To protect him on the journey, his distressed wife provides a sealed lacquer box along with a warning: as long as it remains closed he will be safe, but if it is opened he will never see her again. Back he goes to his native village, a place at once strange and well-known—the hills and stream look familiar, but the trees and fields and faces are different, and the family house is gone. When he speaks his own name, he is told that Urashima Taro drowned four hundred years ago, and in the village graveyard he sees his own tombstone. What *strange illusion* is he victim of, and how to end it? The sealed box—might it be the cause? He opens the box and out bursts a vapor that rises and drifts away. For an instant Taro knows he has destroyed his own happiness, that he will never return to the daughter of the Dragon God. Then his teeth fall out; his face shrivels; his hair turns white; his limbs wither; and he sinks down *crushed by the weight of four hundred winters.*

The tale leads Hearn to memories of pictures, poems, and proverbs based on Urashima Taro; to images of a dancing girl in Matsue performing as the fisher boy; and to reflections on the way everything turns to dust except the truth of such stories. But what truth? That Taro, like all of us, is bewildered by the gods? That in the East those who disobey the gods become enshrined as *kami*, while in the West those who disobey the gods remain alive *to learn the height and breadth and depth* of sorrow? Such questions lead back to the self, and elicit the first childhood memories Lafcadio has ever shared with readers. He recalls that *magical time* when the sea was alive and the touch of the wind could make him *cry out for joy*, and he lived in a country *ruled by one who thought only of ways to make me happy.* She read him stories that made him tingle from head to foot, and sang him to sleep at night, and when the sad day came for them to part, she gave him a charm that for years kept him young and full of hope that he might return to that land. But now, just now in fact, he has come to understand that somewhere, somehow that charm has been lost, leaving him *ridiculously old* and unable to return.

No doubt it is true, as Hearn tells us, that visions of Urashima Taro stay with him during the next day's dusty ride home along the seashore, past parched fields of barley and rice and villages in which naked men beat immense drums to summon the gods of rain. Certainly the tale is very much part of the first letter he writes after getting back to Kumamoto, and the character thoroughly occupies him for the three weeks it takes to get the piece written and off to a publisher. Later it will stand as the first chapter in his second collection on Japan, *Out of the East*. But nowhere—in letter or journal entry—will he attempt to explain why he equates himself with this character. And yet it seems so simple. Lafcadio has always known that, like Urashima Taro, he is a victim of forces that can never fully be understood. Now Nagasaki and the inn at Misumi have moved him to another level of self-awareness. Never before has he seen that he, too, once accidentally happened onto a perfect realm. Never before has he so clearly understood that through his own desires he left that realm to return to an all too human world where things change and decay, and suffering is the price of knowledge. By the very act of writing about Taro and identifying with him, Hearn is showing a recognition—even if not yet conscious—of something that the cumulative experiences of Kumamoto, Hakata, Kobe, Kyoto, Oki, and even Misumi have begun to make very clear: he is now a man who belongs less to either Japan or the West than to some expansive but misty realm of his own imagination.

<>

In January, 1893, Hearn's manuscript—so lengthy it will total seven hundred close-printed pages and be issued in two volumes—goes off to the publishing house of Houghton Mifflin in Boston. Ten months later, Setsu gives birth to their first child, a son named Kazuo. How nice it would be to connect these two events, to say that once the book is done his energy is free for another sort of conception. But, for lack of an appropriate biological theory that could link them, this is just the sort of explanation no biographer can seriously propose. Yet the events must touch and overlap within the reaches of Hearn's mind. Separation and reconnection, death and birth—such experiences are very much part of the emotional turmoil that begins when he sends off the manuscript. Every certainty about East and West, past and future, Japan and himself is called into question. In letter after letter he will ask in so many indirect ways, What does it all mean? What am I doing here? Where am I going? What truth can I now share with the world?

Difficult it is for him—the writer, the enthusiast, the lover of Japan—to accept the limitations (and falsehoods?) of his own well-meant words. The twenty-seven pieces that form the manuscript vibrate with the wonders of Kamakura, Enoshima, Matsue, and Izumo. Yet the moment he sends it off, the moment he allows himself to accept the experiences of the last year and a half, Hearn knows his creation to be an *enormous illusion*, an evocation of a ghost named *Old Japan*. How to account for this? Certainly not through any commercial intent. His unpublished notes are filled with even greater *madness* than that which mars the articles. In the first months here he described *horrible places as gardens of paradise, and horrid people as angels and divinities*. No doubt about it—he was a *fool*. But surely not the only fool in the world; surely anyone can be seduced by the unfamiliar when it is so attractive. Besides, in one important way the manuscript is accurate. During those early days, *Japan was really for me what I thought it*. This is part of an important truth: *To the child the world is blue and green; to the old man grey—both are right*.

And now, what does he really know now? Humility and self-doubt shadow him—*Every day it strikes me more and more how little I shall ever know of the Japanese*—and lack of inspiration becomes his deepest fear. All through 1894 he claims to be dried up, uninspired, wholly unable to experience the kind of *strong sensation* necessary to stir his creativity (or so he says, for in truth he writes most of another book in that year). Much as he would like to blame Kumamoto for this, he knows the problem to be larger. How dreadful to feel *Fairyland is already dead*. But it is true. The country is losing its *Japaneseness*. The constitution, the Diet, the development of industry are all parts of some enormous mistake, one that began with the *crime* of opening the nation. Once Japan was morally *in advance of the West*, but modernization has cast it *backward a thousand years*. No good can come of it. The nation's manners and morals are being irrevocably destroyed. Take the school system: *Monstrosities of brick* have been built at the cost of losing the traditional intimate relationship of pupil to teacher. To substitute the impersonal for the human is a bad bargain, just one more indication that, in another generation, *Japan won't be the best place in the world*.

Becoming critical of Japan does not mean seeing the West in a romantic light. But it does mean seeing the West differently: Japan *opens a man's eyes and mind about his own country, about conventionalisms of a hundred sorts,—about false ideals and idealisms,—about ethical questions*. At home, the struggle for existence as glorified by Spencer may seem to be an irreducible social fact, but a vision of cooperative life as it used to be here—the (imagined?) life of Matsue—leads to this judgment: a civilization based on such a struggle is a *fraud*. Without ever bothering to deny Spencer directly—indeed, he never ceases to call himself a disciple—Hearn begins to doubt the value of *our boasted material progress*. Does it not bring more human problems than benefits? That's what he sees all around him. No longer can he avoid the pain of this paradox: in Japan there is nothing to love *except what is passing away*.

Sobering words, words that might lead to action. But Hearn, like all of us, cannot afford the luxury of living only by words. He has too many daily realities to handle—a family; a son whose future must be secured through a good education; and his own volatile emotions. In 1894 there is public trouble as well. When war breaks out with China that summer, an *immense reaction* against foreign influence sweeps over Japan, or so it seems in Kumamoto, where Lafcadio is sometimes greeted by a *sudden hiss of hatred* from passing strangers. Encounters like this serve only to strengthen the desire to flee Kyushu. But where to go? Manila or Java or some such place with *palm trees, and parrots, and mangoes?* He cannot secure an advance for a book to make such a journey possible. A fishing village on the west coast? That would entail too many discomforts, and besides, *my folks do not share my liking for out-of-the-way nooks and corners.* Back to Matsue? He has no way to support himself there. This problem can be solved only by a decent job offer. Meanwhile, the loneliness of Kumamoto life swells into ever greater nostalgia for the language, customs, and energies of the West. The first signs of this seem trivial enough. After three years of being shaved in *religious silence by a being with a face like Buddha,* Lafcadio one day feels a strange regret for a creature he used to think *frightful,* the American barber, *who parts his hair in the middle and insists on telling you about his girl.* By the summer of 1894, the issue is more serious and open. Worried over the penalty of isolating himself for so long from the *Aryan race,* he begins to feel so hungry for the open ports that in describing them his prose takes flight, soars over the *amethyst hills* of Kobe, the *dreamy luminosity* of Yokohama, the *windy glory* of Nagasaki. Images like this may convince nobody else, but they work on him. Early in July, Lafcadio is on the way north.

By the time he reaches Yokohama Harbor on July 10, Hearn is full of fear. How will he react to men who are *giants?* How deal with a civilization he has been *so long decrying?* By having a revelation, that's how: *Everything seems huge, full of force, dignity, massive potentialities . . . How small suddenly my little Japan . . . What a joy to feel the West! What a great thing is the West! What new appreciations of it are born in isolation!* Ashore, he momentarily slips back four years to that first April day, feels again a *delighted wonder in the radiance of an unknown fairy world.* Illusion. That's what it was. Best to leave it behind and enjoy the company of all these blond men who speak his language. The harsh things he has written about treaty ports—*may the Gods forgive my ignorance*—are wrong; the hard-fisted, coldhearted businessmen of the West are a product of his own mind. In Yokohama he finds a *vast romance* waiting to be written. And he is the man to do it, to capture in words the beautiful stories of these Europeans in exile.

Tokyo is an enormous surprise: the city he detested four years ago, the city which just last month he regarded *with unspeakable hatred*, turns out to be wonderful. The details of what he does here—*I am much too happy to write essays and sketches*—are less important than the impression he takes away. We know that Hearn stays at Chamberlain's house and spends a good deal of time reading in the professor's vast library. We know he takes several outings—to Kamakura, Enoshima, and Otsu—with one of his regular correspondents, W. B. Mason, another American married to a Japanese woman. Together the two men enjoy friendly *debaucheries*, bouts of *beefsteak, whiskey and lemonade, gin and ginger ale and beer*. But their best moment is the *elegant and dainty* dinner at Mason's home—the *shoji* open to *a great big warm moon*, his wife playing the *koto*, the children lighting fireworks in the garden, and the talk in English with someone who understands not just the words, but the silences behind them.

God—how hungry he has been. This kind of sharing, this *sympathy* (how weak this word is to us; how strong to him) is the *supreme delight of life*. Yet moments like this serve to intensify a terrifying thought: I must soon return to Kumamoto. Meeting some *horribly disagreeable foreigners* would make it easier to leave. But how to find this usually ubiquitous species? Back in Yokohama, and even on the five-day boat trip to Kobe and down the Inland Sea, Lafcadio remains enchanted with all sorts of Europeans—scientists, sailors, businessmen, and the normally detestable *globe-trotters*. His good mood cannot last more than three days past the end of the journey: *To write the name Kumamoto now is disagreeable . . . I am tortured by the mere repetition of this question, always recurring. How long can I bear this?*

<>

Let the cycle begin again.

October 1894. Hearn moves to Kobe to take a job as an editorial writer on the weekly *Chronicle* at a salary of one hundred yen a month. The work is intense, but not time-consuming. Only a couple of hours each day are needed to compose a leader on some current topic—educational policy, national character, the Japanese physique, the question of male and female equality, the race problem in America—and then the rest of the time is free for his own writing. But something to do with the return to the close work of journalism, or the tension that has built up over the exile of the last three years, or the simple process of aging, leads in January 1895 to a severe inflammation in his good eye. For three weeks he must remain in a dark room, and when he is well enough to read again, the doctor issues a solemn warning: if Lafcadio wants to keep his sight, he must give up newspaper work. To support himself he will now have to rely on free-lance writing. So worried does this leave him that, when reading galley proofs for *Glimpses of Unfamiliar Japan*, he who has for years denounced missionaries now grows fearful of offending any potential audience and asks Houghton Mifflin to cut some oblique, vaguely antireligious remarks from the preface.

Ask why he is in Kobe and you will learn that he is here to do a *white man's job*, to touch base once again *with men of my own race who, for all their faults, have sympathy and kindness, and who have the same color soul as myself.* Such an attitude does not long endure. Once settled, Hearn avoids the foreign quarter, with its warehouses, shipping offices, clubs, and solid homes. Six months after arriving he claims to be happy only when *out of the sight of foreign faces.* After life in the interior, this world is jarring and unpleasant, and far too full of men who work like slaves *for no other earthly reason than that conventions require them to live beyond their means.* Just listen to the strident voices of Western women, to the gossip and backbiting; just think of carpets, pianos, curtains, brass bands, churches, and white shirts. How awful they all are. What a curse to be in such a place again. Since he cannot get away, his frustration must go into words: *How much I . . . hate all that we call civilization I never knew before. How ugly it is I could never have conceived without a long sojourn in Old Japan—the only civilized country that existed since antiquity.*

Life on tatami—quiet, restrained, and removed, life with plenty of time for writing—that's what he wants and that's what he has. His world is a small one, with few outside contacts and no real friends beyond the family circle. This is by choice. Westerners are too abrasive for companionship, and natives too alien: *I feel unhappy at being in the company of a cultivated Japanese for more than an hour at a time. After the first charm of formality is over, the man becomes ice—or else suddenly drifts away from you into his own world.* Once he hoped to explore the race-soul of these people; now he is convinced they have *no depths to stir.* Not that he really understands what they are about: *I may as well frankly say that the longer I live in Japan, the less I know about the Japanese.* This is no mere conceit. Hearn is coming to feel that the most important events cannot be understood, but only described. Take that day he awakes, full of hatred for Japan and burdened with the feeling that life is not worth living. The mood lasts until the afternoon, when two elderly, blind women balladeers stop at the house to play *samisen* and sing old folk songs in voices so full of *sorrow and beauty,* [and] *all the pain and the sweetness of life* that his despair melts into tenderness. What words can explain this delicious feeling of love recalled? How can one understand this momentary pleasure—for it cannot last—that Japan has become Japan again?

One could go on, as he must, but the redundancy we tolerate in life is less acceptable in art. So maybe it is best to end it quickly by explaining that during two years in Kobe that love-hate pendulum—toward Japan and toward himself—never ceases to swing. More and more his world is an internal one, bounded by the written word, with few external events worthy of being reported by Hearn or his biographer. He publishes two more books—*Out of the East* and *Kokoro*—that are well reviewed back home, but finds he cannot reread his own words once they are in print. He earns a respectable $1,300 in his first year as a freelance writer and expects to do better in the future, but never can stop worrying over finances. He continues to dream of the tropics, but puts off more than one trip to the Philippines because he cannot bear to leave the family. He talks of building a home in Kobe, or buying his former residence in Matsue, but continues to rent a house that is, appropriately enough, half Western and half Japanese in design. He thinks of returning to America, but knows that to leave Japan would be like *tearing one's self in two.* He takes to quoting—as the sum of all he has learned?—this statement made by a friend: *It is only when a foreigner confesses he knows nothing about us that there is some reason to expect he will understand us later on.*

Perhaps. But it's best not to count on it, just as it's best not to count on anything here. Such an attitude underlies the most significant step he takes while in Kobe. Fearful of an increase in feeling against foreigners after the war with China, and worried over possible future economic or political reprisals, Hearn decides at last to apply for Japanese citizenship. The process of naturalization only heightens his suspicions of the government. Out to the house comes an official to ask Setsu the most annoying questions: *whether I had always been kind—whether she thought I would always be good to her—whether she was in earnest—whether she had made the application of her own free will, or under pressure from relations—whether I had forced her to make such an application.* A year later, when granted citizenship, he assumes her family name, and then as a first name chooses *Yakumo* (Eight Clouds), an old poetic label for Izumo. One of the first letters addressed to Y. Koizumi comes from Professor Toyama of Tokyo Imperial University (Edward Morse's old associate). It brings an offer for Lafcadio to return to government service as a professor of literature. As if finally answering a call of fate, or realizing one cannot avoid destiny, Hearn accepts the position. But before moving in the fall of 1896 to the *great capital, so long dreaded* he has one last trip to make.

<>

Not for five years has he seen these glassy waterways between rice-lands, smelled the *blue wood-smoke* and the *clayey odors of the fields,* heard the voices of wild doves and *uguisu* from wooded hills, drawn close to the brown fishermen in boats *shaped like new moons.* The small steamer glides up the Ohashi River, past familiar temple gate and *torii,* white-walled *kura* and balconied houses. Nothing has changed. The same junks are moored in the same old places, as if waiting for his return. Yes, the white bridge does seem *somewhat gray,* and the streets narrower. But not for long; not once Kobe's wide boulevards fade from mind. To wander the town is to find the sunlight and colors of the past, the same shadows trembling in the same lake wind, the same flower odors from walled gardens. He visits his former home and sees the lotus pond, the chrysanthemums, and the little shrine to Inari under the *dove-haunted hill.* He crosses the moat to the castle grounds, climbs the hill, and here's a surprise: the tower has been repaired and the roof tiling is now bright blue, but the raw tints of renovated wall surface are not nearly as beautiful as the *old colors of decay.* Inside he finds a new military museum dedicated to the victory over China in 1895, full of cannon, rifles, swords, and flags captured by Izumo troops during the war.

At a banquet in his honor, Lafcadio finds that a geisha he remembers as a child has grown into a graceful woman. Long ago in Governor Koteda's house, she danced Urashima, and now he requests that she do it again. She dons a mask, the mask of old age, one whose features bear *a faint mocking resemblance to my own.* (Can this be true? Or does he merely wish it true, wish to tell us that he now knows who he is?) Someone raises a cup with the comment *Tonight we must think only of happy things,* and Hearn has to drain his own cup, has to grow cheerful with *sake* even as he knows that happiness can be difficult to distinguish from sadness when visiting *a place once loved and deserted.* Something has vanished, that is certain, and the absence is with him, will always be with him in the years ahead. What can it be? The *queer* street vistas, the shops, the landscape, the birdsongs, the shrilling cicada, the blossom scents are all still here. So the absence must be in him, in his life, in that *first irrevocable illusion of Japan.* Why does this phrase make him think of an old proverb? *Shiranu ga Hotoke—Not to know is to become a Buddha.* Maybe sadness is only part of waking up. Maybe after more than six years only one question really matters—whether in Tokyo, that center of new Japan, *I can be fortunate enough at happy moments to meet with something of the Old.*

Five

REMEMBERING

On a windy day, three Zen monks are looking at a landscape where a huge willow sways gracefully back and forth. "Look at the lovely tree moving," says the youngest monk. "It's not the tree that is moving, but the wind," answers the middle monk. "You are both wrong," says the eldest. "The only thing that's moving is your mind."

—TRADITIONAL STORY

13

Full Circle

Skip fifty-two years. Skip the two years of lecture tours on Japan, the twelve months at Union Theological Seminary, the three congregations (in Schenectady, Boston, and Ithaca), the eight *preaching tours* of Europe. Skip the two marriages, the births of three children (two boys and a girl), the death of his first wife. Skip the sermons, the articles, the reviews, the pamphlets, the books on Japan, Korea, Holland, and the graduates of Rutgers. Skip the awards and testimonials, the memberships in societies honorific and professional, the party for his retirement from the ministry in 1903, the death of Clarkie, once of Shizuoka, in 1907, and of sister Maggie six years later. Skip all the way to a late summer day in 1926. On September 17, his eighty-third birthday, William Elliot Griffis begins a fresh journal. His hand seems a touch shaky, but less so than one might expect. Unlike the many earlier volumes, this one has a title: *The Japan Year*.

After all this time he is going back. What has been for half a century a matter of words and images, or the occasional visiting face seen across a dinner table, will soon become rice fields and mountains, buildings and streets. Half a century has not changed Willie, at least not to judge him by the written word. His diary is as unrevealing now as then. Or perhaps it is more accurate to say that it still reveals only the surface of daily life—names of hotels and restaurants, numbers of people at a reception or lecture. Thoughts, moods, opinions, ideas, and feelings rarely reach the page, except in the most oblique of hints, and the inner man—

but maybe one should say, What inner man? and let the matter go. Maybe it is time to stop expecting him to be self-conscious and self-reflective. Maybe it is time to admire his energy, dedication, and capacity for work despite the problems of age and illness. On his birthday he has been in bed for a week, under the care of a doctor, yet this does not prevent him from reading the proofs of his latest book, *The History of the American Flag.* In Japan he will be plagued by headaches, colds, severe and painful neuritis in the left arm, and the general aches of being eighty-three. But ailments will not interfere with a tour (from Kyushu to Hokkaido, from Honshu to Korea) of two hundred lectures that could easily daunt a younger man.

He is returning at the invitation of the Japanese government; returning to be honored with the Order of the Rising Sun, Third Class; returning to write an official biography of the Emperor Meiji, dead these fourteen years. (Why he has not gone before, why he chooses to go now—neither of these questions does he answer directly, though one suspects *time and money* would likely be his words.) The invitation and honors seem well deserved, not necessarily for what he did in Fukui or Tokyo, but for what he has done since coming home. His first book, *The Mikado's Empire*, published in 1876, has gone through twelve editions and has established him as one of America's leading experts on Japanese history and culture. A huge number of articles in journals popular and serious, religious and secular; subsequent books on Japanese religions, folklore, and art; and a series of biographies of Westerners who helped to shape the new Japan—Matthew Perry, Townsend Harris, Guido Verbeck, J. L. Hepburn, and Samuel Robbins Brown—have helped to underscore his reputation. In the late nineteenth or early twentieth century, when you want to know something about Japan, Griffis is one of the men to ask.

Not that his reputation goes unchallenged. By the twenties, young critics think him a bit of a fool, or even a *humbug.* Perhaps he is one, perhaps both—either would explain so much that can seem shallow in his work. But so would naiveté, earnestness, and simple faith in science, God, and progress of a sort more easily imbibed in the mid-nineteenth century than the twentieth. Simplifying, romanticizing, even plagiarizing—all these charges are made against him. But the most persistent complaint concerns self-promotion and grandiosity. Griffis cannot keep himself out of his own pages. In historical and cultural studies, even in biographies of men like Harris, Verbeck, and Hepburn, Willie always has a cameo role, a paragraph or chapter devoted to his own adventures in Yokohama, Tokyo, or Fukui. Worse yet, for half a century he has tirelessly repeated the same claims: he was the first foreigner called to Japan under the Emperor's Charter Oath (not true); he was the only white man to live and work in a feudal domain (not true); he had a major influence on science education in Japan (problematic); he knew the Emperor (as a private knows a general); he was a major force in the establishment of Japanese Christianity (doubtful).

In this fifty-year flood of words, Griffis has been no neutral interpreter of Japan, but an advocate with an important case to make. Not that he can either see or admit this. Ask and Willie will say that he has *never ceased to criticize the Japanese.* True enough, in a way, but the practices he finds distasteful are predictable, limited, and often enough excusable: these people are not Christian (yet); they don't treat women as equals (yet); their sexual morality is a touch dubious (still). But how much more important it is to recognize them as thrifty, hardworking, progressive, clean, and loyal, ready and willing to shoulder the *civilizing* mission of the Anglo-Saxon race. Griffis applauds the military victories over China in 1895 and Russia ten years later, supports the expansion into Korea, and claims that the Japanese are the most *un-Mongoloid* people in Asia, one with so much *Aryan blood in their veins* that they—unlike the Chinese—are fully capable of becoming *desirable citizens* of the United States.

Now he will see them again, these admirable folk who have helped him more than he has them. We cannot measure the influence of his books, articles, and lectures either on Japan or on the policies of the United States, nor assess the impact of Willie's words on the mind of America (whatever that might be). Yet without the efforts of Griffis, Japan in 1926 would surely be much the same, while without Japan, Griffis would be just another ex-minister, another dabbler in history, another voice in the enormous turn-of-the-century chorus singing hymns of praise for

America's glorious past and more glorious days to come. (He does not see this either, but how could we expect him to? It would be easy to say that what blocks his vision is ego, a fair enough judgment looking back from late in the century. But remember, Griffis always describes himself as the instrument of a higher power. That a later generation cannot invoke such a power, at least not to explain anything historical or personal, may be as much loss as gain. At the very least, it cuts us off from Willie, from the experience of an ego whose boundaries can dissolve into those of a God.)

October 23, 1926. Time to leave Ithaca; time for the journey to commence. He goes by train to Syracuse, Cleveland, Chicago, Los Angeles, San Francisco; by steamer to Honolulu and beyond, to what must be a strange, dreamy moment on Monday, December 13: *Landed at Yokohama about 10 a.m., 56 years after first arrival. Solid and spacious wharves, colossal steamers, etc. & a rebuilt city!* Those are not the only changes. How odd to be greeted by a mob of reporters on the docks, to be dazzled by flash powder, to ride in an automobile along parts of *the old Tokaido* up to Tokyo and to a room at the Imperial Hotel, designed by a young American named Frank Lloyd Wright. At a midday America-Japan Society dinner he is toasted by Prince Tokugawa, descendant of shoguns; at Waseda University that afternoon he lectures to a packed house; at supper he is honored by members of the government. The following days are hectic with lectures, sermons, and meetings; with magazine and radio interviews; with visits from old students, colleagues, missionaries, and various officials. Not until the twentieth is there time for a bit of conscious nostalgia, for *a ride to the old scenes of 1870-74.* One wonders what feelings lie behind that day's journal entry: *All changed! Old Tokyo lost in the new.*

Be content. Such scraps are all he is capable of giving. Griffis is not a sentimental sort, at least not in print. He spends an *Evening (as in 1872) on the Ginza,* and notes only this: *Vast the changes.* He strolls to the temple that once housed the American legation and jots *Zempukuji (of old time Townsend Harris, Pruyn, WEG 1872 etc.).* On New Year's Day, 1927, with the vast city as quiet and the streets as empty as on a Sabbath at home, he writes, *Thoughts of 1873!* (but not what thoughts). On the eleventh of January, he visits his *old stomping grounds* and finds that the campus where he and Verbeck once taught has *changed beyond recognition.* But how he comes to terms with such changes remains a mystery. Nor do we know if he really prefers those remnants of old Japan (he must, he must!), like the narrow streets and shops, teahouses and gardens of Asakusa, the *Same old Vanity Fair and pagan temple as in 1870.* Maybe he just does not have the words. (Occasionally his understatements can be most eloquent. Take this entry: *Kobe. 1871—100. 1927—700,000.*) Or maybe it's enough just to be there, just to be alive. Or maybe he's too busy. Certainly he's too busy, but that is nothing new. He is doing research on the biography of Emperor Meiji, meeting with former students, consulting with missionaries, writing articles, sightseeing, delivering sermons, and lecturing to groups of bankers, reporters, businessmen, government employees, children, students, women, workers, farmers, and members of the nobility in a variety of settings—in high schools, colleges, prefectural offices, factories, Rotary clubs, museums, YMCAs, and churches. The crowds that come to hear him are large—three hundred at the Engineering College of Tokyo Imperial University, six hundred at a church in Shizuoka, fifteen hundred at Doshisha University, two thousand at the Asahi Shimbun hall in Osaka. The lecture, delivered through an interpreter, is always same. He talks of the history of American involvement in Japan; of Perry, Townsend Harris, and the Emperor Meiji; of Verbeck and Maggie Griffis; of his own experiences in Fukui and Tokyo. Especially of his own experiences.

Huge crowds, cheers and applause, reporters asking questions, photographers bombarding him with flashes become so much the norm that descriptions of them in the journal begin to carry the tag *as usual.* Everywhere throughout the country—in the great cities of Tokyo, Kyoto, and Osaka; on the two-month southern swing that takes him all the way to Kagoshima, and the two-week northern swing that reaches Sapporo; and during the month in occupied, colonized Korea—Willie is treated as a most honored guest, a living relic, a man who partook in the nation's most momentous change in two thousand years. Both he and his audiences seem equally determined to enjoy his fame. For him it must be well-earned recognition for a lifetime of devotion to the Lord's work. For them it must be a celebration not just of an important foreigner, but of Japan itself, its growth, its destiny among nations.

An audience on June first with the Emperor Showa caps this happy tour. Griffis marks the occasion by getting ten copies of the next day's *Japan Times*, with its story and pictures of the event, but for him the high point of the trip is already five weeks in the past. On the morning of Monday, April 25, he boards a train in Kobe bound for Fukui. Again we must wonder at the images in his mind, wonder if he is thinking of horseback samurai and snow showers, as he pens *Long ride—to valley. Receptions in Tsuruga & Takefu, officers and hurrahing boys. Enjoyed the glorious scenery first seen in March 1871. ECHIZEN.* Again we must guess at the emotions when, at Fukui station, a little girl he knew in 1871—*now an old lady*—climbs on the train with a delegation of local notables; or when the thousands of people—*adults, boys, girls, school folk*—line both sides of the road, waving American and Japanese flags; or when the car halts for him to hear several hundred schoolboys sing "My Country, 'Tis of Thee."

Four days. That is all the time he has to revel in the feelings and ironies and blank spaces of the past. At the hotel Griffis, for the first time in Fukui, sleeps in a futon on the floor. He meets with his *old boys*, now over seventy years of age. He sees some of his old property, remnants of apparatus from his laboratory, which was destroyed by fire many years before. He attends a *torch light (lantern) procession* given in his honor; goes to a banquet with entertainment by geisha in a restaurant on Atagoyama; and drops in to the local movie house to see a *prolonged Japanese blood and thunder* film. At the Kagaya Theater he lectures to an audience of twenty-three hundred; at the local silk factory, receives a gift of a traditional Japanese suit of *haori and hakama*. He visits shrines, temples, prefectural offices, the middle and technical schools; he meets the governor, the mayor, priests, principals, and teachers. On the last day he explores the *old house*, but whether his Japanese residence or the Western one he does not bother to say. Nor does he sum up the meaning of this return to

Fukui, at least not directly. But three days after departing, while in Kyoto, he makes this entry in the journal: *Began points for a book. Psychology and history. WEG in Japan 1870-1927.* Griffis will never write it. Not enough time, not enough energy. When he goes from Tokyo to Yokohama on June 11, 1927, and boards the steamer amid the now familiar crowds, cheers, flags, and photographers (noting dryly—*contrast with Yokohama and Tokyo of 1870 and 1874*), he has but seven months to live. As always, during this period his days are full with too many things to say and do. He writes articles on his impressions of Japan for publications both secular and religious, for *Current History, National Geographic, North American Review,* the *Nation, Ithaca Journal, Missionary Herald,* and the *Japan Christian Intelligencer.* He reads a large number of books dealing with Japan, past and present, including Frank Tinker's recent biography of Lafcadio Hearn. He begins to sketch notes for an autobiography, then grows more ambitious with an *Idea of a Family History of the U.S.,* one told in terms of his own forebears, who arrived in the mid-eighteenth century. Late in December, he completes the final chapter of the work on Emperor Meiji. At a dinner on January 5, 1928, eleven hundred guests of the Japan Society watch Griffis hand over the manuscript to Japanese Ambassador Matsudaira, a relation of the *daimyo* of Fukui who brought Willie to Japan in 1870.

Full circle—shall we call it that? The final articles underscore the notion, full as they are of dreams that began a long time ago. Fifty-seven years it is since he stepped on the soil of Japan, ready to civilize and Christianize the natives. Fifty-six years, perhaps, since he came to understand they were civilized without being Christian. As they still are. So what is there to say? That their *unmentionable diseases* are gone, and their morals better (though how can he possibly know?); that people who walked are now *flying on wheels*; that stores *rich in stocks of clocks and watches are now in every town*; that two thousand newspapers, and the right to meet and vote and go to public schools, are leading to a new kind of civilization. Christianity? Never count it out. If conversion statistics are not impressive, just remember: faith is not a matter of numbers, but feeling. The best in Shinto and the best in

Buddhism are preparing the ground for the broader *truth of the new religion.* Someday they will know; someday they will accept. And when they do, what a boon for humanity, for *the Americans and the Japanese may, under God and in the spirit of Jesus, evolve a higher type of civilization than any known in the world today.*

That's the final voice of Willie Griffis, who has come a long way from Philadelphia and the Dutch Reformed Church. You can call him naive, unrealistic, and impractical, or denounce him as a visionary. But don't be too harsh. He is, after all, eighty-four and his days are numbered. America, the Lord, and Japan have been with him for almost all of his life, so the desire to blend them into one grand design must finally prove irresistible. Or maybe it's something else. Maybe it's the oddity of those four years in Fukui and Tokyo followed by half a century of attempting to come to grips with what he experienced there. Maybe he has learned that words are not the right medium for dealing with the enormous contradictions of the reality he has lived. Maybe only silence or faith can deal with such contradictions. Maybe that is what he (unconsciously) knows. Maybe.

14

The More Things Change

The last and longest work Edward S. Morse publishes on Japan grows out of a letter from William Sturgis Bigelow. Or so Ned tells us. It is July 1913, and he has just celebrated his seventy-fifth birthday by playing three sets of tennis. His hair white, his beard trimmed short, his glasses thick, Morse is still on a daily schedule that leaves no time for relaxation, rumination, or contemplation. Nelly is gone now, two years in her grave. To say her death was *a shock* is a convention his first biographer can neither violate nor document. No doubt he misses his wife—as he loved her—in his own way, just as he must miss the children, Edith and John, both long married and living with their own families in Concord. Morse remains in Salem, content to dwell alone in the frame house at 17 Linden Street, now dreadfully shabby and run-down, that he built in 1868. He has a housekeeper to take care of domestic chores, a secretary to turn his virtually illegible scrawl into typed manuscripts, and enough shells on the thirty-foot-long table in his study to keep him happy on those days when commitments don't call him off to Boston, Cape Cod, New York, or Washington, D.C.

Fame has long been his. Morse is an imposing figure in scientific and ethnological circles. He has won so many honors and awards and held so many high offices that by now they are merely part of the routine of life. Director of the Peabody Scientific Institute for more than thirty years, Ned is a member of the National Academy of Science and has been president of three organizations:

the American Association for the Advancement of Science, the Boston Society of Natural History (which he joined in 1858), and the American Association of Museums. For twenty years has been keeper of the Japanese pottery at the Boston Museum of Fine Arts, a position created when that institution purchased his collection for $76,000 in 1892. He has served on the pottery jury at international expositions in Chicago, Buffalo, and St. Louis and as a sometime informal consultant for Japanese collections in England, France, and Germany. The Meiji government has twice decorated him, with the Order of the Rising Sun and with that of the Sacred Treasure, and four institutions of higher learning— Bowdoin, Harvard, Yale, and Tufts—have awarded him (or soon will) honorary degrees, with the latter conferring a Doctor of Humane Letters.

Not a bad record for someone who never finished high school or attended college. But no list of honors, however long, is capable of easing Morse toward indolence. Work is still his greatest recreation. After twenty years largely devoted to the pottery, crafts, architecture, roof tiles, sanitation, archery, and manners and morals of Japan, he has, since the turn of the century, given his attention once again to mollusks, including brachiopods. No surprise that they are the subject of his first scientific paper since leaving East Asia in 1882. No surprise either (if one thinks of who he is, has always been) that Ned once again has John Gould involved in his efforts to collect shells. For part of the summer of 1913, the two lifelong friends (a bit stooped now, and slow moving, but no less dedicated) dredge in the harbor, prowl the beaches, and poke through the mud flats of Portland, Maine. Just as they were sixty years ago, they are on the trail of shelled creatures, with Ned especially desperate to know whether one named *Solenomya borealis* buries itself in the ground *siphon or foot downward*.

The more things change, the more they are likely to remain the same. Is that what his old companion from the last Japan trip fears? Bigelow's letter, dated July 1, 1913, is an answer to an earlier note from Morse exulting that a year's leave of absence from the Peabody will provide him with plenty of time to complete new studies of mollusks and brachiopods. What a waste, says the doctor: *The only thing I don't like in your letter is the confession that you are still frittering away your valuable time on the lowest forms of animal life, which anybody can attend to, instead of devoting it to the highest, about the manners and customs of which no one is so qualified to speak as you. Honest, now—isn't a Japanese a higher organism than a mollusc? Drop your damned Brachiopods. They'll always be there and will inevitably be taken care of by somebody or other as the years go by, but remember that the Japanese organisms which you and I knew familiarly thirty years ago are vanishing types, many of which have already disappeared completely from the face of the earth, and that men of our age are literally the last people who have seen these organisms alive. For the next generation of observers the Japanese we knew will be as extinct as Belemnites.*

Indeed! Even the most fanatic and single-minded shell hunter would have to admit the truth of this charge. But what to do and how to do it? Why hasn't he published the big book on Japan he planned so many years ago? Certainly he has the material—no question of that. His thirty-five hundred pages of journals, studded with hundreds of sketches, are a precious record of so much that he did and saw during those three sojourns in Tokyo and his extensive travels from the most northern parts of Yezo (now Hokkaido) to the southern tip of Kyushu. Yet for more than thirty years their author has been unable to come to grips with them. Even now, he remains *perplexed* by the problem of how to handle this mass of material, how to shape it into something of value.

Maybe form does not matter. For a zoologist whose career has been devoted to taxonomy, just as for a literary man (which he has certainly never claimed to be), such an idea is no doubt heretical. But practical, too. That seems to be the message he absorbs from Bigelow. Shortly after the July letter, Morse begins to tackle the notebooks with an eye toward publication. Over the years he has skillfully mined them for information and drawings that have gone into a multitude of lectures, articles, and books. Now he decides to eliminate everything already used and let the original entries stand *as a continuous record* of his travels. Even so, the task is difficult and time-consuming, and Ned must enlist the aid of two helpers: his secretary, who reads and types up the *execrable manuscript*; and his son-in-law, who works to pare away redundancies and straighten tangled prose. More than three years after Bigelow's letter, the job is finally done. In 1917, the notebooks appear in a 900-page, 2-volume edition which contains 777 sketches and is titled, simply enough, *Japan Day by Day*.

The completed work seems to leave Morse a touch uneasy. At least that's the feeling one gets from the preface. No doubt the book's shapelessness and its lack of argument or conclusion trouble his scientific sensibility. Why else begin the manuscript with so many apologies? Ned finds it necessary to explain he could not make the material fit into the headings of that course of twelve lectures he delivered on Japan to the Lowell Institute back in 1881–1882 (as if anyone will remember). He excuses the quality of the sketches on the grounds that so many were made *in jostling crowds* and *bumping jinrikishas*. He worries that the notes may seem too *light and disjointed*. He suggests, ever so tentatively, that the only *value these records may possess lies in the fact that when they were made, Japan had within a few years emerged from a peculiar state of civilization which had endured for centuries*. And he feels the need to justify the whole enterprise on the grounds that since he spent so much time in remote country villages and towns, his observations and sketches are *similar to records made a thousand years ago*.

No need for him to worry. Friends, Japan experts, critics, and the general public—all those who encounter *Japan Day by Day* seem to love it. (Bigelow says that it *brings back the good old days as if they were yesterday,* and William Elliot Griffis, who has never met Morse, calls the work a splendid *permanent record* of the *sights and feelings of Old Japan.*) Readers, then and now, find the book's detailed and evocative descriptions of tools, utensils, clothing, footwear, buildings, dolls, games, country inns, and toys, of habits and practices too common for natives to record and too mundane for most travelers to notice, fresh and immediate; an ethnological gold mine; a unique vision of the daily life of a country still barely touched by modernization. But nobody in print (then or since) seems to notice that *Japan Day by Day* is not just about Japan. It is also about its author and the civilization that he represents. Underlying its universe of details is a clash of cultural styles and meaning, a struggle in which concepts like *civilized, barbarian, progress,* and *tradition* lose their normal sense of opposition and collapse into a realm where the very notion of definition can be elusive. This may be what really troubles Morse. Not that he is capable of saying so, or even recognizing the source of his own disturbance. But the unspoken conflict that pervades *Japan Day by Day* has been troubling him since the late seventies. Remember: he is a scientist whose deepest conviction is that the world can be accurately measured, described, and understood; a Darwinist committed to the idea of evolution for species, civilizations, and nations; an American deeply ingrained with notions of self-help, individualism, and progress. Japan has tested some of these beliefs, shaken others, forced him toward new categories of understanding. But it has always been difficult for him to say what these are. For more than thirty years Morse has confronted the personal and emotional problem of Japan only by indirection. Evidence for this can be found in his career and his writings, but only if one is sensitive to the subjective meaning of the objective word, and to the sound of important things left unsaid.

To read Morse on Japan—the short notices, the reviews, the articles, the books—is to be confronted repeatedly by studies in cultural comparison. Implicitly and explicitly, he is always drawing contrasts between the two countries, contrasts that depict Americans as rude, backward, inartistic, and more than a little uncivilized. Such notions are particularly prevalent in those works obviously prompted by exposure to the aesthetics and behavior patterns of this ancient, sophisticated culture—his first major book, *Japanese Homes and Their Surroundings*; or his Founder's Day address to the students of Vassar on "The Importance of Good Manners"; or his articles on "Japanese Boys and Girls" and "Old Satsuma." But hints of such judgments can also pop up in odd, unexpected places—say, a scholarly treatise on *Terra-Cotta Roofing Tiles*, or the article "Latrines of the East," in which his evolutionary views are carried to some sort of logical conclusion with the solemn assertion that the progress of a civilization, indeed, its very *intellectual status*, may best be gauged by *the advance it makes in disposing of waste matters in a clean, wholesome and economical way.*

Whenever comparisons unfavorable to America reach Morse's

consciousness, he justifies them as constructive, a way of learning from another culture and thus helping to improve the quality of life at home. But *Japan Day by Day* seems to go too far. The cumulative effect of nine hundred pages of contrasts apparently startles him, for the book ends with a curious tacked-on paragraph that begins with the admission that readers may wonder *what my attitude is regarding my own people*. The answer is a touch oblique. After terming the endless comparisons detrimental to the United States *not invidious* but only *plain statements of facts as I saw them forty years ago*, Morse offers a profession of loyalty for his native land. But not one written in his own words. The conclusion of *Japan Day by Day* is a flag-waving passage, taken from another author, which cheers Americans as the freest, most industrious, earnest, active, moral, religious, chivalrous, and sober people in the world.

Odd, certainly. And disappointing too. The modern reader would rather have him grapple with the issue of what these contrasts mean to him, or explain why he has never incorporated those Japanese values that he loves—neatness, delicacy, politeness, and formality—into his own brusque, cluttered life. But in *Japan Day by Day* Morse once again disappoints us. He neglects to say what we wish he would say, is incapable of revealing those inner truths that so interest us. Just what are his feelings while he rereads and reworks the journals? Is it a shock to come face-to-face with himself of almost forty years before? Does he reexperience the joys and liberation of discovering the world to be much more various and beautiful than he had ever imagined? Apparently not. Certainly not if one is to judge by the letters to his best friend, Gould. During the years of labor on the notebooks, his only comments on the process are factual (how many pages transcribed, how many left to go) and wholly devoid of nostalgia. Typical, of course. The past is clearly a different country from the one he dwells in today. His own experiences may just as well belong to someone else, or be those of a character in a novel read a long time ago.

This same attitude means that Morse never acknowledges the decisive role of Japan in his life, never mentions—at least in print—that without that land he might still be a fairly obscure natural scientist. Sturgis Bigelow can write to Ned that, for good or ill, his own trip to Japan in 1882 was *the turning point of my life*, but such self-understanding is alien to Morse. In his seventies as in his teens, he deals with the world in terms of things, not feelings. The enormous influence of Japan upon his opinions and ideas is there not just there in the works on pottery, architecture, and archeology, or in the ethnological writings on archery in different cultures, but it also underlies his social criticism. Listen when he wonders about the confusion and disorganization of city life, or crusades against steam whistles as a menace, or condemns the growing masses of vagabonds and criminals, or urges the creation of public art museums to raise the cultural level of the masses, and you are transported back to a land where people bow hello and crowds are well behaved, where rickshas spin silently over country roads and gardens are lovely and free of refuse, where the tatami is sweet underfoot and a single, exquisite scroll hangs in the *tokonoma* and the world is growing larger than you ever knew it could be.

He may never say it, but we can. Ever after Japan, Morse is condemned to live in a state that may best be described as one of comparative cultural discomfort. Being Morse, he is incapable of recognizing, dwelling upon, or even naming such a feeling. Besides, it is only situational, something that arises from time to time and can be exorcised by writing articles and books, or by fondling a lovely piece of pottery, or that—if he just waits a bit—will vanish into the busyness of a life where there is always another project to plan and pursue. The best bit of evidence for this recurrent psychic state is negative. Despite all the money he makes selling his collection to the Museum of Fine Arts in 1892, Ned never returns to Japan. He has the time and the good health (not until the age of eighty-two will he begin to complain of physical ailments) and now he certainly has the money. Of course there is nothing special for him to do in Japan, but Morse has always been capable of cooking up things to occupy his time. Is it too extreme to suggest that he somehow instinctively understands that going back would be too painful? That it would be like once again encountering a love which can never be consummated because it is for something of the spirit and not of the flesh.

15

No European Can Understand

The invitation from Cornell University is a godsend. Twenty-five hundred dollars for a series of lectures on Japanese civilization. How long has he been hoping, praying, working, writing letters to friends to get something, anything that will take him back to America? Now it is autumn, 1902. Difficult to believe he's been in this land for more than twelve years. Time to get out, at least for a little while. Time to take Kazuo somewhere to begin that much-needed Western education. Time to leave this land where each day the future becomes increasingly difficult to avoid. Why, just six months ago he had to move farther from the center of Tokyo, and all because of those fools at Kobudera temple. Imagine chopping down a grove of ancient cedars just to raise money, and doing this despite his offer to pay more to keep the trees standing. But no. To the new head priest he is no more than an unknown foreigner. Besides, it really wouldn't make much difference. The paddies, the fields, the bamboo groves behind his house in Ushigome—so recently the far edge of town—had been disappearing too, buried beneath ugly wooden tenements. Fewer birdsongs in the morning, fewer frogs at twilight, and everywhere the confusion of roads torn up to install water mains. Just as well that Setsu was ready for a larger house. Now they are in Nishi-Okubu, a region still rural and green and lovely enough to encourage this awful thought: How long can it stay that way?

Never has Hearn grown to like the city. It is more accurate to say he tolerates the great capital for the money it brings him;

makes use of some of its cultural opportunities (chiefly craft and art shows); and enjoys—though he will not admit this—some of the foreign company that it provides. Ask and he is still likely to call it *this detestable Tokyo*, a place where *there are no Japanese impressions to be had*. So vast and varied is this urban landscape that he finds it *utterly impossible* to describe. And yet he cannot keep from attempting to portray its sprawl—the quarter of foreign embassies that resembles an American suburb; the endless regions of low houses of *indescribable squalor*; the vast military parade grounds *trampled into a waste of dust, and bounded by hideous barracks*; the dismal *turmoil* of factories and railroad stations; the *horrid* miles of telegraph poles; the streets, torn up for seven years now to build an underground, that become swamps in the rainy season. What an awful place for a writer; what a *dead waste and muddle* in which to *think of art or time or eternity*.

And yet Tokyo is home, the setting for a life that proceeds with monotonous routine. Six times a week Hearn—smoking a cigar, hatless no matter what the weather, books wrapped in a purple *furoshiki*—rides off in a ricksha to the university to teach for half a day. Back home in the afternoon, he tutors Kazuo in English, then takes a two- or three-hour walk away from the city. Along country lanes he marches at a brisk pace, stopping occasionally to scrawl in a tiny notebook, or to explore shrines and mossy wells, or to rest at thatched houses, where he drinks tea with farmers and converses in his grade-school Japanese. Dinner, like all his meals, is Western: he likes roast beef and chicken, bread, plum pudding, coffee and milk. Then it is family hour, an interlude of simple games and songs with the children, Kazuo, Iwao, and their tiny brother Yukichi. Evenings are a time for work and contemplation. Rarely does he leave the writing desk before midnight.

If Hearn's daily round includes few social activities, this is by choice. Every Thursday he takes Setsu out for dinner and an afternoon of shopping, and once in a very long while he spends an evening at the home of another Western faculty member. But mostly he prefers to remain at home. All random visitors—students (unless from Matsue or Kumamoto days), people from America who know his writing, newspaper reporters on the track of a feature story—are turned away from his door, and rarely does he accept invitations. Yet Lafcadio is no hermit. Chamberlain (who teaches at the same school) and Mason may both vanish mysteriously from his life, but two others take their places as friends: James Foxwell, a Cambridge graduate and fellow professor, and Mitchell McDonald, a paymaster in the U.S. Navy and part-owner of Yokohama's Grand Hotel. With Foxwell he occasionally takes dinner at a downtown hotel or at the Seiyokan, a Western-style restaurant in Ueno Park. To meet with McDonald, a bluff type with no expertise in literature, Hearn goes down to Yokohama for a day or a weekend of *extravagant and very naughty things*—whiskey, cigars, *imperially and sinfully splendid dinners*, and *wonderful chats until ghost-time, and beyond it!*

His reactions to such occasions explain why they are not more frequent. After a meal at the Metropole Hotel, where he has been annoyed by meeting some friends of Foxwell, Lafcadio bursts out, *Why should I lose an evening of (to me) precious work, and tire myself . . . What do I care for Mr. G. or Mr. M.? . . . What do I care for the whole foreign community of Tokyo?* Similar complaints pepper the notes to McDonald, even (especially!) when the occasion has been most agreeable: *That supper at the Grand Hotel! I am awfully demoralized to-day—feeling gloriously well, but not in a working mood. A week more of holidays would ruin me!* There is a lesson here that, when it reaches consciousness, must be shared with friends. The world contains too much temptation, and too many enticements that are a threat—nay, a mortal danger—to the serious literary temperament. Pleasure, recognition, admiration, and friendship—yes, he craves them all. That is exactly why he must renounce them and disappear from the world into his study. Solitude is what he most needs. To write well, to say the things he has to say, it is necessary for him to remain *humble, obscure, and earnest.*

No doubt about it—Hearn in these years seems a desperate man, full of an odd terror over each moment stolen away from his work. Shall we name this anxiety, say he is haunted by some strange demon or ridden by an unknown guilt? His wife has different words. She, after all, has to deal with Lafcadio's quirks and demands. She is the one who must make sure the children are quiet when he is working, who must rise early to dust and straighten his room in order to avoid his complaint, *You have a mania for cleaning.* She is the one who must worry that he may suffocate from smoke or burn the house down by the way he neglects the wicks on the oil lamps late at night; the one who in the morning must sweep up the fat bodies of mosquitoes bloated with blood that he forgets to brush away; the one who must call him from his desk repeatedly to meals and forgive his absent-minded remark, *Haven't I had dinner yet?* She is the one who— when he pours whiskey into a wine glass, or puts salt in his coffee, or drifts off while slicing the bread—must gently say, *Papa-san, wake up from your dream.* She is the one who must endure the way he endlessly paces the corridor, weeping or laughing to himself. So maybe her simple explanation of Hearn's obsession is as good as any we can provide: *His greatest pleasure was to live and write in the world of his imagination.*

Such pleasure has a practical side: it pays off in both money and recognition. Regular as the turning of the seasons, books by Hearn roll from first-rate American presses—Houghton Mifflin, Little, Brown, and Macmillan. At the time of the Cornell invitation, nine volumes have been published—*Glimpses of Unfamiliar Japan*; *Out of the East*; *Kokoro*; *Gleanings in Buddha Fields*; *Exotics and Retrospectives*; *In Ghostly Japan*; *Shadowings*; *A Japanese Miscellany*; and *Kotto*—and the completed manuscript of a tenth, *Kwaidan*, is on the way to America. Like the first, each book is a loosely organized collection of essays, sketches, philosophic speculations, and prose poems that tend to the suggestive rather than the definitive. None of them argues a thesis, though in a single volume—and indeed over the years—certain themes or topics do recur: Hearn is perennially fascinated by Buddhism, local rituals, ghosts, animal life, old tales and legends. What grows increasingly rare in his pages is personal experience, those fresh visions of people, landscapes, artworks, and architecture that fill so many early articles. Time and location are the obvious culprits here. They force him toward work that derives less from the senses and more from the written word.

Summer is the only time when he abandons writing. This season for play and relaxation, for sun and sea and a taste of what was once Japan comes to mean Yaizu, a fishing village on the Tsuruga coast, near enough to Tokyo (just over a hundred miles) for Hearn initially to propose the family go there by ricksha. Setsu refuses any such ordeal and insists on the train, but try as she might, she can never dissuade him from vacationing in this town where there are no other tourists and the accommodations are distinctly primitive. Year after year the Hearn family occupies rooms with low ceilings and poor ventilation above Otokichi's general store, rooms that smell of fish, swarm with fleas, and have no view of the ocean. In Yaizu there is nothing to do but eat, stroll, loaf, swim in the deep harbor, sit on the breakwater, watch the fishing boats, and swap stories with the poor, simple, semiliterate inhabitants. That is just the point. Here no one reads his books and everyone calls him *sensei* and he can wear *yukata* day and night. No wonder he insists, *I* *like* *roughing it among the fisher-folk. I love them.* No wonder that only once in seven summer vacations does he leave here, and then to complete that important Japanese ritual—to climb Mount Fuji.

That climb should be a personal pinnacle. Hearn's life, after all, seems full and good. Surely that is the appropriate judgment, then or now. He has a lovely family, a fine home, a good job, a steady income, regular vacations, an opportunity to be creative, and a great deal of recognition for his art. But all of this cannot stop his worries, nor cause his restlessness to cease. He fears losing his teaching job, fears not being able to provide for the family. He worries over Kazuo, who seems so timid, so frail, so unwilling to learn. He longs to touch Western civilization once again, to visit Europe and—especially after Foxwell and McDonald both depart Japan in 1900—to see friends in America. He wants to flee Tokyo, a city where he can get no peace and quiet. Often he suggests to Setsu that they relocate in the Oki Islands, or in Matsue. But she knows him well now, well enough to reply that only when he is a Buddha (that is to say, after he dies) will he achieve peace. And while Hearn, in all his love for the old culture, can report this as a piece of traditional Japanese wisdom, it sounds much like the words of any practical woman, unwilling to let a husband forsake a good position because of a lifelong itch that can never be scratched away.

The prospect of Cornell serves both to calm the restlessness and to make him wonder what he can say of significance to an American audience. Not much, if one is to believe what he tells a friend: *I am quite sure that I do not know anything about Japanese art, or literature, or ethnology, or politics, or history.* All Hearn can do is what he has always done—*be suggestive,* convey some *psychological, religious, social, and artistic impressions,* with the aim of producing in the minds of listeners an *idea of Japan different from that which is given in books.* Even so, his work on the lectures is unlike anything he has done before. Now he plays the scholar; undertakes a good deal of systematic reading and research; organizes ideas and chapters in logical progression; strips his language and seems to reach for the precise rather than the evocative word. As always, he works in a kind of fury. Eight months after the invitation, a six-hundred-page rough draft of a volume that grows out of the lectures is almost complete.

What irony lies behind this accomplishment. In these same months, he must struggle daily against despair as he watches his carefully constructed world begin to crumble. Problems start late in 1902, when a blood vessel bursts in his throat during an attack of bronchitis. The man who returns to his students a few weeks later has aged many decades, and it is this gray, bent, slow-moving figure who must confront a harsh new university policy. Just before the annual contract renewal, Hearn is informed that beginning the next term he will no longer be paid as a foreigner but as a Japanese. When he objects to the drastically reduced salary, an official brusquely tells him that he should learn to eat rice. A *strong protest* by students on his behalf may warm the heart, but it can neither put bread on the table nor prevent his resignation as of the end of March. The insult and pain may be eased by the prospect of America, but not for long. During the spring of 1903 the president of Cornell withdraws the offer because a typhoid epidemic on campus has caused a curtailment of expenditures.

Writing is for Hearn even more a refuge, a consolation, a therapy, and ultimately a source of meaning during this period of great troubles and in the few remaining months he has left to live. To the observer distant in time and space, the last year and a half of his life add nothing new. The position at Tokyo University is replaced by one at Waseda, a private university; the invitation to Cornell by one to Cambridge, England. But he never does manage to leave Japan. In the fall of 1903 his wife gives birth to their first daughter, Suzuko. In the summer of 1904 he goes to Yaizu with the two oldest boys for a very short season of seventeen days, while Setsu remains at home with the two tots. A heart attack takes him early on the evening of September 26, 1904, while he sits at his writing desk, pen in hand. Later his wife will say his death was prefigured by portents: the ill omen of a late-blooming cherry tree; the sad song of an insect named *matsu-mushi*; and his last dream of a journey not to any known land, but to some *strange place.*

The book that begins as the lectures for Cornell, *Japan: An Attempt at Interpretation*, is published the same month that he dies, but Hearn never sees a bound copy. Surely this is his strangest work, at least in part because it is on the surface so unstrange, so unlike all the others. Distanced, measured, and analytical, it is strange not just because he can, for the first time, stand back from his own experience to analyze the charm and allure of Japan. And not just because of his orderly attempt to impose upon the nation's history and religion the gospel of social evolution as preached by Herbert Spencer. And not just because he can at last see and admit that everything he has loved about this culture—its arts, manners, morals, and even its women—is not the product of some sweet period of pastoral freedom, but the result of an incredibly controlled, oppressive, despotic social order that has endured for two thousand years. And not just because he can admit that, despite his findings, this society still bewitches him, and that *to witness its gradual destruction* has brought him grief. And certainly not just because he now realizes that the elf land, the paradise he thought he found here in the past, has turned instead into a vision of a *higher future*, a world in which humanity may achieve *those ethical conditions prefigured by the ideals of Old Japan: instinctive unselfishness, a common desire to find the joy of life in making happiness for others, a universal sense of moral beauty.*

No. *Japan: An Attempt at Interpretation* is most strange because of what Hearn seems to tell us unconsciously. He is a man who has bowed before images of Buddha with no faith in Nirvana;

clapped his hands before Shinto shrines while judging the gods they hold to be no more than myths; written on reincarnation with no belief in it. He has spent fourteen years living with the Japanese and studying them. He has devoted his intellectual and artistic energies to capturing and expressing their traditions and culture. Now he insists for the first time in print upon some words spoken years before by his friend Nishida: *When you find, in four or five years more, that you cannot understand the Japanese at all, then you will begin to know something about them.* Call this conceit and paradox, but Hearn now sees it as a kind of wisdom that makes one free. When he insists over and over in this final tribute to his adopted homeland that no European can ever comprehend the Japanese, he seems on the edge of another idea, one that he does not live long enough to voice. Yet his life and writings suggest it: the real problem is not that Japan cannot be understood, but that words can only take you part of the way toward such a goal.

After

A Zen monk and a Hindu holy man, hiking together through the spring countryside, come to a swollen river. Without a word, the Hindu starts to walk across the top of the water, but the Zen monk calls him back, saying, "That's not how to get across." The holy man returns and the monk leads him to a spot where they can wade through the water to the far shore. "There," says the monk, "that's the proper way to cross a river."

—TRADITIONAL STORY

How to conclude? With the personal and the historical. The history and the historian. With the author at his desk in Pacific Palisades, California, sometime in late November 1985. And with Townsend Harris in an armchair in the lounge of the Union Club, at the corner of Twenty-second Street and Fifth Avenue in New York City, on an autumn day in 1875. The author's gaze wanders from a stack of more than four hundred neatly photocopied pages to the computer screen before him. What, he wonders, does his manuscript do, say, explain? And why has he given almost a decade to this project, these three men, that foreign land? For Harris, seventy-five and usually referred to as the *Old Tycoon* by other members of the club, today is special. With him is an admiring visitor named William Elliot Griffis, recently back from Japan. When the young man hands over as a gift two copies of a visitor's map to Tokyo that he published in Yokohama just the year before, the former diplomat is clearly more interested in something else. Eagerly Harris presses questions on the younger man about whether the Japanese view his role in the opening of their country in a positive light and if they hold him in high esteem.

The attitude is understandable. For men like Harris, history

272

was an arena which held the possibility for a kind of worldly redemption. When on that first day in Kakisaki he wrote *beginning of the end*, Harris was undoubtedly thinking of himself, wondering if this time he could achieve that success which had always eluded him. A failure in his own eyes, he had at the age of forty-three fled his home in New York City to spend the next seven years wandering on the margins of Western civilization, picking up odd jobs in the ports of Asia—Penang, Manila, Calcutta, Singapore, Macao, Hong Kong. Japan was the last chance for this childless man to become a person of consequence and leave his name in the history books. How else to explain the fact that, just a few weeks after becoming the first Westerner ever to stand erect in the presence of the Shogun, Harris ceased to make entries in the journal that he had kept ever since his appointment as consul. For three more years in Japan and eighteen years at home, he would pen nothing about his accomplishments, evidently content to await the verdict of history. There is no doubt that he would be immensely pleased at the many kind words about him from generations of historians and biographers, both American and Japanese. Perhaps he would even appreciate the rare sort of immortality he achieved when that later American hero, John Wayne, portrayed him in a motion picture entitled *The Barbarian and the Geisha*.

The concerns of the author as he stares at the almost completed manuscript have nothing to do with the opinions of people in Japan. Less interested in his role in history than with the problem of writing it, he has publishers, the historical profession, and the meaning of his own work on his mind. Am I, he wonders, the same man who landed in Yokohama more than a decade ago, knowing little of Japan beyond what could be (dimly) remembered from the war or learned from Kurosawa films and Mishima novels? This is an impossible question to answer. Certainly I know more about the land and its culture from so much looking, hearing, tasting, reading, and writing. I have seen Mount Fuji now, seen its shape from the window of the bullet train, rising so stark and startling into a clear spring sky that it became easy to understand its status as a *kami*. Seven years after leaving, I was in Japan again, on a pilgrimage called research—there to walk the Yokohama Bluff, stand before the huge Daibutsu at Kamakura, visit the shrine to Benten at Enoshima (the sacred cave has been closed as too dangerous for tourists), enjoy the crowds at the great temple complex at Asakusa, admire the Tokugawa tombs at Nikko, and plunge into the sulfurous baths at Yumoto (on my forty-sixth birthday). This time I rode the train through the long valleys that lead from Lake Biwa to Fukui, inspected the French dissection models in the Municipal Museum at the summit of Atagoyama, ate dinner in a restaurant built on the site of Griffis's house. This time I strolled along the willow-draped moat in Kitabori, removed a tiny ceramic fox from Hearn's favorite shrine to Inari (as insurance that I would someday return), and stood atop Matsue Castle to gaze upon Lake Shinji and the peaks that circle it.

All these experiences are part of the author's words now, part of that journey of self-exploration that leads through the past and back to myself. To write about Griffis, Morse, and Hearn has been to learn that my choice of them was more personal than I could have known or guessed, to confront the fact that all three men are really part of me. Despite my self-awareness and my strong belief in cultural relativism, there can be no doubt that, as professor of American Studies, I played for Japanese students and colleagues the role of missionary (cultural, not Christian), scientist (bearing the critical techniques of Western scholarship), and, perhaps belatedly, romantic writer (witness this book). Yet if it is interesting to find that in intercultural attitudes we have improved upon our predecessors only in our self-consciousness, it hardly seems to justify the effort that has gone into writing (for me) and reading (for you) this book. Somehow I still want more from my subjects. I still want them to articulate openly that Japanese critique of Western culture that has remained buried and implicit in their stories. I still want them to explain the dissonance that Japan created in their lives (and mine), to elucidate the pain, confusion, and ecstasies, the lessons of the culture that can never be named or quantified.

To make such demands of the dead—whether one is writing or reading about them—is surely to seek disappointment. They do not, after all, live outside the boundaries of the author's written words. One breathes life into them, and they give back the wisdom of perpetual incompletion. Not much of a bargain, but maybe it's only to be expected. Admit it: there is something else as well, something that becomes apparent only as these lines emerge. If the goal has been exorcism, then it has been accomplished. The passion for Japan is gone now, replaced by the kind of fondness with which we remember a sweet love affair; what lingers is a special feeling for the shapes, tastes, and colors of that culture, for its polite forms of speech and ceaseless bowing, for its sensitivities of gesture and its ideas that cannot be rendered directly into but only suggested by our words. So maybe it is true that my three subjects—along with the obvious passage of time—have reconciled me to work, culture, and country after all, and have done this by showing the similarity of past and present, life and art.

Men of the nineteenth century, and certainly men of action like Townsend Harris, would be startled by a reading of the past in terms of the present, the personal, the problematic. They had more faith in the solidity of intellectual structures and the enduring meaning of words than any historian can maintain in the last decades of the twentieth century. Too many wars, isms, and ideologies have come between us, too many movements in science, art, and scholarship that underline the limitations on our ideas and our ability to assert them, that suggest every evocation and every representation is at best a partial truth. This sense of partiality connects to another lesson that arises from the attempt to understand and render the experience of these three Americans in nineteenth-century Japan. The author has been forced to learn a good deal about the limits of words, and scholarship, and the entire apparatus of the tradition in which he has been trained— which means that he has been pushed toward fresh visions and new ways of understanding the seamless reality of past and present that we call our world. He has also had to learn to write a book in a spirit which insists that you cannot at the conclusion summarize a story—even one constructed from the remains of the past that historians like to designate as facts—as if synopsis, rather than experience, were its meaning, goal, and very end.

Sources

Notes

Acknowledgments

Index

Sources

Here I indicate the research collections and books most useful to me in writing this book. Thus I focus largely on personal materials produced by my three subjects during their sojourns in Japan, and list only the most important of the many memoirs and scholarly works I read in an effort to understand the lives of foreigners living in Meiji Japan.

William Elliot Griffis

Primary Sources

The William Elliot Griffis Papers in the Special Collections and Archives of the Rutgers University Libraries comprise fifty-two manuscript boxes and twenty-eight scrapbooks, which contain a huge amount of personal material, including his diaries; correspondence with family members, friends, associates, and publishers; manuscripts of works published and unpublished; and clippings from newspapers and magazines. Also located here are the letters and the Japanese journal of his sister, Margaret C. Griffis. For a guide to this collection, rich on the whole topic of Westerners in Japan, see Ardath W. Burks and Jerome Cooperman, "The William Elliot Griffis Collection," *Journal of Asian Studies*, 20 (Nov. 1960), 61–69. There is also a small Griffis collection at the Fukui Municipal Historical Museum in Fukui, Japan.

Some of Griffis's books also provide insights into his stay in Japan: *The Mikado's Empire* (New York: Harper, 1876), *Verbeck of Japan: A Citizen of No Country* (New York: Revell, 1900), *Hepburn of Japan and His Wife and Helpmates* (Philadelphia: Westminster, 1913), and *Townsend Harris: First American Envoy in Japan* (Boston: Houghton Mifflin, 1895). The closest Griffis ever came to autobiography is *Sunny Memories of Three Pastorates* (Ithaca: Andrus and Church, 1903).

279

Secondary Sources

The only attempt at a biography of Griffis is Edward Beauchamp, *An American Teacher in Early Meiji Japan* (Honolulu: University of Hawaii Press, 1976). Francis Y. Helbig, "William Elliot Griffis: Entrepreneur of Ideas" (M.A. thesis, University of Rochester, 1966) attempts to chart his shifting beliefs.

For the context of Fukui, see Kanai Madoka, "Fukui, Domain of a Tokugawa Collateral *Daimyo*: Its Tradition and Transition," and Motoyama Yukihiko, "The Education Policy of Fukui and William Elliot Griffis," both in Ardath Burks, ed., *The Modernizers: Overseas Students, Foreign Employees, and Meiji Japan* (Boulder: Westview, 1985). The volume also contains two other articles that analyze Griffis's ideas and impact: Hazel T. Jones, "The Griffis Thesis and Meiji Policy towards Hired Foreigners," and Umetani Noboru, "William Elliot Griffis' Studies in Japanese History and Their Significance."

Bibliographies

The M.A. thesis by Helbig has the best (but by no means complete) list of Griffis's works. Beauchamp's biography has a shorter bibliography, and the Burks and Cooperman article gives some indication of the range of his writings.

Edward S. Morse

Primary Sources

The Edward Sylvester Morse Papers, in the Phillips Library of the Peabody Museum of Salem, Massachusetts (catalog no. E-2), consist of ninety-nine boxes of material, and include copies of publications, manuscripts, diaries, the voluminous and virtually lifelong correspondence with John Gould, and the journals that form the basis of *Japan Day by Day* (Boston: Houghton Mifflin, 1917) and provide the chronological backbone for my work. Because Morse's handwriting is so difficult to decipher, and because the published volumes include most of the material from the original journals, I cite from the published version.

Of his many published works, those most useful for understanding the Japan period and its long-range influence on him include: *Japanese Homes and Their Surroundings* (Boston: Houghton Mifflin, 1885); "Science Lectures in Japan," *Popular Science Monthly*, 14 (Jan. 1879), 388–389; "Health Matters in Japan," *Popular Science Monthly*, 12 (Jan. 1879), 280–286; "Notes on Hokusai," *American Art Review*, 1 (1879), 145–148; "Japanese Boys and Girls," *Wide Awake*, 22 (June 1886), 55–57; "Old Satsuma," *Harper's New Monthly Magazine*, 77 (Sept., 1888), 512–528; *Terra-Cotta Roofing Tiles* (Salem, Mass.: Essex Institute, 1892); *Museums of Art and Their Influences* (Boston, 1892); "If Public Libraries, Why Not Public Museums?," *Atlantic Monthly,* 37 (July 1893), 112–119; *On the Importance of Good Manners* (Boston: Hastings, 1894); "Latrines of the East," *American Architect and Building News,* 39 (March 18, 1893), 170–174; *Can City Life Be Made Endurable?* (Worcester, Mass.: M. S. Davis, 1900); *The Steam Whistle: A Menace to Public Health.* (Salem, Mass.: Newcomb and Gauss, 1905).

Secondary Sources

Dorothy G. Wayman, *Edward Sylvester Morse: A Biography* (Cambridge, Mass.: Harvard University Press, 1942), the only book-length work on the man, is more of a chronological homage than a critical biography, but it does have the virtue of containing long extracts from his diaries. The briefer memorials, J. S. Kingsley, "Edward Sylvester Morse (1883–1925)," in *Proceedings of the American Academy of Arts and Sciences,* vol. 61 (Boston: Academy of Arts and Sciences, 1926), 549–555, and L. O. Howard, "Biographical Memoir of Edward Sylvester Morse," in *Biographical Memoirs* (Washington, D.C.: National Academy of Sciences, 1937), vol. 17, 3–29, can do no more than provide overviews of his life and career.

Anyone interested in Morse as pottery collector should take a look at his *Catalogue of the Morse Collection of Pottery* (Cambridge, Mass.: Museum of Fine Arts, 1903; new edition, Rutland, Vt.: Tuttle, 1979). For the high opinion of the collection during Morse's life see Sylvester Baxter, "The Morse Collection of Japanese Pottery," *American Architect,* 12 (May 28, 1887), 5–16. More recently the value of his collection has been called into question. See Soame Jenyns, *Japanese Pottery* (London: Faber, 1971), which not only casts considerable doubt upon Morse's "eye" for pottery, but also deplores his baleful influence on collections of Japanese pottery in the Western world.

Bibliographies

"Bibliography of Edward Sylvester Morse," compiled by Albert P. Morse for the Peabody Museum, lists 558 publications. The Howard memoir contains a bibliography of 124 titles; Merrill E. Champion, "Edward Sylvester Morse, with a Bibliography and a Catalogue of his Species," *Occasional Papers on Mollusks,* 1 (Sept. 20, 1947), 129–144, focuses on his scientific works.

Lafcadio Hearn

Primary Sources

The largest collection of Hearn material, including notebooks and letters, is in the Lafcadio Hearn Collection (no. 6101), Manuscripts Department,

University of Virginia Library. Other repositories of important Hearn material are the Houghton Library, Harvard University; the Henry W. and Albert A. Berg Collection of the New York Public Library, which holds his letters to Ellwood Hendrick; and the Henry E. Huntington Library, San Marino, Calif., where one can find the letters to Henry Alden. In Japan, the Lafcadio Hearn Museum in Matsue contains some letters, books, and manuscripts.

Happily, a large number of Hearn's letters have been published; unhappily, some have been edited, occasionally to delete material that an early-twentieth-century editor thought either too risqué or somehow damaging to Hearn's reputation. In the Notes, I cite published letters unless the quotation is from a letter that has not been printed or a passage that has been deleted. The published collections of his letters are as follows: Elizabeth Bisland, ed., *The Life and Letters of Lafcadio Hearn* (Boston: Houghton Mifflin, 1906), 2 vols.; Elizabeth Bisland, ed., *The Japanese Letters of Lafcadio Hearn* (Boston: Houghton Mifflin, 1910); Milton Bronner, ed., *Letters from the Raven: Being the Correspondence of Lafcadio Hearn with Henry Watkin* (New York: Brentano, 1907); Sanki Ichikawa, ed., *Some New Letters and Writings of Lafcadio Hearn* (Tokyo: Kenkyusha, 1925); *Letters from Shimane and Kyushu* (Kyoto: Sunward Press, 1934); Ichiro Nishizaki, ed., "Newly Discovered Letters from Lafcadio Hearn to Dr. Rudolph Matas," *Studies in Arts and Culture*, 8 (1956), 85–118; and Ichiro Nishizaki, ed., "New Hearn Letters from the French West Indies," *Studies in Arts and Culture*, 12 (1960), 59–110. (This journal is a publication of Ochanimizu University in Tokyo.)

All of Hearn's articles and books written in Japan are full of clues to his life and beliefs, but the best for the early years are *Glimpses of Unfamiliar Japan* (Boston: Houghton Mifflin, 1894), 2 vols.; *Out of the East* (Boston: Houghton Mifflin, 1895); and *Kokoro* (Boston: Houghton Mifflin, 1896).

Two memoirs by family members are most important—that by his wife, Koizumi Setsuko, *Reminiscences of Lafcadio Hearn* (Boston: Houghton Mifflin, 1918), and that by his eldest son, Koizumi Kazuo, *Father and I: Memories of Lafcadio Hearn* (Boston: Houghton Mifflin, 1935).

Secondary Sources

Of several Hearn biographies, Elizabeth Stevenson, *Lafcadio Hearn* (New York: Macmillan, 1961) is by far the best. Nina H. Kennard, *Lafcadio Hearn* (New York: Appleton, 1912) is interesting only because it contains some letters from Hearn to his long-lost relatives in England. Oscar Lewis, *Hearn and His Biographers* (San Francisco: Westgate, 1930) details the early controversies over Hearn's origins, character, and originality.

The critical literature on Hearn as a literary artist is substantial. Surely the most detailed study is Beongcheon Yu, *An Ape of the Gods: The Art and Thought of Lafcadio Hearn* (Detroit: Wayne State University Press, 1964).

Bibliographies

P. D. Perkins and Ione Perkins, *Lafcadio Hearn: A Bibliography of His Writings* (Boston: Houghton Mifflin, 1934) is an exhaustive and, to its time of publication, virtually complete list of writings by and about Hearn. For more recent items, see the decent bibliography in Stevenson's biography and the bibliography of critical works listed in Yu.

General Works

For a broad overview of the encounter between America and East Asia, one can do no better than Akira Iriye, *Across the Pacific: An Inner History of American–East Asian Relations* (New York: Harcourt Brace, 1967). Supplementing this by detailing relations with Japan are two similar and rather pedestrian works, both of which have useful bibliographies: Foster Rhea Dulles, *Yankees and Samurai: America's Role in the Emergence of Modern Japan, 1791–1900* (New York: Harper, 1965), and William L. Neumann, *America Encounters Japan: From Perry to MacArthur* (Baltimore: Johns Hopkins University Press, 1963).

For an overview of Japan's development during the period, Chitoshi Yanaga, *Japan Since Perry* (New York: McGraw-Hill, 1949) is useful. Scholarly insights into the the social, political, and attitudinal changes in Japanese life during the Meiji period can be found in two collections of essays: Donald Shively, ed., *Tradition and Modernization in Japanese Culture* (Princeton: Princeton University Press, 1971) and Marius B. Jansen, *Changing Japanese Attitudes towards Modernization* (Princeton: Princeton University Press, 1965). Ardath W. Burks, ed., *The Modernizers: Overseas Students, Foreign Employees, and Meiji Japan* (Boulder: Westview, 1985) contains articles by both Japanese and American scholars about foreigners and the modernization of Japan. Hazel Jones, *Live Machines: Hired Foreigners and Meiji Japan* (Vancouver: University of British Columbia Press, 1980), is a most detailed study of the *o-yatoi*, those foreigners who worked for the Japanese government.

To get a feeling for the lives and adventures of Westerners in Meiji Japan, one can begin with two anecdotal, uncritical volumes by Pat Barr, *The Coming of the Barbarians: The Opening of Japan to the West, 1853–1870* (New York: Dutton, 1967), and *The Deer Cry Pavilion: A Story of Westerners in Japan 1868–1905* (New York: Harcourt Brace, 1969), or three chatty, journalistic ones by Harold Williams, *Tales of Foreign Settlements in Japan* (Rutland, Vt.: Tuttle, 1958); *Shades of the Past, or Indiscreet Tales of Japan* (Rutland, Vt.: Tuttle, 1960); *Foreigners in Mikadoland* (Rutland, Vt.: Tuttle, 1963). For the feel of that first port open to Westerners, see N. B. Dennys, ed., *The Treaty Ports of China and Japan* (London: Trubner, 1867); Paul C. Blum, *Yokohama in 1872* (Tokyo: Asiatic Society of Japan, 1963); and Otis Manchester Poole, *The Death of Old Yokohama in the Great Japanese Earthquake of September 1, 1923* (London: Allen & Unwin,

1968). The changes in both Yokohama and Tokyo are chronicled in John R. Black, *Young Japan* (London: Trubner, 1880); the capital alone is covered in Edward Seidensticker, *Low City, High City: Tokyo from Edo to the Earthquake* (New York: Knopf, 1983). For the look of the people, countryside, and towns of Japan, see *The Far East*, a well-illustrated Yokohama weekly published in the seventies. More accessible is Clark Worswick, ed., *Japan: Photographs, 1854–1905* (New York: Knopf, 1979). To understand the notions of Japan that foreigners brought with them, see Jean-Pierre Lehmann, *The Image of Japan: From Feudal Isolation to World Power, 1850–1905* (London: Allen & Unwin, 1978).

There are surprisingly few scholarly studies of foreigners in Japan. By far the best work on a single individual is F. G. Notehelfer, *American Samurai: Captain L. L. Janes and Japan* (Princeton: Princeton University Press, 1985). Also of some use are Lawrence W. Chisolm, *Fenollosa: The Far East and American Culture* (New Haven: Yale University Press, 1963), and Sandra C. Taylor, *Advocate of Understanding: Sidney Gulick and the Search for Peace with Japan* (Kent, Ohio: Kent State University Press, 1984). Of firsthand accounts, memoirs, and hagiographies there are many (see bibliographies of Barr volumes and Notehelfer). Those most interesting or useful to me were Henry Faulds, *Nine Years in Nipon: Sketches of Japanese Life and Manners* (London: Alexander Gardner, 1885); Alice Mabel Bacon, *A Japanese Interior* (Boston: Houghton Mifflin, 1893); Horace Capron, "Memoirs" (typescript, University of Florida Library, Gainesville), vol. 2; E. Warren Clark, *Life and Adventures in Japan* (New York: American Tract Society, 1878); Charlotte B. DeForest, *The Evolution of a Missionary* (New York: Revell, 1914); Isaac Doonan, *A Missionary's Life in the Land of the Gods* (Boston: Richard Badger, 1914); Edwin Dun, "Reminiscences of Nearly Half a Century in Japan" (Ann Arbor: University Microfilms); Henry T. Finck, *Lotos-Time in Japan* (New York: Scribner, 1895); Townsend Harris, *The Complete Journal* (New York: Doubleday, 1930); Henry Heusken, *Japan Journal* (New Brunswick: Rutgers University Press, 1964); Edward H. House, *Japanese Episodes* (Boston: Osgood, 1881); George Trumbell Ladd, *Rare Days in Japan* (New York: Dodd, Mead, 1910); John La Farge, *An Artist's Letters from Japan* (New York: Century, 1897); Percival Lowell, *Noto* (Boston: Houghton Mifflin, 1891), *Occult Japan, or the Way of the Gods* (Boston: Houghton Mifflin, 1895), and *The Soul of the Far East* (Boston: Houghton Mifflin, 1888); Arthur Collins Maclay, *A Budget of Letters from Japan* (New York: Armstrong, 1886); Rufus B. Peery, *The Gist of Japan* (New York: Revell, 1897); Mary Pruyn, *Grandmamma's Letters from Japan* (Boston: James Earle, 1877); Raphael Pumpelly, *Across America and Asia* (New York: Leypoldt and Holt, 1870); Clara Whitney, *Clara's Diary: An American Girl in Meiji Japan* (New York: Kodansha, 1979).

Notes

The following notes provide the original sources of direct quotations. Consecutive quotations from the same source within a paragraph of text are grouped. I do not note a specific source for single words or descriptive phrases used commonly by one of my subjects; if readers dip into the works of the person in question, they will easily find such words and phrases.

The following abbreviations are used:

BHC Basil Hall Chamberlain
MCG Margaret C. Griffis
WEG William Elliot Griffis
LH   Lafcadio Hearn
ESM Edward S. Morse

Before

1 *I shall be . . . Grim Reflections*: Mario E. Cosenza, ed., *The Complete Journal of Townsend Harris* (New York: Doubleday, Doran, 1930), 196, 225.

1. Seductive Temptations

9 *fitting temple*: *Christian Intelligencer*, March 2, 1871. The article is signed "Curio," as were all of WEG's pieces from Japan published in this newspaper.

10 *fancy creatures*: Ibid.

10 *clothing mother Nature*: WEG, *The Mikado's Empire* (New York: Harper, 1876), 331.

12   *treasures of knowledge . . . silent conquering force*: *Christian Intelli-gencer*, March 2, 1871.
13   *land of seductive temptations*: Ibid.
13   *a neglected set*: Ibid.
13   *Blue sky*: *Mikado's Empire*, 353.
14   *naked as when . . . real Japan . . . poet to express*: Ibid., 354.
14   *flourishing . . . splendid road . . . The maid*: Ibid., 356, 358.
15   *a wheelbarrow . . . bloody code*: Ibid., 361, 362.
15   *Rambles*: The word is scrawled in huge letters across the printed pages of WEG's unpublished journal that correspond to his first week in Tokyo. The journal is located in the WEG Collection, Rutgers.
16   *wilderness of a million . . . monotonous and gloomy*: *Mikado's Empire*, 363, 397.
16   *loathsome . . . doleful*: Ibid., 369.
16   *the human form . . . Religion and innocent*: Ibid., 364, 378.
16   *built in European*: Handwritten English version of contract with Echizen, WEG Collection, Rutgers.
17   *emblems and tokens*: WEG, *Verbeck of Japan* (New York: Revell, 1900), 247.
18   *paganism, feudalism . . . scores of men . . . long since forgotten*: *Mikado's Empire*, 403.
18   *For a man's*: WEG to MCG, Feb. 4, 1871.

2. Christian Virtues

19   *world of delight*: ESM, *Japan Day by Day* (Boston: Houghton Mifflin, 1917), I, 2.
20   *waste of time*: Ibid., 4.
20   *No chairs*: Ibid., 7-8.
20   *like various . . . You really travel*: Ibid., 6.
22   *no matter how crazy*: Ibid., 40.
24   *animated . . . more complex . . . proverbs, good precepts*: Ibid., 50, 54.
24   *I must confess . . . in a New England*: Ibid., 72, 78.
25   *On discovering that . . . wonderful conception . . . devotion*: Ibid., 83, 93.
25   *trace of brutality*: Ibid., 107.
26   *like little children . . . what would be*: Ibid., 99, 100.
26   *I hope to get*: ESM to John Gould, July 11, 1877, quoted in Dorothy G. Wayman, *Edward Sylvester Morse: A Biography* (Cambridge, Mass.: Harvard University Press, 1942), 238.
27   *Thus far in . . . Little by little*: *Japan Day by Day*, I, 125, 131.

3. Demons and Gods

28 *surely the realization*: LH, "My First Day in the Orient," *Glimpses of Unfamiliar Japan* (Boston: Houghton, Mifflin, 1894), 7.
29 *the beauty of*: Ibid., 15.
29 *of some beautiful . . . Illusion . . . I am beginning*: Ibid., 19, 24.
30 *creature of circumstances*: LH to Henry Watkin, April 25, 1890, in Milton Bronner, ed., *Letters from the Raven* (New York: Brentano, 1907), 93.
31 *intangible and volatile*: "My First Day," 1.
31 *taking part in*: LH to William Patten, November 28, 1889, quoted in Edward L. Tinker, *Lafcadio Hearn's American Days* (New York: Dodd, Mead, 1924), 328–330.
32 *land of dreams . . . to see into the heart*: LH to Henry Watkin, April 25, 1890, in *Raven*, 94.
33 *with crowds of pilgrims . . . something infinitely*: LH to Joseph Tunison, June 10, 1890, in Oscar Lewis, *Hearn and His Biographers* (San Francisco: Westgate, 1930), 10.
33 *about to melt*: LH, "A Pilgrimage to Enoshima," *Glimpses*, 95.
34 *fear the gods*: LH, "Jizo," Ibid., 35.
34 *laws of progress*: "A Pilgrimage," 103.
34 *I've been living*: LH to Elizabeth Bisland, n.d. (1890), in Elizabeth Bisland, ed., *The Life and Letters of Lafcadio Hearn* (Boston: Houghton Mifflin, 1906), II, 5.
35 *extraordinarily difficult . . . at least five . . . I must resign*: LH to Joseph Tunison, June 10, 1890, in *Hearn and His Biographers*, 9–12.
35 *higher life*: "A Pilgrimage," 78.
35 *domesticated nature . . . as far in advance*: LH to Elizabeth Bisland, n.d. (1890), in *Life and Letters*, II, 3.
36 *I only wish*: Ibid.
36 *I resolve to . . . under big trees*: LH to Henry Watkin, April 25, 1890, in *Raven*, 93.

4. With the Help of the Lord

39 *Providence so ordered*: WEG, "Japan at the Time of Townsend Harris," in *Japan: A Comparison* (New York: Japan Society, 1923), 12.
40 *the Kingdom*: WEG, diary, Dec. 20, 1863. Almost all his life WEG made daily entries in a diary. These diaries are located in the WEG Collection, Rutgers.
41 *acres of trash*: WEG to MCG, Dec. 24, 1871.

42 *Mother's twenty-eighth*: Diary, April 11, 1865.
43 *time passed heavy . . . Rose up . . . performing the prodigy*: Diary,
    Sept. 5, 1859; Sept. 24, 1864; Sept. 9, 1864.
44 *As the strangers*: Diary, June 9, 1860.
44 *Civil War commenced*: Diary, April 13, 1861.
45 *quakers and niggers*: Diary, Nov. 7, 1861.
46 *the handmaid*: George H. Cook, quoted in Frances Y. Helbig, "Wil-
    liam Elliot Griffis: Entrepreneur of Ideas" (M.A. thesis, University
    of Rochester, 1966), 19.
47 *I heard considerable*: WEG quoted in newspaper clipping, n.p., n.d.,
    pasted into Diary, Feb. 2, 1867.
47 *new worlds . . . exhilarating and joyous . . . the weapons . . . social
    pleasures . . . ingratitude to God*: Diary, June 4, 1867.
49 *good week*: WEG to MCG, March 16, 1870.
49 *I wish I could*: WEG to MCG, January 13, 1870.
49 *short course . . . penny-wise plan . . . better prepared*: WEG to
    MCG, Feb. 10 and May 26, 1870.
50 *grappling with doctrines . . . Whatever the result*: WEG to MCG,
    March 30, 1870.
50 *thronged with pretty*: WEG to MCG, Jan. 5, 1870.
50 *purest and strongest*: WEG to MCG, April 8, 1870.
50 *VENI! VIDI! VICI! . . . Love's labor won*: WEG to MCG, Jan. 29,
    1870.
50 *a quick and brilliant . . . no home brighter*: WEG to MCG, April 8,
    1870.
51 *freely all that . . . would be hard . . . sunny . . . marriage and its
    train*: Ibid.
51 *inexorable and hopeless . . . experiences of poverty*: WEG to MCG,
    May 31, 1870.
51 *Were it not*: WEG to MCG, Sept. 6, 1870.
52 *There is no*: WEG to MCG, Sept. 26, 1870.
52 *splendid offer . . . money and travel . . . a duty to*: Ibid.
52 *that you believe*: Anna M. Griffis to WEG, Oct. 10, 1870.
52 *to a land without . . . It would be*: MCG to WEG, Oct. 10, 1870.
53 *I can study*: WEG to MCG, Sept. 26, 1870.
53 *Unable to do*: WEG to MCG, Oct. 3, 1870.

5. The World of Nature

55 *a distinct species*: Augustus Addison Gould, quoted in Dorothy G.
    Wayman, *Edward Sylvester Morse: A Biography* (Cambridge,
    Mass.: Harvard University Press, 1942), 13–14.
56 *Must I give up*: ESM, diary, April 27, 1858. ESM Papers, Peabody
    Museum, Salem, Mass.

56 *accomplished lady . . . skate, dance, ride*: ESM to Jane B. Morse,
     Jan. 28, 1860.
57 *God teaches us*: Diary, March 6, 1858.
57 *I will be*: Diary, March 22, 1858.
57 *free thinkers*: Diary, April 10, 1859.
58 *which saves the . . . I intend taking*: ESM to John Gould, Nov. 10
     and Oct. 10, 1858.
59 *Prof has given*: ESM to John Gould, Jan. 1, 1860.
60 *You need not*: ESM to Jane Morse, Jan. 29, 1860.
60 *intellectual and refined*: Diary, April 6, 1860.
60 *There is no*: ESM to Jane Morse, Dec. 10, 1859.
60 *Prof spoke to . . . a close student . . . that one can*: Diary, Jan. 20
     and 21, 1860.
61 *Two Years*: Diary, Feb. 8, 1858.
62 *There are thousands*: ESM to Jane Morse, Dec. 21/22, 1859.
62 *Don't you perceive . . . Darwin's struggle*: ESM to John Gould,
     March 11, 1860.
63 *Stupid lecture . . . He regarded cats*: Diary, May 22 and Oct. 4,
     1861.
63 *an old bachelor*: Diary, Oct. 31, 1860.
63 *Nellie is just*: ESM to Jane Morse, Oct. 1860.
64 *do anything but . . . She is the one*: Diary, June 17 and Oct. 31,
     1860.
64 *ignerant regarding*: Diary, Jan. 20 and April 16, 1861.
64 *What a delightful*: ESM to John Gould, March 29, 1863.
65 *just the man*: Asa Gray to ESM, Dec. 17, 1872, quoted in Wayman,
     Morse, 228.
66 *What a wonderful*: Charles Darwin to ESM, quoted in Wayman,
     Morse, 222.
66 *It isn't every day*: ESM to John Gould, Oct. 25, 1873.
66 *I should rather . . . My chief care*: Ibid.
67 *aside from describing*: J. S. Kingsley, "Edward Sylvester Morse," in
     Proceedings of the American Academy of Arts and Sciences, vol.
     61 (Boston: Academy of the Arts and Sciences, 1926), 554.

6. Leucadia to Martinique

68 *Real life is*: LH to Henry Mills Alden, July 17, 1888. LH Collection,
     Huntington Library. Published in Elizabeth Bisland, ed., "Some
     Martinique Letters of Lafcadio Hearn," *Harper's*, 142 (March
     1921), 520.
68 *The wish to*: LH, "Of Moon Desire," *Exotics and Retrospectives*
     (Boston: Little, Brown, 1898), 177.
71 *rigid, grim face*: LH to James Hearn, Jan. 6, 1890, in E. C. Beck,

ed., "Letters of Lafcadio Hearn to His Brother," *American Literature*, 4 (May 1932), 169.

71 *It is the mother*: LH to James Hearn, n.d. (1889 or 1890), in ibid., 169.

71 *of prayers*: Quoted in Elizabeth Stevenson, *Lafcadio Hearn* (New York: Macmillan, 1961), 20.

73 *the shadow*: LH, "My First Romance," in Elizabeth Bisland, ed., *The Life and Letters of Lafcadio Hearn* (Boston: Houghton Mifflin, 1906), I, 45–46.

73 *dropped into*: LH to Minnie Atkinson, n.d., quoted in Nina H. Kennard, *Lafcadio Hearn* (New York: Appleton, 1912), 67–68.

74 *in exchange for*: Quoted in ibid., 69.

74 *published in cheap*: Ibid.

75 *ghoul . . . thrusting*: LH, "Giglampz," *The Enquirer*, Oct. 4, 1874. Reprinted in Albert Mordell, ed., *An American Miscellany: Articles and Stories Now First Collected* (New York: Dodd, Mead, 1924), I, 16.

75 *a hideous adhesion*: LH, "Violent Cremation," *The Enquirer*, Nov. 9, 1874. Reprinted in *American Miscellany*, I, 35.

75 *a healthy, well-built*: LH, "Some Strange Experience," *The Commercial*, Sept. 26, 1875. Reprinted in *American Miscellany*, I, 62.

76 *I love her*: LH to Henry Watkin, n.d., quoted in Stevenson, *Hearn*, 69.

76 *He would have*: H. E. Krehbiel to Joseph Tunison, quoted in Oscar Lewis, *Hearn and His Biographers* (San Francisco: Westgate, 1930), 110–111.

76 *the inner life*: LH to H. E. Krehbiel, 1878, in Bisland, ed., *Life and Letters*, I, 196.

77 *the American disposition*: LH to H. E. Krehbiel, 1882, in ibid., 241.

77 *It is time*: LH to Henry Watkin, 1878, in Milton Bronner, ed., *Letters from the Raven* (New York: Brentano, 1907), 46.

77 *curious, crooked*: LH, "At the Gate of the Tropics," *The Commercial*, Nov. 26, 1877. Reprinted in Albert Mordell, ed., *Occidental Gleanings: Sketches and Essays Now First Collected* (New York: Dodd, Mead, 1925), I, 167.

78 *the sweetest of all*: LH, "The South," *The Commercial*, Nov. 29, 1877. Reprinted in *Occidental Gleanings*, 187.

78 *a five-cent*: LH to Henry Watkin, April, 1878, in *Raven*, 53.

78 *starvation, sickness . . . gigantic shoulders . . . something decently . . . a most damnable*: LH to Henry Watkin, Feb. 1878, in ibid., 47–52.

78 *rattle off . . . long, golden . . . one without*: LH to H. E. Krehbiel, 1878, in *Life and Letters*, I, 176.

79 *a man of letters*: Quoted in Stevenson, *Hearn*, 107.

80 *I would give . . .*: LH to H. E. Krehbiel, Dec. 1883, in *Life and Letters*, I, 294–295.

80 *to find the Orient*: LH to Elizabeth Bisland, April 7/14, 1887, in ibid., 390.

80 *A man must*: LH to W. D. O'Connor, June 29, 1884, in ibid., 328.

80 *I have no*: LH to Henry Mills Alden, July 17, 1888. LH Collection, Huntington Library.

81 *the great number*: LH to Rudolph Matas, April 30, 1888, in Ichiro Nishizaki, ed., "Newly Discovered Letters from Lafcadio Hearn to Dr. Rudolph Matas," *Studies in Arts and Culture*, 8 (March 1956), 113.

82 *No one thinks*: Ibid., 114.

82 *simply heaven*: LH to Rudolph Matas, July 30/Aug. 15, 1887, in ibid., 93.

82 *forever*: LH to Elizabeth Bisland, 1887, in *Life and Letters*, I, 420.

82 *If you try*: LH to Rudolph Matas, Sept. 6, 1887, in "Newly Discovered Letters," 105.

83 *tremendous . . . the blaze of*: LH to Annie Alden, winter 1887, Huntington Library.

83 *Slowly, you begin*: LH to George M. Gould, June 1888, in *Life and Letters*, 424.

83 *Heaven and Sea . . . stupid beyond*: LH to Rudolph Matas, July, 1887, in "Newly Discovered Letters," 92.

83 *I am not sure*: LH to Henry Mills Alden, Feb. 8, 1888, Huntington Library.

83 *bewilders*: LH to Henry Mills Alden, Nov. (?) 1888, Huntington Library.

83 *does not allow*: LH to George M. Gould, June 1888, in *Life and Letters*, I, 423.

83 *you get tired*: LH to Henry Mills Alden, Jan. 5, 1888, Huntington Library.

84 *Like tearing my*: LH to Rudolph Matas, June 5, 1888, in "Newly Discovered Letters," 117.

84 *Civilization*: LH to Joseph Tunison, 1889, in *Life and Letters*, I, 444.

84 *My friends advise*: LH to Elizabeth Bisland, 1889, in ibid., 44.

7. Feudalism in Fukui

88 *singing girls*: WEG, diary, Feb. 25, 1871.

88 *caterwauling . . . probably the most*: WEG to MCG, Feb. 26, 1871.

88 *Yonder is Fukui . . . something vaguely grand*: WEG, *The Mikado's Empire* (New York: Harper, 1876), 423–424.

89 *I thanked him*: Ibid., 425.

90 *The houses of wood . . . I was disgusted . . . the cud*: Ibid., 430.
91 *homesickness . . . dejection . . . magnitude . . . the dirt*: WEG to MCG, March 12 and March 23, 1871.
91 *From early morn*: WEG to MCG, March 26, 1871.
91 *Dear Intelligencer*: WEG, "In the Heart of Japan," *Christian Intelligencer*, April 27, 1871.
91 *at the ends of the earth*: WEG to MCG, April 28, 1871.
93 *in the heart . . . help these people*: "In the Heart of Japan."
93 *proud to perform . . . newspapers, Churches*: Ibid.
93 *to make Fukui college*: WEG to MCG, March 23, 1871.
94 *an old family . . . small boys . . . so large that*: WEG, "The Rutgers Student in Japan," *The Targum*, 3 (Oct. 1871), 1.
94 *unearthly yells . . . a picture*: *Mikado's Empire*, 433–434.
95 *First day*: Diary, March 7, 1871.
95 *Japs speak the truth*: Diary, June 26, 1871.
95 *99 out of a hundred*: WEG to MCG, July 5, 1871.
95 *clear and beautiful*: WEG to MCG, March 9, 1871.
96 *I am very busy*: WEG to MCG, March 26, 1871.
96 *some sort of omelette*: WEG to MCG, Dec. 3, 1871.
97 *Exciting work to teach . . . Very tiresome to teach*: Diary, March 23 and May 2, 1871.
97 *In teaching physical*: WEG, clipping in "Fukui Scrapbook," Rutgers Library.
97 *Three or four . . . the governments of*: WEG to MCG, April 28, 1871.
98 *Industry is my happiness*: WEG to MCG, Sept. 3, 1871.
98 *under all the lights*: WEG to MCG, April 2, 1871.
98 *It never satiates*: WEG to MCG, April 10, 1871.
98 *I feel more*: WEG to MCG, April 2, 1871.
98 *I spent the evening*: WEG to MCG, April 10, 1871.
99 *Mr. Lucy and I . . . We rode out*: WEG to MCG, April 10, 1871.
100 *Reproduce some of*: Diary, July 3, 1871.
100 *living green*: WEG to MCG, June 5, 1871.
100 *glorious with autumn*: Diary, Nov. 19, 1871.
100 *ploughs as old . . . reaping hook*: WEG to MCG, Oct. 28, 1871.
101 *dusky gold of October*: Diary, Oct. 12, 1871.
101 *the dignified samurai . . . the prettiest*: WEG, "A Damio's Government," unpublished manuscript, Rutgers Library.
101 *I am beginning . . . genuine Japanese*: WEG to MCG, April 28, 1871.
101 *blushing piece*: WEG to MCG, June 18, 1871.
102 *It must be remembered*: WEG to MCG, Aug. 17, 1871.
102 *Pagan, heathen, Asiatic*: *Mikado's Empire*, 437.

102   *where ancestral tablets ... everything human ... shut in from ...*
     new civilization ... Why not leave: Ibid., 439–440.

102   *So in this*: Diary, July 16, 1871.

102   *perhaps as good*: WEG, "Japanese Theatricals," *The Home Journal*,
     clipping in WEG's "Fukui Scrapbook," Rutgers Library. The arti-
     cle is datelined Fukui, May 27, 1871.

102   *How much better*: WEG, "A Japanese Funeral," *Christian Intelli-
     gencer*, n.d., clipping in "Fukui Scrapbook," Rutgers Library.

103   *evils that disfigure ... full of the happiest ... It gives one*: WEG to
     MCG, June 5, 1871.

103   *I don't know*: WEG to MCG, June 18, 1871.

104   *utter unconsciousness*: WEG, "A Philadelphian in Japan," Philadel-
     phia *Evening Telegraph*, clipping in "Fukui Scrapbook," Rutgers
     Library. The piece is dated Jan. 15, 1871, but must be from a
     year later, because WEG was not yet in Fukui on the former date.

104   *Stepped inside*: Diary, May 3, 1871.

104   *beast-like innocence ... afraid of a foreign ... We were sitting*: "A
     Philadelphian in Japan."

105   *I have told them*: WEG to MCG, March 23, 1871.

105   *singing girls, dancing ... headache after last night's folly ... Felt, as
     usual*: Diary, April 16, 1871; Jan. 20, 1872; July 31, 1871.

105   *In all the city*: WEG, "In the Land of Buddha," *Christian Intelligen-
     cer*, n.d., clipping in "Fukui Scrapbook," Rutgers Library. The ar-
     ticle is datelined Fukui, Nov. 4, 1871.

105   *strong ethical sense*: Ibid.

106   *simple ceremonies*: WEG to MCG, April 2, 1871.

106   *a family at prayer*: Diary, Nov. 30, 1871.

107   *Thank God for Buddha ... humane creed*: "In the Land of Buddha."

107   *faiths and history*: WEG to MCG, July 5, 1871.

107   *Away off in this land ... My mother's son ... I hope to stand*:
     WEG to MCG, May 28 (?), 1871.

107   *must teach nothing ... Our master's cause ... I know well*: WEG
     to MCG, Oct. 28, 1871.

108   *Oh my poor*: Edward Warren Clark to WEG, Nov. 24, 1871.

109   *into the slime ... human weaknesses*: WEG to MCG, May 28 (?),
     1871.

110   *I am very*: WEG to MCG, March 26, 1871.

110   *my saddest and sorest*: WEG to MCG, June 25, 1871.

111   *one of these*: WEG to MCG, Aug. 12, 1871.

111   *I must take on*: WEG to MCG, Aug. 17, 1871.

111   *Rose at 6*: Diary, Aug. 28, 1871.

111   *Nor can any*: WEG to MCG, Sept. 4, 1871.

111   *Consulted with*: Diary, Sept. 7, 1871.

111 *In my own household*: WEG to MCG, Sept. 9, 1871.

113 *day after day*: Ibid.

113 *general conception* . . . *really well grounded*: WEG to MCG, Dec. 7, 1871.

113 *close, hard, consecutive*: WEG to MCG, Oct. 28, 1871.

113 *under other systems* . . . *sharp angles of*: *Mikado's Empire*, 539.

114 *A higher position*: WEG to MCG, Oct. 1, 1871.

114 *a golden day*: WEG, "The Sea Empire," *The Independent*, n.d., clipping in "Fukui Scrapbook," Rutgers Library.

114 *solemn burial*: *Mikado's Empire*, 534.

114 *It is a new era* . . . *I shall be*: WEG to MCG, Oct. 1, 1871.

115 *Fukui or Tokyo*: Diary, Dec. 16, 1871.

116 *with a salary* . . . *as well as* . . . *whether I am lost*: WEG to Murata Ujihisa, Jan. 12, 1872. A draft of the letter is in the WEG Collection, Rutgers; it is not clear if a copy was actually sent to Murata.

116 *barbed arrows*: WEG to MCG, Feb. 4, 1872.

117 *the awful mountain solitudes*: Ibid.

117 *I go away*: WEG to MCG, Jan. 20, 1872.

117 *not a little* . . . *the scene of*: Ibid.

117 *pride, dignity* . . . *they were quite able* . . . *found some truth*: *Mikado's Empire*, 434, 540.

118 *with thrills of* . . . *silent flashes* . . . *to the native*: WEG to MCG, Feb. 4, 1872.

8. Enoshima Weeks, Tokyo Years

120 *fairly good* . . . *very agreeable*: ESM, *Japan Day by Day* (Boston: Houghton Mifflin, 1917), I, 144.

120 *give no value* . . . *hammer into*: Ibid., 181, 180.

121 *willing to do* . . . *astonishment and delight*: Ibid., 181, 183.

121 *number of new*: Ibid., 227.

123 *indescribable* . . . *beautiful cove* . . . *conveniently level*: Ibid., 188.

124 *There is too*: Ibid., 189.

125 *two civilizations* . . . *vulgar curiosity* . . . *active American*: Ibid., 177, 195.

125 *general intelligence* . . . *a hackman at home*: Ibid., 191, 192.

125 *primitive fishing village*: Ibid., 235.

126 *whys and wherefores* . . . *asked a question*: Ibid., 212.

126 *laughing and pleasant* . . . *interest or importance*: Ibid., 157, 212.

127 *just the reverse* . . . *are a much older*: Ibid., 221.

127 *a set of overgrown*: Ibid., 229.

128 *I have spent*: Ibid., 245–246.

129 *Edo is*: Quoted in Edward Seidensticker, *Low City, High City: Tokyo from Edo to the Earthquake* (New York: Knopf, 1983), 26.

131 *prepared to take . . . I am in: Japan Day by Day*, I, 257.
131 *scatter things . . . not to touch . . . catch-all . . . these people*: Ibid., 285, 317, 318.
132 *would have done credit*: Ibid., 282.
132 *pure and simple . . . without running*: Ibid., 284, 340.
132 *peculiar socialistic views*: A missionary writing in *The Heathen Woman's Friend* (Feb. 1879), as quoted in Dorothy Wayman, *Edward Sylvester Morse: A Biography* (Cambridge, Mass.: Harvard University Press, 1942), 248.
132 *entirely out of proportion*: WEG to John Gould, July 14, 1878.
133 *greedy to learn: Japan Day by Day*, I, 284.
135 *astonished . . . purity of design . . . truthfulness to nature . . . It is such violations . . . to make a study*: Ibid., 254, 261, 258.
136 *bent on business . . . beat us out . . . to collect every kind*: Ibid., 275, 270.
136 *walking along*: Ibid., 325.
136 *never ending source*: Ibid., 343.
136 *You are sure*: Ibid., 262–263.
137 *my point of view . . . getting accustomed . . . acquiring a taste . . . dietetic laboratory . . . things that I*: Ibid., 315, 391, 387, 441.
138 *May 1, 1878*: Ibid., 371.
139 *too much absorbed . . . roaming the city*: Ibid., 307, 375.
140 *There was no plea*: Ibid., 378.
140 *who lives in . . . the simple beauties*: Ibid., 386, 390.
141 *how staid and sober*: Ibid., II, 94.
142 *chock full of sketches*: ESM to John Gould, Sept. 2 (21?), 1878.
142 *great dredging . . . tropical shells . . . difficult to concentrate . . . magnificent views: Japan Day by Day*, II, 137.
143 *How natural it seemed*: Ibid., 166.
144 *what there . . . unconsciously . . . passion . . . natural born*: Ibid., 104.
144 *never so systematic*: Ibid., 106–107.
144 *little collection . . . representative pieces*: Ibid., 104, 106.
145 *expressed his amazement . . . making stuff . . . slapping it out . . . exquisite reserve*: Ibid., 157–158, 185–187.
146 *a large addition*: Ibid., 190.
146 *I want to get out*: ESM to John Gould, May 2, 1879.
146 *no time for such affairs . . . touch a drop of wine . . . the infernal slanders: Japan Day by Day*, II, 200–201.
147 *familiar with the plants*: Ibid., 205.
147 *The class was divided*: Ibid., 205–206.

9. Magic Matsue

148 *Dear Professor Chamberlain*: LH to BHC, 1891, quoted in Elizabeth Bisland, ed., *The Life and Letters of Lafcadio Hearn* (Boston: Houghton Mifflin, 1906), II, 31–32.

149 *the land of*: LH, "Bon-Odori," *Glimpses of Unfamiliar Japan* (Boston: Houghton Mifflin, 1894), 120.

149 *tenderest . . . loftier . . . ghosts riding . . . night-black*: Ibid., 120, 121.

149 *unknown in other*: Ibid., 130.

150 *out of old . . . in a bark . . . Here I am*: Ibid., 128–129.

150 *vaster than the*: Ibid., 131.

150 *unrecorded beginnings . . . visions of archaic . . . simple country girls*: Ibid., 134, 137.

153 *a vast and sinister*: LH, "The Chief City of the Province of the Gods," *Glimpses*, 162.

155 *commonplace Western garb . . . old Japanese heroes*: LH, "From the Diary of an English Teacher," *Glimpses*, 431.

155 *much larger . . . much handsomer*: Ibid.

156 *a much more agreeable*: Ibid., 432.

156 *whose hearts have*: "The Chief City," *Glimpses*, 170.

156 *I am being*: LH to BHC, Oct. 1890, in *Life and Letters*, II, 14.

156 *my first really*: LH to BHC, Sept. 1890, in ibid., 8.

156 *infinite bubbling . . . magnificent . . . grand avenue . . . astonishing . . . majesty . . . massive . . . immense . . . colossal*: LH, "Kitzuki: The Most Ancient Shrine in Japan," *Glimpses*, 180–188.

157 *a vast . . . majestic, bearded figure . . . clumsy barbarian . . . into the dwelling . . . sob and shrill*: Ibid., 190–191, 202.

158 *delightfully natural . . . antique world*: LH to BHC, Oct. 1890, in *Life and Letters*, II, 13–14.

158 *dainty*: LH, "In a Japanese Garden," *Glimpses*, 343.

159 *comfortable with a friend . . . the form of . . . discovered, developed*: "Diary of an English Teacher," 463, 453–454.

159 *was made for . . . the most beautiful*: Ibid., 458.

160 *strangely pleasant . . . psychic comfort . . . clear, free, living air*: Ibid., 476, 477.

161 *stupendous ghost*: "The Chief City," *Glimpses*, 153.

162 *mere shadows . . . touched where I*: LH to BHC, Jan. 1891, in *Life and Letters*, II, 24.

162 *astonishingly kind . . . A few more*: Ibid.

162 *a delusion . . . beloved concubine*: LH to Ellwood Hendrick, Oct. 7, 1891, in Berg Collection, New York Public Library.

163 *When I went*: Koizumi Setsuko, *Reminiscences of Lafcadio Hearn* (Boston: Houghton Mifflin, 1918), 6.

164 *nearer and nearer . . . There are many*: Koizumi, *Reminiscences*, 6.

164 *How fine a*: LH to *Japan Weekly Mail*, May 14, 1891. Reprinted in *Letters from Shimane and Kyushu* (Kyoto: Sunward Press, 1934), 30.

165 *lofty, spacious*: LH, "In a Japanese Garden," *Glimpses*, 344.

165 *I am able*: LH to Page Baker, Aug. 1891, in *Life and Letters*, II, 43.

165 *like a queen*: LH to Ellwood Hendrick, 1891, in ibid., 61.

166 *commonplace . . . doomed to pass away . . . Impermanency*: "In a Japanese Garden," 384.

167 *funny little cries . . . a merry tumult*: LH, "Of a Dancing Girl," *Glimpses*, 526, 527.

167 *love mixed with*: Ibid., 530.

170 *It gave me*: LH to BHC, Aug. 1891, in *Life and Letters*, II, 53.

170 *little drowsy sea*: LH to Nishida Sentaro, Aug. 1891, in ibid., 54.

170 *after the fashion . . . I have discovered . . . Some detestable missionary*: LH to BHC, Aug. 1891, in ibid., 46, 48.

171 *get at the*: LH to BHC, Sept. 4, 1891, in Elizabeth Bisland, ed., *The Japanese Letters of Lafcadio Hearn* (Boston: Houghton Mifflin, 1910), 17.

171 *if it were possible*: LH to BHC, April 1891, in *Life and Letters*, II, 26.

171 *vast, extraordinary . . . It is not . . . the irrefragable obstacle*: Ibid., 26–27.

172 *no mind for*: Koizumi, *Reminiscences*, 15.

172 *the folks of the Hamlets*: LH, "By the Japanese Sea," *Glimpses*, 507.

172 *they cast aside*: Koizumi, *Reminiscences*, 17.

174 *magnificent exception*: LH to BHC, May 22, 1891, in *Japanese Letters*, 10.

174 *impersonality . . . individuality . . . the great march . . . disappear before*: Percival Lowell, *The Soul of the Far East* (Boston: Houghton Mifflin, 1888), 195, 226.

175 *individualism . . . a desirable tendency . . . unbounded opportunities*: LH to BHC, Aug. 1891, in *Life and Letters*, II, 40.

175 *never hated any . . . religion of love*: LH to BHC, Aug. 27, 1891, in *Japanese Letters*, 14.

175 *oppression . . . objects of idolatry . . . diamond hard*: LH to BHC, 1891, in *Life and Letters*, II, 36.

175 *What is really*: LH to BHC, Sept. 27, 1891, in *Japanese Letters*, 14–15.

176 *depth does not*: LH to BHC, Aug. 1891, in *Life and Letters*, II, 40.

176 *unspeculative . . . the suggestions of . . . relations of things*: LH to BHC, May 22, 1891, in *Japanese Letters*, 10.

176   oscillation . . . There are times: LH to BHC, Aug. 1891, in *Life and Letters*, II, 56.

176   the Japanese are: LH to BHC, May 22, 1891, in *Japanese Letters*, 10.

176   the best people: LH to BHC, Aug. 1891, in *Life and Letters*, II, 57.

177   romances nobody else . . . When I get rich: LH to Ellwood Hendrick, Oct. 1891, in ibid., 64.

177   impertinence: LH to BHC, 1891, in *Life and Letters*, II, 36.

178   pen of fire . . . I've lost it . . . It is all soft: LH to Ellwood Hendrick, Oct. 1891, in ibid., 63.

178   dry, bony, hard: LH to BHC, 1891, in ibid., 35.

178   I must try: LH to Ellwood Hendrick, Oct.(?) 1891, in Berg Collection, New York Public Library.

178   for nothing in: LH, "Notebook: Japan" (ca. 1890–1891), item 29 in LH Papers, University of Virginia.

178   to take the shape . . . It does not: LH to Ellwood Hendrick, 1891, in Berg Collection, New York Public Library.

179   try to take: LH to Ellwood Hendrick, Oct. 1891, in *Life and Letters*, II, 65.

179   About seeing Japan: LH to BHC, Aug. 1891, in ibid., 58.

180   quaint old city . . . single ungenerous word . . . Could I have: LH, "Sayonara," *Glimpses*, 684, 691.

180   peaked host . . . sky and earth . . . more and more: Ibid., 691–693.

10. To Be a Literary Man

186   blistered, weary . . . dear old music: WEG to MCG, Feb. 4, 1872.

186   see as the Japanese: WEG, *The Mikado's Empire* (New York: Harper, 1876), 549.

186   great changes and improvements: WEG, Diary, Feb. 3, 1872.

186   the more serviceable: WEG, "Letter from Yedo," *Christian Intelligencer*, clipping in "Fukui Scrapbook," Rutgers Library. The letter is dated March 23, 1872.

186   the pleasure: WEG to MCG, Feb. 12, 1872.

187   best teachers . . . I should be: WEG to MCG, March 10, 1872.

187   nothing special to write: WEG to MCG, March 22, 1872.

187   Much of the charm: WEG to MCG, March 10, 1872.

188   too much like home . . . something more primitive: WEG, "Inside Japan," *Lippincott's*, 12 (Aug. 1873), 174.

189   all the comforts . . . good society . . . my love and admiration: WEG to MCG, Feb. 12, 1872.

189   American mail in: Diary, March 26, 1872.

189   the untold and secret . . . amid the grand . . . too heavy to bear: WEG to MCG, April 21, 1872.

190 *I must have company*: WEG to Martha Griffis, April 15, 1872.
190 *one in a million . . . asking her to*: WEG to MCG, April 21, 1872.
190 *I want someone*: WEG to Martha Griffis, June 6, 1872.
190 *I could do*: Ellen Johnson to WEG, Oct. 19, 1872.
191 *occupy a position*: WEG to MCG, April 21, 1872.
191 *polite deference rather*: WEG to MCG, June 12, 1872.
191 *Began teaching Nanko*: Diary, April 19, 1872.
191 *bright, eager*: WEG to MCG, April 21, 1872.
191 *my chief joy*: WEG to Martha Griffis, June 6, 1872.
191 *Usual day at school*: Diary, April 23, 1872. This is the first of many
      such entries.
191 *several sources*: WEG to MCG, Feb. 4, 1872.
191 *professing Christians . . . who have not*: WEG, "A Christian Church
      in Yedo," *Japan Gazette*, Dec. 4, 1872.
192 *old and ugly*: MCG to sisters, March 29, 1874.
192 *not our old Willie . . . superior to all*: MCG to sisters, Oct. 30,
      1872.
192 *independent of everybody's . . . needs to get married*: MCG to sis-
      ters, Sept. 28, 1872.
193 *He has grown*: MCG to sisters, Oct. 30, 1872.
193 *first interpreter to*: WEG to sisters, Sept. 9, 1872.
193 *no work . . . Everybody lives*: MCG to sisters, Sept. 28, 1872.
194 *accustomed to life . . . much happier*: Ibid.
194 *Japan does not*: MCG to sisters, Nov. 27, 1872.
194 *I see . . . whom we know wear*: MCG to sisters, Jan. 4, 1873.
194 *in its glory*: MCG, "Japan Journal," Oct. 13, 1872.
195 *high flung . . . Lords & Ladies . . . often read of . . . It will be*: MCG
      to sisters, Jan. 8, 1874.
195 *He will not*: MCG to sisters, Aug. 18, 1872.
195 *committed for life*: WEG to sisters, July 9, 1873.
196 *fine feather*: WEG to sisters, Oct. 28, 1873.
196 *Made plan*: Diary, Sept. 25, 1873.
196 *I shall make*: WEG to sisters, Oct. 28, 1873.
196 *in true civilization*: Clipping, n.p., n.d., in "Fukui Scrapbook," Rut-
      gers Library.
197 *extraordinary progress . . . that modern cosmopolitan*: WEG, "Ja-
      pan: Extraordinary Progress in the Empire during 1872," Clip-
      ping probably from New York *Tribune*, datelined Jan. 22, 1873.
197 *honorable with history . . . that was old*: WEG, "The First Christian
      Church in Yedo," clipping, possibly from the *Christian Intelligen-
      cer*, in "Fukui Scrapbook," Rutgers Library.
198 *the priceless value*: WEG, "A Railroad Ride in Japan," *Targum*,
      Nov. 1873.
198 *outrageous messes . . . freshness of surprise . . . bleeding their vic-

tims: WEG, "A Trip to Kioto, by the Tokaido," clipping, date-lined July 28, 1873, in "Fukui Scrapbook," Rutgers Library.

199 *Paris of Japan*: Ibid.

199 *perpetual holiday . . . numerous wives . . . sacred countenance*: MCG, "Japan Journal," Aug. 13, 1873.

199 *Fine views*: WEG, Diary, July 29, 1873.

199 *Willie's particular friend . . . Great pleasure*: MCG, "Japan Journal," Aug. 13, 1873.

199 *mere sheds . . . 24 days in the wilds . . . never looked so good*: Ibid.

200 *superficial . . . great revenue*: WEG to *Japan Herald*, May 8, 1873.

200 *forbidding students*: WEG, "Ebb and Flow in Japan," New York *Independent*, n.d., clipping in "Fukui Scrapbook," Rutgers Library.

200 *advance . . . positive regression*: Ibid.

200 *Was notified today*: Diary, July 15, 1873.

201 *treachery*: WEG, *Verbeck of Japan* (New York: Revell, 1900), 270–271.

201 *I dropped a note*: Ibid.

201 *I wouldn't stay*: WEG to sisters, Oct. 28, 1873.

201 *The influences here*: WEG to sisters, July 29, 1873.

201 *I shall return*: WEG to Tanaka Fujiro, Oct. 13, 1873.

201 *I would not*: WEG to sisters, July 29, 1873.

202 *life's best fruits . . . ingratitude and neglect . . . unrequited love . . . I don't want*: WEG to sisters, Oct. 28, 1873.

202 *like bushes*: WEG, "A Sabbath in Yedo," clipping datelined Dec. 1, 1872, in "Fukui Scrapbook," Rutgers Library.

203 *Disappointed*: Diary, Jan. 1, 1873.

203 *fit of anti-Caucasianism . . . sweet simplicity . . . starch or sawdust . . . alimentary . . . a Japanese meal*: WEG, "Inside Japan," *Lippincott's*, 174, 179, 181.

204 *golden flushed horizon . . . Lovely day*: Diary, March 19, 1874.

204 *Glorious weather*: Diary, Nov. 22, 1873.

204 *Saturday, July 18*: Diary, July 18 and 19, 1874.

11. Chanoyu and Utai

207 *What a constant*: Charles Darwin to ESM, Oct. 10, 1879. Quoted in Dorothy Wayman, *Edward Sylvester Morse: A Biography* (Cambridge, Mass.: Harvard University Press, 1942), 251.

207 *No other*: Boston *Evening Transcript*, quoted in ibid., 176.

208 *changes in fauna . . . antiquity of man*: ESM, *Japan Day by Day* (Boston: Houghton Mifflin, 1917), II, 214, 219.

208 *lulled to sleep . . . a little of*: Ibid., 214.

209 *for at least*: Ibid., 239.

209 *We shall have*: Ibid.
209 *Quaker-like simplicity . . . vases, pictures, plaques*: ESM, *Japanese Homes and Their Surroundings* (Boston: Ticknor, 1886), 309. A facsimile edition of this work was issued by Tuttle Publishers, Rutland, Vt., and Tokyo, 1972.
210 *It was difficult*: ESM, *Japan Day by Day*, II, 243.
210 *ransack . . . as a thing . . . A Koyashi*: William Sturgis Bigelow to ESM, Sept. 3, 1883.
211 *Dealers were coming*: *Japan Day by Day*, II, 247.
211 *The experience*: Ibid., 266.
212 *remarkable atmospheric effects . . . mists slowly rising . . . dark thatched roofs*: Ibid., 274.
212 *merry groups . . . Nearly every town*: Ibid., 263.
212 *One has*: Ibid., 267–268.
213 *afford a greater*: Ibid., 270.
213 *overwhelming gratitude . . . as it was . . . Idyllic*: Ibid., 274, 269.
213 *seven flowers . . . sweet singing insects*: Ibid., 416–417.
214 *leave this angelic*: ESM to John Gould, Nov. 11, 1882.
215 *this sanitary process . . . no loud cries . . . good-natured, witty . . . have much to learn*: *Japan Day by Day*, II, 338, 370, 353, 435.
216 *I have neither . . . bull in the china . . . rude*: Ibid., 342–343.
216 *I have begun*: Ibid., 344.
216 *grotesque . . . uselessly absurd*: *Japanese Homes and Their Surroundings*, 150.
217 *simplicity and absolute . . . kneeling upright*: *Japan Day by Day*, II, 249, 253.
218 *after a fashion*: Ibid., 355.
218 *natural and easy*: *Japanese Homes and Their Surroundings*, 150–151.
218 *I took my*: *Japan Day by Day*, II, 401.
219 *a fair ear . . . one constant wail . . . I have as*: Ibid., I, 360, 295–296.
219 *The performance began*: Ibid., 399–400.
220 *inspiration or thrill . . . with no ear for music . . . We thought certain . . . It may be*: Ibid., 401–402.
220 *musical and catchy . . . delicious contrasts . . . impressive . . . the power of music*: Ibid., I, 422; II, 224, 237.
221 *He sang a line*: Ibid., II, 401.
221 *a constant strain . . . two consecutive notes . . . rich and sonorous . . . It is by taking*: Ibid., 407, 401, 402.
222 *contemptuous laughter . . . humiliating experience*: Ibid., 407.
222 *Lately I have*: Ibid, 395–396.

222 *puzzling pieces . . . I am pretty sound . . . It may be interesting to record*: Ibid., 396, 399–400.

12. The Cost of Exile

224 *scraggy*: LH to Japan *Weekly Mail*, Nov. 11, 1891, in *Letters from Shimane and Kyushu* (Kyoto: Sunward Press, 1934), 54.

224 *Dismal. Depressing.*: Ibid., 53–54.

224 *fish out of water*: LH to BHC, Nov. 1891, in Elizabeth Bisland, ed., *The Life and Letters of Lafcadio Hearn* (Boston: Houghton Mifflin, 1906), II, 77.

225 *wilderness*: LH to Japan *Weekly Mail*, Nov. 11, 1891, in *Letters from Shimane*, 54.

225 *magnificence*: LH to Masanubo Otani, Nov. 1891, in *Life and Letters*, II, 70.

225 *outrageously expensive*: LH to Nishida Sentaro, 1891, in ibid., 67.

225 *not nearly so*: LH to Ellwood Hendrick, Jan. 1892, in ibid., 81.

225 *horribly ugly*: LH to Nishida Sentaro, Nov. 11, 1891, in Sanki Ichikawa, ed., *Some New Letters and Writings of Lafcadio Hearn* (Tokyo: Kenkyusha, 1925), 21.

225 *extraordinary . . . last twenty years*: LH to Otani Masanubo, Nov. 1891, in *Life and Letters*, II, 69.

225 *One must travel*: LH to BHC, Nov. 1891, in ibid., 76.

226 *Kumamoto doesn't seem*: LH to Nishida Sentaro, Nov. 1893, in ibid., 154.

226 *modernized . . . too big . . . a stranger*: LH to Nishida Sentaro, Feb. 19, 1893, in *Some New Letters*, 81.

226 *here the Gods*: LH to Nishida Sentaro, June 7, 1893, in ibid., 94.

227 *Western manners*: LH, "With Kyushu Students," *Out of the East* (Boston: Houghton Mifflin, 1895), 29.

227 *most unpleasant*: LH to Nishida Sentaro, June 27, 1892, in *Some New Letters*, 34.

227 *a prison*: LH to BHC, Nov. 11, 1894, in Elizabeth Bisland, ed., *The Japanese Letters of Lafcadio Hearn* (Boston: Houghton Mifflin, 1910), 379.

227 *What an education*: LH to BHC, May 12, 1893, in ibid., 97.

227 *beastly . . . I won't stay*: LH to Nishida Sentaro, Dec. 13, 1892, in *Some New Letters*, 61.

228 *If I once*: LH to Nishida Sentaro, Aug. 5, 1894, in ibid., 125.

228 *a sort of factory*: LH to Nishida Sentaro, June 27, 1892, in ibid., 35.

228 *never speak to me*: LH to Ellwood Hendrick, Nov. 1892, in *Life and Letters*, II, 100.

228 *I do not yet*: LH to Nishida Sentaro, April 21, 1893, in *Some New Letters*, 89.

228 *despised as hirelings*: LH to BHC, June 15, 1893, in *Japanese Letters*, 120.

228 *intellectual machine . . . every official*: LH to BHC, Jan. 27, 1894, in ibid., 236.

228 *silent as death*: LH to Nishida Sentaro, Sept. 18, 1892, in *Some New Letters*, 48.

229 *no mental company . . . There is my*: LH to Ellwood Hendrick, Nov. 1892, in *Life and Letters*, II, 100.

229 *There are nearly*: LH to BHC, Jan. 19, 1893, in *Japanese Letters*, 40.

229 *haven from dangerous . . . emotion and suffering*: LH to Ellwood Hendrick, Nov. 1892, in *Life and Letters*, II, 98–99.

230 *odd or pretty . . . working too hard . . . It is late . . . ancient custom . . . After all*: LH to BHC, Oct. 11, 1893, in *Japanese Letters*, 181–182.

230 *I used to think*: LH to BHC, June 27, 1894, in ibid., 333.

231 *millions of individualities . . . There is nothing*: LH to BHC, Sept. 9, 1893, in ibid., 163.

231 *My first enthusiasm . . . tradition and race feeling . . . the human heart*: LH to BHC, June 27, 1893, in *Some New Letters*, 123.

231 *Here the peasants*: LH to W. B. Mason, Nov. 11, 1892, in *Japanese Letters*, 434.

231 *infernally dull*: LH to Nishida Sentaro, April 21, 1893, in *Some New Letters*, 89.

231 *nervous lonesomeness*: LH to BHC, Aug. 12, 1894, in *Japanese Letters*, 368.

232 *well worthy . . . Oriental picturesqueness . . . to assimilate*: LH to Japan *Weekly Mail*, April 3, 1892, in *Letters from Shimane*, 59–65.

232 *booths glimmering*: Ibid.

232 *extraordinary stories*: LH, "From Hoki to Oki," *Glimpses of Unfamiliar Japan* (Boston: Houghton Mifflin, 1894), 53–54.

233 *sharp, indescribable sensation . . . fairy world . . . a little odd*: LH to W. B. Mason, July 24, 1892, in *Japanese Letters*, 402.

233 *I can't think*: LH to W. B. Mason, July 30, 1892, in ibid., 403.

233 *I have become*: Ibid., 403–404.

233 *primitive west coast*: LH to W. B. Mason, Aug. 1892 (?), in ibid., 410.

234 *thrill of pleasure . . . With what hideous*: LH to W. B. Mason, Aug. 6, 1892, in ibid., 412.

234 *Primitive*: LH to W. B. Mason, Aug. 24, 1892, in ibid., 418.

234 *gentle . . . quaint*: "From Hoki to Oki," 609.

235 *Oh, we used*: Ibid., 607.

235 *From a romantic . . . the far–reaching influences:* Ibid., 585, 625.

235 *as I was going . . . steam-laundry . . . stupid convention:* LH to BHC, July 22, 1893, in *Japanese Letters*, 140–141.

236 *In a Japanese . . . so atrocious . . . nice girl:* Ibid., 141–142.

236 *the blaze of summer:* LH, "The Dream of a Summer Day," *Out of the East*, 2.

236 *suddenly reborn:* LH to BHC, July 22, 1892, in *Japanese Letters*, 142.

236 *the sorrows . . . that enchanted land . . . strange illusion . . . crushed . . . to learn the height . . . magical time . . . cry out . . . ruled by one . . . ridiculously old:* "Dream of a Summer Day," 7, 11, 19, 20, 21.

239 *enormous illusion . . . Old Japan:* LH to BHC, Feb. 16, 1894, in *Japanese Letters*, 255.

239 *horrible places . . . Japan was really . . . To the child:* LH to BHC, May 25, 1894, in ibid., 313.

239 *Every day:* LH to Nishida Sentaro, Nov. 1893, in *Life and Letters*, II, 159.

239 *strong sensation:* LH to BHC, Feb. 6, 1893, in *Japanese Letters*, 60.

240 *Fairyland is already:* LH to BHC, Feb. 12, 1894, in ibid., 249.

240 *in advance of . . . backward a thousand:* LH to BHC, Jan. 14, 1893, in ibid., 32.

240 *Monstrosities in brick:* LH to BHC, Feb. 25, 1894, in ibid., 259.

240 *Japan won't be:* LH to BHC, June 16, 1893, in ibid., 138.

240 *opens a man's eyes:* LH to BHC, May 12, 1893, in ibid., 97.

240 *fraud:* LH to Ellwood Hendrick, Feb. 1893, in *Life and Letters*, II, 108.

240 *our boasted material:* LH to BHC, Feb. 5, 1893, in *Japanese Letters*, 57.

240 *except what is:* LH to BHC, Feb. 16, 1894, in ibid., 254.

240 *immense reaction:* LH to Page M. Baker, 1894, in *Life and Letters*, II, 175.

240 *sudden hiss:* LH to BHC, n.d., in *Japanese Letters*, 227.

240 *palm trees, and parrots:* LH to BHC, Feb. 5, 1893, in ibid., 57.

241 *my folks do not:* LH to BHC, May 16, 1894, in ibid., 310.

241 *religious silence . . . who parts his hair:* LH to BHC, April 19, 1893, in ibid., 87.

241 *Aryan race . . . amethyst hills . . . dreamy luminosity . . . windy glory:* LH to BHC, May 16, 1894, in ibid., 310.

241 *giants . . . so long decrying . . . Everything seems huge:* LH to BHC, July 16, 1894, in ibid., 341.

241 *delighted wonder in:* LH, "In Yokohama," *Out of the East*, 326.

241 *may the Gods . . . vast romance:* LH to BHC, July 17, 1894, in *Japanese Letters*, 345–346.

242 *with unspeakable hatred*: LH to Nishida Sentaro, June 2, 1894, in *Some New Letters*, 113.

242 *I am much too happy*: LH to BHC, July 20, 1894, in *Japanese Letters*, 350.

242 *debaucheries . . . beefsteak, whiskey*: LH to BHC, July 15, 1894, in ibid., 340.

242 *elegant and dainty . . . a great big*: LH to BHC, July 20, 1894, in ibid., 350.

242 *sympathy . . . supreme delight . . . horribly disagreeable foreigners*: Ibid.

242 *To write the name*: LH to BHC, Aug. 12, 1894, in ibid., 368.

243 *white man's job*: LH to Ellwood Hendrick, Sept. 30, 1894, Berg Collection, New York Public Library.

243 *with men*: LH to Nishida Sentaro, Oct. 23, 1894, in *Some New Letters*, 133.

243 *out of sight*: LH to Ellwood Hendrick, April 1895, in *Life and Letters*, II, 252.

243 *for no other*: LH to BHC, April 1895, in ibid., 249.

243 *How much I hate*: LH to BHC, Jan. 1895, in ibid., 200.

243 *I feel unhappy . . . no depths to stir*: LH to BHC, March 1895, in ibid., 217, 215.

244 *I may as well*: LH to Page M. Baker, Jan. 1896, in ibid., 288.

244 *sorrow and beauty*: LH to BHC, March 1895, in ibid., 220.

244 *tearing one's self in two*: LH to BHC, Feb. 1895, in ibid., 203.

244 *It is only*: LH to Page M. Baker, Jan. 1896, in ibid., 288.

245 *whether I had*: LH to Nishida Sentaro, Dec. 1895, in ibid., 278–279.

245 *great capital . . . blue wood-smoke . . . clayey odors . . . shaped like new . . . somewhat gray . . . dove-haunted hill . . . old colors*: LH, "Notes of a Trip to Izumo," *Atlantic Monthly*, 79 (May 1897), 678–687.

246 *a faint mocking . . . Tonight we must . . . a place once . . . first irrevocable illusion . . . Not to know . . . I can be*: Ibid.

13. Full Circle

251 *never ceased to*: WEG to Ambassador Takahira, May 7, 1908.

251 *un-Mongoloid . . . Aryan blood . . . desirable citizens*: Quoted in newspaper clippings, unsigned, n.d., in WEG Collection, Rutgers.

252 *Landed at Yokohama*: WEG, Diary, Dec. 13, 1926.

252 *ride to the . . . All changed*: Diary, Dec. 20 and 24, 1926.

252 *Evening . . . Zempukuji . . . old stomping . . . Same old*: Diary, Dec. 27, 1926; Jan. 1, 2, 11, 1927.

253 *Kobe*: Diary, April 24, 1927.

254   *Long ride*: Diary, April 25, 1927.
254   *torch light . . . prolonged Japanese blood . . . Began points for*: Diary, April 27 and 29, May 2, 1927.
255   *contrast with Yokohama . . . Idea of a Family*: Diary, June 11 and Nov. 4, 1927.
255   *unmentionable diseases . . . flying on wheels . . . rich in stocks*: WEG, "Japan's Progress in Rebuilding an Empire," *Current History*, 27 (Feb. 1928), 682–683.
256   *truth of the new religion . . . the Americans*: WEG, "Christianity in Japan: Surface Breezes and Deep Sea Currents," *Christian Intelligencer*, 2 (Oct. 10, 1927), 170.

14. The More Things Change

257   *a shock*: Dorothy Wayman, *Edward Sylvester Morse: A Biography* (Cambridge, Mass.: Harvard University Press, 1942), 404.
258   *siphon or foot*: ESM to John Gould, Sept. 3, 1913.
259   *The only thing*: William Sturgis Bigelow to ESM, July 1, 1913.
259   *perplexed*: ESM, *Japan Day by Day* (Boston: Houghton Mifflin, 1917), I, ix.
259   *as a continuous . . . execrable manuscript*: Ibid., x, xiv.
260   *in jostling crowds . . . bumping jinrikishas . . . light and disjointed . . . value these records . . . similar to records*: Ibid., xi, viii, ix.
260   *brings back the*: William Sturgis Bigelow to ESM, Nov. 15, 1917.
260   *permanent record . . . sights and feelings*: WEG to ESM, Nov. 5, 1917.
261   *intellectual status . . . the advance it makes*: ESM, "Latrines of the East," *American Architect and Building News*, 39 (March 18, 1893), 170–174.
262   *what my attitude . . . not invidious . . . plain statements*: ESM, *Japan Day by Day*, II, 435.
263   *the turning point*: William Sturgis Bigelow to ESM, Nov. 15, 1917.

15. No European Can Understand

265   *this detestable Tokyo . . . there are no Japanese . . . utterly impossible . . . indescribable squalor . . . trampled into a waste . . . dead waste and muddle . . . think of art*: LH to Ellwood Hendrick, Aug. 1897, in Elizabeth Bisland, ed., *The Life and Letters of Lafcadio Hearn* (Boston: Houghton Mifflin, 1906) II, 333–334.
266   *extravagant and very naughty . . . imperially and sinfully*: LH to Mitchell McDonald, Jan. 1899, in ibid., 423.
266   *Why should I lose*: LH to Ernest Foxwell, Nov. 1899, in ibid., 457.

266   *That supper*: LH to Mitchell McDonald, Aug. 1898, in ibid., 392–
      333.
266   *humble, obscure, and earnest*: LH to Mitchell McDonald, Sept.
      1899, in ibid., 452.
267   *You have a mania . . . Haven't I had dinner . . . Papa-san . . . His
      greatest pleasure*: Koizumi Setsuko, *Reminiscences of Lafcadio
      Hearn* (Boston: Houghton Mifflin, 1918), 33, 44–45.
268   *I like roughing it*: LH to Mitchell McDonald, June 1899, *Life and
      Letters*, II, 448.
269   *I am quite sure . . . be suggestive . . . psychological, religious . . . idea
      of Japan*: LH to Elizabeth Wetmore, Nov. 1902, in ibid., 486–
      487.
269   *strong protest*: LH to Elizabeth Wetmore, 1903, in ibid., 493.
270   *strange place*: Koizumi, *Reminiscences*, 79.
270   *to witness its . . . higher future . . . those ethical conditions*: LH, *Ja-
      pan: An Attempt at Interpretation* (New York: Macmillan, 1904),
      502, 504–505.
271   *When you find*: Ibid., 9–10.

Acknowledgments

An earlier version of Chapter 7 was published as "Griffis in Fukui" in *Ploughshares*, vol. 10, nos. 2 and 3 (1984). I am grateful to the following publishers and institutions for granting permission to quote from various materials: Houghton Mifflin Company, for passages from *Japan Day by Day*, copyright 1917 by Edward S. Morse, renewed 1945 by the Estate of Edward S. Morse; the Huntington Library, San Marino, California, for letters of Lafcadio Hearn; the Henry W. and Albert A. Berg Collection, Astor, Lenox, and Tilden Foundations, New York Public Library, for letters of Lafcadio Hearn; the Peabody Museum, Salem, Massachusetts, for materials from the Edward S. Morse Papers; Special Collections/Archives of the Rutgers University Libraries, for materials from the Griffis Papers; and the Manuscripts Department, University of Virginia Library, for material from the Lafcadio Hearn Collection. The photograph of Griffis is reproduced courtesy of the Fukui Municipal Historical Museum, Fukui, Japan; of Morse, courtesy of the Peabody Museum, Salem, Mass.; and of Hearn, courtesy of the University of Virginia Library.

Words cannot convey my full gratitude for the help and generosity extended to me by a variety of institutions and individuals: The Committee on the International Exchange of Scholars and the Japanese Fulbright Commission for the Senior Lectureship that led to this book. The National Endowment for the Humanities for both a Summer Stipend and a Senior Fellowship, which helped with travel, research, and writing. The Open Grants Division of the East-West Center, which gave me a congenial place to live and work for a year. The Division of Humanities and Social Sciences at Caltech for time off and generous financial support. Librarians Jeanne Tatro at Caltech and Clark Beck at Rutgers. Professors Takuwa Shinji, Ohara Nakagazu, Yamamoto Shuji, Noguchi Kenji, Kawakami Seisaku, and the late Ueno Seiichiro, colleagues at Kyushu University who helped me begin to feel at home in Japan. Chinami Kyoko, Ishibashi Chiharu, Sakamoto Hitomi, Sakamoto Jun, Nunomura Yumiko, Kayama Fujio, Kubota Yuko, and Tae Yasuhiro, students who were teachers too. Yamada Miyoko and her family in Yanagawa; Atsumi Ikuko, Donald Shults, Ueda Jun, Nakamura Keiji, and Nakamura Shoko, friends in Japan whose deeds were lessons. Caroline Yang, Otis Cary, Murakata Akiko, Yamashita Eiichi, Jeff Blair, Kajitani Yasuyuki, Ichikawa Hiroki, Miyazaki Masaaki, Janet Jencks, and Alan Casebier, generous with their time as hosts, guides, and interpreters. Clayton Koppes, Lou Breger, Richard Hertz, Jimmy Fisher, Nick Dirks, and Will Jones, friends who urged me onward with criticism and support, and who kept the faith even when I lost mine. Eri Yasuhara, who labored to keep down the number of my errors with the Japanese language. Aida Donald of Harvard University Press for support at the two most crucial periods, the beginning and the end. Jennifer Snodgrass for saving me from some of my worst literary impulses. Irene Baldon, who with a remarkably even temper got me through the many visions and revisions. And Cheri Pann, who created a world with space for the bird to fly.

Index